Under the Rainbow

Under the RAINBOW

An Intimate Memoir of Judy Garland, Rock Hudson and My Life in Old Hollywood

John Carlyle

Foreword by Robert Osborne
Edited and Introduced by Chris Freeman

CARROLL & GRAF PUBLISHERS
NEW YORK

Under the Rainbow

Carroll & Graf Publishers
An Imprint of Avalon Publishing Group, Inc.
245 West 17th Street, 11th Floor
New York, NY 10011

AVALON
publishing group incorporated

First Carroll & Graf edition 2006

Interior photograph of John Carlyle reproduced courtesy of John Paul Davis

Library of Congress Cataloging-in-Publication Data is available.

ISBN-13: 978-0-78671-853-5
ISBN-10: 0-7867-1853-6

9 8 7 6 5 4 3 2 1

Interior design by Maria E. Torres
Printed in the United States of America
Distributed by Publishers Group West

Contents

"MY GARLAND TIMES"

My Garland times, the most heightened hours and, God knows, the heterosexual heights of my life, began in earnest when I took Judy to bed. Or was it the other way around for a lady who was accustomed to conquest?

"You're not going to get rid of me."

I knew she meant it, curled beside me in the Hillman Minx that had replaced my Oldsmobile, as we twisted out Sunset toward Rockingham.

"Don't drive too fast, darling." That would become her whispering, unnecessary entreaty whenever I was behind the wheel. The chance of Judy getting injured while a passenger in my car terrified me—as did the thought of discovering her dead beside me in bed, which was, unfortunately, never an unlikely possibility.

We were finished with a midnight meeting with some dealmaker-lawyer at the Polo Lounge in the Beverly Hills Hotel. Such persons abounded. They were seldom able to pin Judy down and usually vanished, befuddled by her night owl's time clock and confounded in the face of her greatest weapon: vagueness. Sid Luft, the most effective chargé d'affaires she ever had (not counting Louis B. Mayer), once told me, in a moment of pique, that "Judy couldn't do anything right, except sing a song." But, unless supine on Seconal or crashing from Ritalin, she could do absolutely anything she set her mind to, from concocting her own hats and cooking Thanksgiving dinner, to being the most careful and caring mother in show business—or, on the night in question, wooing me.

Lionel, her houseman, went drowsily back to bed after closing the electronic gates behind us in the driveway. "Obey Mama!" was chalked on the pantry blackboard. Joey and Lorna were asleep in their room beside Lionel's. I nervously filled an ice bucket to take to the bar in the living room while Judy went to change. I vacillated between fear and determination in my certainty that I was at that moment, at last, the more than willing—and hopefully able—object of her affections.

She returned, an alluring child in her chiffon peignoir, her aroma the seductive scent of her favorite fragrance, White Shoulders, her eyes waiting, like a calf's. We sipped, we talked, we embraced, and I told her that, yes, I would stay with her until she went to sleep. Her fingers were like the wings of a small bird against my cheek and around my waist as we walked down the hall to her bedroom. The only light came from outside and we went to her bed, where I need not have been afraid.

MEMORIES OF JOHN CARLYLE

Who's that?

The first time I saw John Carlyle was at dusk on Norma Place in Los Angeles in the early '60s, just as the sun had faded and night was about to take over. I had been visiting a friend who had recently moved to the area, not far from where I lived on Hammond. But whereas my street was like a thousand and one others in the area, Norma Place had personality. It was a street where one expected to see colorful, eccentric theatrical people, a place where it was readily evident that you weren't in Kansas any more.

Dorothy Parker lived (and drank) there with her husband Alan Parker. The great writer would regularly pass out in the bushes when she was out walking her dogs. Estelle Winwood, Tallulah Bankhead's best pal, lived in the lower half of a two-story dwelling. Tuesday Weld and her mother, who was always referred to as Wednesday out of her ear-shot, lived in back. John Dall was just down the street. Nina Foch and Carleton Carpenter, separately, also lived there. They were all familiar names in the 1960s, all exceptionally interesting people.

But I'd rarely seen anyone as fascinating as the one I saw looming a block away. I swear he was wearing a cape, but common sense tells me that that probably wasn't true at all. But he should have been. There in the far off distance, he looked like Heathcliff on the moors, determinedly walking against fierce winds (although, mind you, it was a serene, warm summer night in West Hollywood). He was unsmiling, intense, on a mission. He might have been Edgar Allan Poe hurrying home to an attic to shiver as he wrote about a raven or a premature burial. Whoever he was, he was an intensely dark and intriguing presence.

"That's John Carlyle," my friend told me. "They call him 'The Black Star.' I think it's because he seems to only come out of his house at night."

Perfect! That seemed an ideal description for someone who lived on Norma Place, and John Carlyle was implanted in my brain then, and forever after, as "The Black Star." Never mind that he wasn't black—instead, Baltimore-society white—nor was he a star by Hollywood's definition. He certainly had star presence, and as the years ticked by and we became great friends, it was apparent that he possessed enough of a dark side to make him a terrifically interesting person to know.

"Interesting" hardly covers it. He was colorful, classy, and worthwhile, and few people have been funnier than he. Genuine wit flowed with his blue blood. He also possessed impeccable manners that could, and did, give him the freedom to comfortably mix with anyone, in any sphere. And, despite what my friend had said, "The Black Star" did often venture out in the daytime. I've seen it with my own eyes.

He had enough money that he didn't have to grub to get work like most of us, but he was always trying to find work and he wanted to work. He was an actor and, as long as I knew him, he was hopelessly stage-struck. He did auditions, attended acting classes, did workshops, and was especially devoted to Theatre West. I think his problem was that he wanted to be an actor so much that he was never comfortable enough on stage or in front of a camera to be as effective as he could have been. The charm and personality that he had in person never traveled well from the stage or through a camera.

But whenever he'd get an acting job, he was in heaven. After he was cast in the first Los Angeles production of *Bent*, which turned into a long run for him—one with numerous critical raves—John felt as if he had, at last, found the end of the rainbow. He never did find that ultimate pot of gold he was searching for—becoming a star in the Hollywood scheme of things—but his success in *Bent* went a long way in forever bolstering his own sense of worthiness and accomplishment. The low point, he always said, was when he sold subscriptions via telephone for *Life* magazine. But he did it. He was a survivor.

In his younger days, he drank too much, partied too intensely, popped too many pills, participating in that well-traveled ritual that people are expected to go through when youth is on their side. It didn't help, of course, that he was intensely handsome, a Hollywood bachelor with a disposable income and charm to burn, so the welcome mat was always out for him at parties. Then as now, good looks opened doors, but back then pills were plentiful, and they hadn't been around long enough for people to find out how damaging they could be.

Stories about John and Judy Garland on Norma Place were legendary at the time. "Madame Gumm," as he called her, was a perfect playmate for "The Black Star." During the period they partied and pilled together, he was mad about her, as he had been for years; she adored him and his razor-sharp wit. A dangerous combination, those two, but for the most part their relationship seemed to be as much about laughter, pranks, mischievousness, and affection as it was about all the wine and roses that were also a part of it.

I was in on some of those Carlyle–Garland rides on that merry-go-round, including the night at Judy's in Brentwood when all was friendly and fun between the two of them until Judy, buoyed by some pills kicking in, suddenly turned into Lady Macbeth, threw a drink in John's face and ordered him out of her house. It was an ugly moment, but by the next morning Judy had forgotten it, and for John it became a crazy addition to his endless Garland lore.

I also remember a madhouse night at John's in which Judy started out sweetly low-key but became more manic by the minute, then began disappearing into the bathroom with Hedy Lamarr, the two of them giggling uncontrollably, each time emerging wearing one another's clothes. Soon after, Lana Turner's daughter Cheryl Crane arrived with some friends, prompting John to pick up the phone and order more booze from a neighborhood liquor store; it was delivered by the ex-husband of Nina Foch, complicated by the fact that Nina was at the party and was not on friendly terms with the ex. That party lasted well into the next afternoon.

One of the great things about John was that he didn't embrace only those who'd join him in romancing the pills or the vodka. He never pushed anyone to join him in another drink. Everyone was free to do their own thing; in turn, he also wanted to be allowed to do his. It is also an indication of the high regard his friends had for him that we liked being around him even at those times he'd be under the influence and at his most impossible.

Then came the time when he decided enough. And he meant it. He stopped the pills—like that. He quit drinking altogether. After drawing many a sober breath and getting his act and his life together over a period of years, he did go back to having an occasional cocktail, but he never again overindulged. Sense and sensibility kicked in. We all suspected it would.

And it was about that time that he began writing. He discovered that he had a great flair for it. I think he felt a great freedom in finding something he could do on his own. Unlike with acting, now he didn't have to wait until someone invited him to ply his craft. The written word suited his lifestyle, and his wit, extremely well. Almost immediately, he became as dedicated a writer as any I've known. He wrote every day, long hours at a time. And he certainly had the stories to tell. One he wrote, for example, was based on an Academy Award–winning actress and the son she inadvertently destroyed, but the best is the one you're about to read, covering his own life in a Hollywood that no longer exists, about those nights with Madame Gumm, and the other famous people with whom he partied, worked, and, on occasion, lived. On paper, he captures moments in time with a panache and uniqueness that had always eluded him as an actor. True nirvana, at last!

John Carlyle is someone I always admired for his bright mind, quick wit, friendship, and immense loyalty, but I never had more reason to respect him than when he was ill and nearing the end of his life. Despite pain, frustration, anger, confusion, and fear, he never complained. Or if he did, it was his loyal pal John Paul Davis who bore the brunt of it. John always seemed optimistic, always had a joyful lilt in his voice whenever we'd talk. He constantly gave the future, including his own, a positive spin. In those final days, he truly was a hero of towering proportions.

John Carlyle is one of the best friends I've ever had, an irreplaceable force of nature to all of us who loved him. I couldn't be happier that his story and his writing are at last seeing publisher's ink. I guarantee that if "The Black Star" was still with us, he'd be overjoyed, too.

—Robert Osborne, May 2006

A STAR IS CUT

He got his big break in 1954, with the help of Henry Willson, the movie star idol-making agent he shared with Rock Hudson. New in town, the twenty-three-year-old John Carlyle (born Carlyle Fairfax Posey—as he asks, "can you imagine?") was cast as the "assistant director" of the movie-within-a-movie in George Cukor's remake of *A Star is Born*. But, in John's case, not only was a star not born, a star was cut.

The only audience ever to see John Carlyle in *A Star is Born* was the one at its first preview in Huntington Park, California—and John wasn't even there. After that initial three-and-a-half-hour screening, every frame of John's performance was among the thirty minutes of footage that wound up on the cutting-room floor. The shortened version of the film was shown at its quintessentially Hollywood premiere on September 29. John Carlyle was at the historic Pantages Theatre that night, with his friend actor Tom Irish and a few others, to witness—along with a nationwide audience watching live on NBC—the likes of Marlene Dietrich, Humphrey Bogart and Lauren Bacall, Elizabeth Taylor, Joan Crawford, Groucho Marx, Jack Warner, and, of course, Judy Garland gathering among photographers and swarms of screaming fans to experience the opening night of a movie that he was no longer in. I don't think he ever really recovered from the impact of that profound disappointment.

John Carlyle's is a story of the one who didn't make it, but his story is more complicated—and much more interesting—than that. He had, as he readily, even proudly, admits, "fringe benefits": beauty and a modest trust fund. Indeed, John was so blessed by those benefits that he considered using that for the title of his memoir. He also had a hunger to be admired, especially by the sexy young men (and a few young rebels famous for more than their beauty) in New York, Los Angeles, and elsewhere. There are stories about assignations with the likes of James Dean and Marlon Brando—among others—that John chose not to write about, but he has told plenty of others. He had a fondness for the same booze and drugs that undid his dear friend and sometime lover, Judy Garland. The one thing that was born for him on the set of Cukor's film was a friendship with the woman he'd idolized since 1939, when he went, as a kid in Baltimore, to see her in *The Wizard of Oz*. From that moment on, John was under the spell of the rainbow. Much of his fantasy life about Hollywood and the movies began on that fateful afternoon. And in John's case, many of those fantasies were realized.

In addition to his obsession with Judy was John's reverence for the formidable Joan Fontaine. As he relates in *Under the Rainbow*, he was able to get Miss Fontaine to agree to sponsor the drama club at his prep school, Christchurch School in the bucolic countryside of Virginia. In Hollywood in the '50s and later, John entered into an intricate relationship with his cinema goddess. It seems that he was somewhere between her friend and her number-one fan, although her work and her relationship with her sister, Olivia de Havilland, were not to be discussed, as John later found out, much to his chagrin.

John's life story takes the reader back into a way of life that has for the most part disappeared from American culture, except perhaps for a small segment of the patrician East Coast. The Posey family and the Boone family—yes, Daniel's progeny—had old money in Baltimore, and, as old money seems to do best, it produced its share of eccentrics and dreamers. From the Boone family manse, Oak Hill, with Uncle Herbert's peacocks, to John's father, Rowland Posey, an oft-married, hard-drinking, discontented lawyer who wanted to be a playwright like his hero, Eugene O'Neill, John's family has its share of upper-crust American gothic elements. He takes his readers through those early years—his youth, as well as his time spent as a struggling actor in New York and in regional theater—as a prelude to his Hollywood life. The details of John's life read like a time capsule: People don't live like that any more, and few of us have seen such a vivid account of that long-ago lifestyle.

The great tragic event of Rowland Posey's life began at the outset of his son's life: The beautiful Carlyle Posey, Rowland's young wife and John's mother and namesake, harbored a secret about her health—the complicated aftermath of rheumatic fever—in order to try to have a child. But she couldn't withstand the trauma to her body and died shortly after her son was born. It doesn't take a Freudian to imagine the reverberations of such a tragedy, and John confronts some of those circumstances and tremors with admirable candor and bravery. In his memoir, he uses his most treasured possession, a beautiful portrait of his mother, as a memento mori. His attractive young mother remained a watchful witness to her son's every move. After John's death, the portrait by Trafford Klots was donated to the Maryland Historical Society.

As a boy, young Carlyle Fairfax Posey struggled with his stepmother and stepbrother, but he and his father remained close, and their relationship is movingly described in the book. Particularly resonant for gay readers will be the "coming out" scene in his father's den. It shows a loving and understanding father comforting his troubled son in a way that, fifty years later, many parents are still unable to do. John always loved his father for that, despite their other differences, not the least of which was the father's embrace of Alcoholics Anonymous while the son continued to overindulge in his favorite pills and liquor.

• • •

Under the Rainbow is ultimately a story about chasing your dreams and about dreaming big. John didn't go to New York or Hollywood to be an actor; he went to be a star. He had beauty on his side, to be sure, and some measure of talent, but he didn't have enough in the way of dedication or serious ambition. His is a cautionary tale about a young man—and a middle-aged man—who aspired to stardom but didn't do the work it required. He openly describes his enjoyment of the hunt and the concomitant distractions, and says that he was more interested in carousing the night before an interview than in being fresh and prepared for the morning after. That behavior, he recognizes, cost him any real shot at success in Hollywood. He worked, off and on, in commercials, in television, and on the stage, but his credits leave a lot to be desired, and it's a good thing that he didn't have to rely on his modest income from acting to pay his mortgage. He could thank Mum—his Grandmother Posey—for that pot of gold.

John sometimes found love on the hunt and worked at maintaining relationships, but he wasn't especially good at it. In his forties, though, he'd had enough of the side effects of his indulgences and joined AA. At the first meeting, he met the man he'd spend the rest of his life with, another struggling actor turned realtor, John Paul Davis. The two shared their lives together in West Hollywood for over twenty-five years, until John's death from cancer in May 2003. I had the pleasure of meeting John and J. P. in the summer of 2001, when I lived across the street from them, housesitting for their dear friend and mine, actor/comedian Taylor Negron, whose love of John and his milieu comes through in his heartfelt Afterword, "To the Left of the Rainbow." Taylor's remembrance of John serves as a postscript, providing a moving account of the last years of John's life.

John and J. P. were wonderful companions for five o'clock cocktails—they started drinking again in the '80s, a rather delicate process John relates almost as a confession in *Under the Rainbow*. John was a wonderful raconteur and pleasant company. He was never bitter, as far as I saw, but he certainly enjoyed reminiscing about the past, and I know from some of his friends that he did, in darker moments, always go back to the 1950s and '60s as his "best of times."

In his biography of Judy Garland, Gerald Clarke suggests that meeting and befriending Judy was the best thing that ever happened to John Carlyle. John gently—or optimistically—disagreed with Clarke's assessment, but John recognized that Judy was a great source of joy and sorrow for him. He knew, though, that he could never have saved her. Had he married her, he was pretty sure that he would have faded out prematurely along with her. He was not, after all, a great reformer and was always more than happy to see her indulgences and raise them a level.

Joan Fontaine notwithstanding, John kept many dear friends for a half-century or more. Robert Osborne, who has kindly written a Foreword for *Under the Rainbow*, had known John since their days in Los Angeles in the early 1960s, when both of them were struggling actors. Mr. Osborne went on to make a name for himself as a film historian and as the engaging, informative host of Turner Classic Movies.

One of John's friends from his one-year cameo appearance in college, at the University of North Carolina at Chapel Hill, was Chuck Williamson. After struggling with emphysema and other ailments over several months, Chuck passed away while I was in the process of writing this introduction. I know he was thrilled that one of John's dying wishes—to see his book published—had come to pass. On their grand tour of Europe in the early 1950s, Chuck and John had quite the adventure. For Chuck, it was a life-defining time, as he met and fell in love with the handsome Tucker Fleming, who still, at eighty, turns heads and turned out to be much more than John's first impression of him as a "marked-down Gary Cooper." Chuck and Tucker lived up the hill from John for about forty years; their friendship was a wonderful record of gay relationship and the families we choose.

I was deeply saddened to learn, from Taylor, that John had been diagnosed with lung cancer early in 2003. He struggled valiantly, but it was a losing battle. His loss was devastating for J. P. and for the rest of us who knew and loved John. As it happened, I was going to be living in Los Angeles on sabbatical for about seven months beginning in January 2004, so Taylor persuaded J. P. to let me rent John's space in their lovely West Hollywood home. J. P. was reluctant at first, feeling the need for privacy and, really, seclusion in his mourning, but he agreed to take me in on a month-by-month basis. A few weeks into it, we had dinner, and he asked me if I would be around to take care of the cats—don't get me started on all the cats!—in August, when he had planned to go to Montreal for a vacation. That solidified our arrangement, and we developed a very close friendship in our time together.

I knew that in the 1990s John had started writing. He'd written a couple of novels and a memoir. J. P. asked me if I would read some of John's work to see if it was worth publishing. Of course he had great stories to tell, but up until this point I wasn't sure how well he had told them. I was enthralled with *Under the Rainbow* from the very beginning. It was clear to me immediately that it was a book worthy of publication and would be of interest to anyone who cared about the movies, about mid-century (and later) gay life, and about Hollywood in general. In editing the book, I wanted to keep John's voice alive and to be careful not to insert my voice into his memoir, so what I wound up doing was cutting about ten percent of the manuscript (John could some times go on—or off on tangents), rearranging a few sections, and providing chapter titles. I occasionally rewrote a sentence or two or added a transition, but otherwise the words—like the stories—are John's. A few of the names have been changed—to protect the guilty.

To my mind, perhaps the central question of John Carlyle's life—and maybe it's the central question of all of our lives—is whether his was a fulfilled life. Certainly, it was a full life—full of travel, of adventures, of love, of the wonders and the struggles of Hollywood—but he leaves the issue of fulfillment unresolved. Maybe it's for the reader to decide, or maybe it's John's final secret, the story he kept to himself. I don't know how "happy" John was. I don't think he thought of himself as a "failure," in spite of his star never quite rising, but in writing his story and now having it go out into the world, he has made a mark and left a legacy that I am sure he would be proud of. There is, I think, a fulfillment in writing a memoir, in seeing that one's life has generated a story that might be entertaining or even instructive to others. John was a gentleman; he had, in the words of our friend Stephen Bellon, a "generosity of spirit." He may have loved life more than he enjoyed it, and he has left this record behind to tell part of his tale.

One of my favorite memories of my time with John took place during dinner at Mark's, a favorite restaurant in West Hollywood. We were all in good form that night after a cocktail or three. Late in the evening, John regaled us with the story of his absurd audition for *Rebel Without a Cause*. It was a very funny story—one related in *Under the Rainbow*—and at the end of the story, as he paused for a sip of his drink, I said, "You did all that work, and Nicholas Ray had the nerve to give Natalie Wood your part!" John laughed out loud, delighted to participate in poking fun at himself and happy to share the punch-line of one of his best stories.

I am honored to have been part of the publication of *Under the Rainbow*. It is a gift to John, to J. P., and to everyone who knew John and who recognized what he had to share with those of us lucky enough to benefit from being on the inside of John's life—or just on the fringe.

—Chris Freeman, May 2006

CHAPTER ONE

NEW YORK, 1951–52

A MANHATTAN TAXI could not take me fast enough from the pier across town to the Palace Theatre. I waited in the lobby after asking the black man who was sweeping up cigarette butts if he could direct me to the manager. I asked Mr. Herb Bonus for a job as an usher. He introduced me to my first agent, Turner—the theatre janitor—and then led me into the box office where I filled out an employment application. He checked my uniform size, asked no questions, and said I could park my luggage inside the glass doors that led to the inner lobby. Mr. Bonus looked amused as he watched me set off to find a place to live. I bought a New York *Herald Tribune* to check the rental ads over lunch in the Automat opposite Bryant Park.

It was December 1951. I should have been in my home at 617 West University Parkway checking employment offers in the *Baltimore Sun*. My next address turned out to 29 East 38th Street, within walking distance of the Palace. I rented one room that faced the rear, with a shared bath on the third floor of a brownstone run in liberal fashion by a boozy former showgirl. The once-pretty Mrs. Harmony tended to drift off to sleep (in front of one of the first television sets ever manufactured) before any late arrivals, in or out of residence, entered her building. That was fine for me. My frequent callers came late and left early, preferably before dawn. It's an ordeal to wake up with a stranger.

After Mrs. Harmony gave me a key to the front door of her brownstone, I went out to a pay phone to call my surprised family collect. My sweaty palms were like eels. I held the receiver with both hands to promise that I would report my new location to the New York draft board. I said that of course I would come to Baltimore for Christmas, provided Mr. Herb Bonus gave Judy Garland and me the holiday off. My little sister Ann squealed and giggled in the pleasure of talking to me again. Mother and Dad said they still loved me; they were glad to have me back in the United States after my extended stay in Europe. My stepbrother Jimmy was not at home.

I was always eager to get to work. My new cadre of uniformed friends in the men's and ladies' locker rooms beneath the Palace lobby shared the same enthusiasm. We shined our shoes, tested our flashlight batteries, stood side by side while Mr. Bonus inspected our lapels and shirts and seams, and then sprang to our positions at the head of whatever aisle in balcony, mezzanine, or orchestra he had assigned us to seat the privileged public. None of us wanted to miss a second of the first drumbeat of even the preliminary overture for the opening acts. Those were the crème de la crème of newly revived vaudeville: the European adagio dance team Giselle and François Szony; Spanish ventriloquist Señor Wences; the strutting Nicholas Brothers (they were the cat's meow); and the half-century old but still young comedy team of Smith and Dale. After they performed, the houselights came up for intermission. The crystal chandeliers twinkled over last-minute, stylishly late celebrity arrivals. The occupants of the red and gold boxes strained to see the most famous stars of the day who came to pay homage, as thrilled and expectant as the rest of us. The warning bell sounded. We ushers took our places again. When the house lights dimmed to darkness once more, there were no other latecomers.

During the pulsating overture, the applause escalated at the sound of each refrain of every beloved song Judy Garland had originated. It exploded when her twelve tuxedo-clad boys came on to sing of "Babes on Broadway" and "Dear Old MGM." When Judy herself crouched on stage behind them and miraculously appeared center stage in their midst, the audience was up for grabs. Her ushers — flashlights clamped under our arms — clapped harder, with more frenzied love, than anyone. Then she was lifted, tossed and turned by her boys. She danced; she sang gloriously for her supper. She was a wailing wanton in the guise of a child. She laughed that bubbling, abandoned laugh. She adored us for our affection that she could not — would not — ever get enough of. When she sat, tiny and wet-eyed, upon the apron, her lovely legs dangling from her damp white robe, to finish with "Somewhere Over the Rainbow," she transported every soul in the theatre back to innocence. Our thanks for the journey was thunderous.

When the Palace went dark for Christmas vacation, there was no excuse not to board the train for Baltimore and 617 West University Parkway. Mr. Bonus promised to reinstate me when I returned to Manhattan.

Twelve-year-old Ann was now scrawny-adorable in her Roland Park Country School uniform. She offset the covert gloom at home. My father had one collapsed lung from tuberculosis, an increased appetite for alcohol with a lower threshold for it, and a decreased tolerance for my stepmother, whom I always called "Mother." Mother attempted to cope with the knowledge that the occasional other woman distracted him. She tried to believe his indifference to her would diminish with his return to stronger health. Both knew Ann was the ballast that kept their marriage afloat. Mother's son Jimmy concentrated on rising to greater scholastic and athletic heights at my former Waterloo, St. Paul's School for Boys. All four were pleased to have me home — for a holiday visit. My brief stay shored up the creaky foundation of the unified family picture Mother struggled to present to Baltimore friends.

I need not have been fearful of my father's reaction to my extended travels or to my life in New York. He listened, he made allowances, and he began to withdraw. He was hopeful for my happiness and my future. The important conciliation he offered was in the form of moderate financial aid. This, after my gallop off to Europe for two summer months on his gift horse of one thousand dollars. I agreed to accept more loot on a temporary basis. I meant it when I said I would repay him one day. He let me know, without words of autocratic wisdom, that I was otherwise on my own. His new hands-off strategy nurtured old fears and bolstered my guilt. These were feelings he was well aware of—feelings he could no longer remedy—which began to distance our relationship.

When I was a child and looked woebegone over some transgression or slight, my father had snapped: "Get that hangdog look off your face!" When he implored me to return from Europe, he ended a letter I received in Paris by writing: "I'm afraid, however, that I'm wasting pen and paper, for you are hypersensitive to criticism and have been for many years."

He was correct. But why? Why, always? Should he have taken a belt strap to me regularly as a child? He knew he could not take such recourse when I returned from Europe. Perhaps he was wary. He did not want to reproduce that hangdog expression on the face of a youth who had learned to use it as a weapon. Were his feelings toward me subconsciously ambivalent because of his wife Carlyle's death when I was born? That tragic circumstance surely produced the hangdog look in the first place. My birth mother's death evoked instant consolation early on from every sympathetic elder—flurries of affection, too bewildering to last, to pleasure the only child. So much for open arms, except to search for others.

Along the alarming course of growing older, I continued to see what my father already knew: We were much alike. He could be quick to anger, thin-skinned too; weepy, possibly, when he drank, and just plain sad when he could no longer drink. His sense of humor and honorable nature did not always countermand his melancholia. This was the kid who had placed his father's unloaded revolver—in lieu of dropping a courtly pocket-handkerchief before a prospective partner—in the circle of alarmed little girls in dancing class; the adult who gave only to the panhandler who admitted he wanted the money to buy himself a drink. He managed to temper, through too many sessions in psychoanalysis, those and other traits that made him more interesting to me in the first place. What I call his flattening out was just beginning when I took my sabbatical from the Palace. For my father, laying off the sauce, years of analysis, and one more marriage were still to come. We laughed together. I rejoiced in his intellect and understanding, but his own changing needs were already paramount to everyone's, save Ann's.

The day after the 1952 New Year, Dad sent me a check for my twenty-first birthday. I celebrated my coming of age back at the Palace. I would not have had it any other way. Each night, tired, I would change out of my uniform, walk through Bryant Park, stop at a deli for a ham and cheddar on rye and a container of milk, and go home to my brownstone. Sometimes giddy, skinny Ben and the more serious, pockmarked Harry would ask me in to eat my sandwich in their room at the front of the building. They liked to gossip and to bitch about their ribbon-clerk jobs in the garment district, and they always wanted to get the nightly lowdown on my job at the Palace. I described every star Judy introduced from the stage—from June Allyson to ballerina Vera Zorina. No, Miss Garland had not been late, and her voice had been magnificent. Yes, she was still costumed in the same unbecoming dresses by Pierre Balmain and Irene Sharaff. No, Betty Hutton, the star they both adored, had not been in the audience.

We three shared the same bathroom in the middle of the hallway. When they had finished their long preparations for bed, I said good night to take my turn. I bought a swatch of fabric that Ben made into curtains for me on his sewing machine so I could cover the neighboring view of the adjacent brownstone's peeling trim and crumbling brick wall. Over my bed, in the small room I kept as immaculate as I had my boarding school cubicle at Christchurch, I hung a framed print of John Singer Sargent's charcoal sketch of John Barrymore — to anchor my course toward the acting profession.

In the mornings, I made the rounds of the casting offices carrying my first airbrushed glossy photographs. They key-lighted my large brown eyes under a pompadour of dark hair and backlit my high cheekbones. Ben and Harry thought, correctly, that they made my handsome face too "pretty." But I was thrilled by them. How many millions of headshots have been tossed into wastebaskets, I wonder? Other than one or two callbacks, my results were negligible. My face and veneer of youthful vigor were not enough to deliver the goods, especially without an Actors' Equity card. I should have had the guts to audition — again and again — for the Actors Studio, where I would have been made to do the groundwork to begin to learn my craft. Instead, afraid to compete, I yanked off my tie in resignation and dreamed of Hollywood, where agents, I naïvely thought, could be the foot soldiers.

The prospect of my Army physical, which had been transferred from the Fifth Regiment Armory in Baltimore to Local Board #6 at Madison Square Garden, was ten times more terrifying than making the audition rounds. At dawn on the dismaying day that I had to answer my summons, my clothing was clinging to me. I discarded everything, neatly folded, alongside a football field of other damp piles. When it was my turn to be interviewed, I talked of the barely discernible tuberculosis scar on my obligatory chest X-ray, emphasized a family history of that disease, mentioned my fluid-filled eardrums that had had to be punctured in childhood, and told of my very real sinus problems. Baring my buttocks to have a flashlight poked up my ass was almost as agitating as telling a nudnik psychiatrist that I was sexually attracted to men. My father had mailed me a letter from a family physician, Dr. Manfred Guttemacher, corroborating this fact, which was such a stigma in the 1950s. Turning the letter over to the draft board was up to me. I did. Eventually, I received in the mail a 1-Y draft deferment card, which I lost long ago and never had cause to show to anyone.

The only person who knew the truth of that day's admission and classification was my unflinching father, who would have been struck by the irony of a meeting I had some forty years after that draft physical with the other person who knew the truth about me. At a cocktail party, a Baltimore lady beckoned to her husband. Her married name had made me blanch. Over he came—my very first dalliance, the shrunken remnant of the Prince in *Snow White*. He had shown me the ropes, so to speak. He blinked at me through tortoiseshell frames. I thought of bolting to my sister's guest room and locking the door. Certainly he recalled me as a schoolmate, he told his wife. He smiled dully. I stood, rooted to the spot, staring, searching in vain for the Prince. He patted his sparse gray hair, fiddled with his regimental tie and a gold navy blazer button. His sorrowful eyes were polite. I wondered how old he was now—seventy-something? I prayed that I looked unchanged. That would have been something. We silently sipped our drinks while his wife extolled serendipity. My pulse gradually returned to normal. I wondered if he remembered—I never forgot.

Judy Garland's nineteen-week Palace engagement ended on February 24. The spit-and-polish demeanor of the ushers belied our turmoil at her closing; our bright eyes masked the melancholy awareness that she would no longer be singing for us. We flexed our white-gloved hands to applaud her into the stratosphere for the final time. She sang encore after encore, begging us to let her go. She was stunned with love and reciprocated the emotion with jubilant sobs. When we stood collectively to sing "Auld Lang Syne" to her, all dams burst, and her ushers crumpled into tears.

Coat-hanger-thin Turner, my first acquaintance at the Palace, had been the theatre's janitor from headliners Bojangles Robinson through the soft-shoe team of Buck and Bubbles. He circulated through the Garland closing night party, sweeping up cigarette butts and discarded cocktail napkins into his long handled, copper-lidded dustpan. We were gathered in the large marble-walled foyer that stretched between the rest rooms beneath the lobby. Turner—did I care then about any black man's last name?—sniffled and muttered to himself and any guest who would listen, "They ain't been nothin' like her; nobody, anytime, like that lady!" Composer Hugh Martin, whose obsessive health-food dependency and hypochondriacal nature were less well known than his "Meet Me in St. Louis" songs, was a delicate white counterpart of Turner. At the party, the two men threw their fragile arms around one another and smiled toothy, matching grins.

Hugh was Miss Garland's piano accompanist. He had been kind to this Garland devotee when we met, and the devoted Hugh was probably the single partygoer actually celebrating his star's last stand. His soft-spoken sensibilities were not always the match for Judy Garland's volatility. Judy, as I would later learn, could indulge in hyperbole as well. Once during my tenure at the Palace, she had been more than overly medicated and could not complete one performance. Hugh had helped her into the wings. Years later, she reported to her fan club magazine that I had taken my job as an usher to be "closer to her" and that I had "bonked" patrons over the head with my flashlight for yelling that she was drunk. And that I had been fired. She added that she had collapsed from one too many sodium pentothal shots for "heart palpitations." The truth is that Mr. Bonus did not fire me and I merely threatened the patrons with the flashlight. I told them to shut up or leave the theatre. And Lord knows what really was in Judy's system.

The bar was set up outside the usher locker room, where we had hurried to change into our street clothes. There was no need to rush. We drank champagne (domestic, alas), chatted with Turner and Hugh, gawked at the waiting celebrities, and felt more sentimental than when the great gold curtain had rung down upstairs, when, finally, after more than an hour, Judy Garland entered on the arm of her producer-fiancé, Sid Luft.

Still unaccountably wearing her orange stage makeup and dressed in a black bolero jacket outfit, Judy acknowledged the room's applause by throwing her head back and laughing and blowing kisses with her left hand. We all revolved around her, and, though a few guests paid their respects and departed, most of us lingered, circling to get a closer look. Spotting Hugh, she started to move toward him when Turner crossed her path to say goodbye. She hugged him; he dropped his sweeper and went to pieces. "Oh, darling, darling," she said as she hugged the old man, "I'll be back." "You promise?" choked Turner, tears streaming down his face. She did promise, then turned to stroke Hugh's thin, sallow cheek. And, because he was a well brought up young man from Alabama, he introduced her to me.

"It's been such a pleasure, Miss Garland," I managed, a boa constrictor at my throat. "We'll miss you so much." Usherette Kathy Nolan, who aspired to a singing and acting career of her own and emulated Ethel Merman, boomed over my shoulder, "You're Miss Show Business, Judy! A legend!" But Judy, pretending she did not hear her, kept her eyes on mine. She thanked me, gently brushed back my hair, and kissed me on the cheek. When I finally got home that night, I woke Ben and Harry to tell them about actually meeting Judy Garland. They were bug-eyed, and so was I.

Feeling aimless and almost bereft after Judy's run ended, I nonetheless stayed on at the Palace through the March and April weeks that other headliners such as opera star Lauritz Melchior, comedian Ben Blue, flamenco dancer Jose Greco, and the comedy team of Olsen and Johnson took her place. Their acts were old and stale, and the atmosphere was no longer charged. I spent most of my time standing outside on Broadway, wearing a fancy cape and an operetta hat, offering programs to the thinning crowds still willing to pay to get in. In the noisy classroom of Times Square, I learned how to raise and project my voice.

Singer Johnnie Ray walked by one night while I was bellowing show times. He looked about thirteen and walked like a sightseeing bumpkin dazed by his new stardom. This remembrance is recorded because of our later friendship during his Ciro's days in Los Angeles, because of his sweetness and the tragic shortness of his fame, which dazed him all the more. His funeral, like Judy's, would be like the old days: SRO. He adjusted his hearing aid as I watched him disappear at Forty-seventh Street into greater fanfare, misfortune, and ignominy.

CHAPTER TWO

BALTIMORE BOYHOOD

MY MOTHER CARLYLE'S hazel eyes follow me in my West Holly-wood living room. Her dark brown hair is drawn back in the androg-ynous style of the '30s. One shoulder is highlighted beneath a deep blue Spanish shawl. A long strand of pearls trails from her patrician neck, entwined in the hand resting in her lap. Behind her are rus-sets and ambers and a muted Boone family coat of arms. The portrait's frame is rococo and elegant, the way frames used to be. Her delicate mouth conveys the youthful hint of snobbery that would squirm to manifest itself in me. Hers is a look of complacent certainty that the world would be her oyster. She was, in the shrugged-off words of my Aunt Camilla, "a perfect beauty, and that's all there was to it." I was named after her. Her maiden name was Carlyle Fairfax Boone; I was christened Carlyle Fairfax Posey. Can you imagine?

There was no limit to my father's grief when his wife, sick with rheumatic fever, hemorrhaged and died one hour after my birth. She was twenty-five. I was delivered at 2:29 A.M. on January 5, 1931. And she was dead long before sunrise.

My father, Charles Rowland Posey, Jr., was a twenty-two-year-old law student whose privileged world would be profoundly troubled following my birth. His life would be marked by three more marriages, alcohol, and a basic disinclination toward anything other than writing unproduced plays and listening to Dixieland jazz. Tuberculosis and his strained efforts to be a too-loving and overly permissive father would also take their toll. He fostered my aversion to abject affection. On my early birthdays, his maudlin yearnings for his dead wife prompted my own lifelong struggle not to cry too easily. I have not yet cried for my mother, nor have I harbored guilt for her death. I have fantasized about her, searched as my father did for her substitute, and, because she did not live to reveal her imperfections, I have probably held her in higher esteem than I should have.

Aunt Camilla wrote on the back of a surviving snapshot of her sister: "In one of Carlyle's eyes there was a brown spot which left when she was pregnant. We wondered if it would come back. You know—it still hurts." Her beauty in her portrait always turned my head. That accidental hereditary attribute has enabled a whole parade of people to possess my attention for too long a time. Good looks are a weapon I was allowed to wield for the forty-odd years I resembled my mother. After that, the tables turned and I began to look more like my father, who was handsome in his youth, distinguished in middle age, and gaunt with illness in later life. I have kept my hair; Dad was balding by his late twenties. My characteristic preoccupation with appearance continues, but vanity hangs by a thread.

Mine was a spoiled security destined to be blown out of the water with the infringement of stepmothers, a stepbrother, and interfering relatives. I remember long drives through the Maryland countryside with dear Mum, my father's imperious mother, who once asked me: "Who loves you the most?" "You!" I replied, snuggled against her in the back seat. We rode to Druid Ridge Cemetery where Carlyle and my Grandfather Posey were buried. Dalcour, her chauffeur, helped me feed the swans on the cemetery lake. Mum was my great-grandfather Brigadier General Winfield Scott Featherston's only daughter Eloise from Holly Springs, Mississippi. She had closely waved, marcelled white hair and my father's hawkish nose, and she looked like what she was: a high priestess of the Daughters of the American Revolution. Her large, indecipherable handwriting—in weekly letters from Baltimore to wherever I was—might have been Queen Victoria's.

I also remember audiences with my maternal Grandmother Boone on the long wooden porch at Oak Hill, the house Grandfather Boone had built of stone on seemingly endless grounds. Grandmother Boone was an august vision of grays and whites seated in an imposing, high-backed wicker chair. When I was handed to her, she would squint her pale blue eyes and murmur gratefully that I had Carlyle's large brown ones. Her sight was dimming, and she died in my unclear early years. I cannot remember my Grandfather Boone, who, as my Uncle Herbert would say, "went off to the races" before his wife. But his Oak Hill was a grand haven with its cavernous entrance hall and a fireplace in every tapestry-laden, high-ceilinged room. I was fascinated by the dumbwaiter that went down to the good-smelling kitchen. In the basement kitchen, ample, black-haired Marie, a first cherished servant, treated Cousin Gordon and me to her homemade raisin hot-cross buns with glasses of cold fresh milk. When Marie was killed in a car accident, she kindled my earliest awareness that someone I knew could be irrevocably lost.

At Mum's table, my father remonstrated that I was his domain, damn it, when stern Colonel Dale, Mum's second husband, attempted to make me sit up straight. Colonel Dale was the late Charles Rowland Posey, Sr.'s successor. Grandfather Posey was an insurance executive who died before I was born. My father, who was about to be classified 4-F in World War II, tolerated the Colonel for Mum's sake. Whether or not Colonel Dale approved, permissive Mum, assisted by her doting maid Louise, gave me elaborate birthday parties. At these affairs she had clowns that made me laugh and other children and puppet shows that bored me.

Estelle Bolling materialized, as if by *black* magic, on my father's arm when I was three. A former dress model from Montreal, my father's new wife was a handsome woman with upswept, prematurely gray hair and a schizophrenic personality. Her large green eyes were by turn cool or adoring. She was, in her bizarre manner, scary to me then, a tantalizing mystery later. It is a puzzle that my second mother was the first woman to exemplify my penchant for the mercurial and forceful woman.

I no longer had my lonely father to myself. Did his marriage to Estelle teach me to resent and even dismiss that person who no longer held me at the center of his attention? Their chaotic six-year union was surely my first tutorial in the necessary art of self-preservation. I did not know what to expect from Estelle, and I reacted accordingly. I giggled and sighed when she tickled and kissed me to sleep. I screamed with pain and hatred when she "accidentally" sat me on a red-hot stove. I learned the power of sulky silence after she punished me for some infraction by plunging my head into a tub of cold water.

She told me a bedtime story about her being alone in a twilit barn as a young girl. A bat zoomed at her out of the dusk and sent her into such a frenzy that its moist, sticky body got tangled in her hair. She swore the revolting tale was true and that the bat had to be cut out of her hair. With pleasure I pictured her bald.

There was a day at Maryland's Eastern Shore with "Daddy," as I called him then, and Estelle, broad-shouldered and striking in a black one-piece bathing suit. I stuck my tongue into my sand bucket to torment a turtle I'd found on the beach. The small creature clamped down. I ran in hysteria to my elders with the turtle dangling from my mouth. Daddy bellowed for a doctor; Estelle calmly rushed me to the water's edge. This time she forced me face first into the cold of the ocean. My bleeding tongue was freed, but I am still leery of turtles. And stepmothers.

Once I startled her while she was dressing for a dinner party. I poked my head into her bathroom and hollered "Boo!" Instead of the reaction of laughter I expected, a half-dressed madwoman confronted me. She turned me upside down upon the tile floor. I was sped to the hospital to get stitches in my gashed-open scalp, which left a scar where no hair ever grew again. At least I had the consolation of having ruined her evening. My enraged, fledgling lawyer father took to his highballs after such scenes. He did the same during contretemps with his wife that had nothing to do with me. I know their quarrels were dramatic to eavesdrop on, and I always prayed for my father to win. The battles were loud and monstrous—glasses broke and furniture smashed behind their closed door. A lexicon of filth and profanity seeped forever into my vocabulary.

Mum looked down her aristocratic nose at Estelle. When she was able to rescue me from the Posey apartment, Mum was my clucking, probing ally, whether over delicious chicken croquette lunches at the Women's Exchange downtown on Baltimore's Charles Street, or during brief summer trips she managed to take me on to Rye Beach, New Hampshire.

She put a stop to my playing in a Rye Beach barn after I climbed into the loft to dive into the hay and promptly tumbled down the stack's slippery surface to the earthen floor below. I landed beside a pitchfork that lay—tines up—three inches from my head. The wind was knocked out of me. A farmhand carried me to the old country inn where we were staying. Mum's thin, penciled eyebrows rose toward her hairline. She turned paler than the white powder she wore. She never told my father that her grandson had narrowly missed being an early contender for brain surgery, at best.

My mother's intimidating family did not care for Estelle either. Perhaps they thought that because she had been a model, she was common, or that Carlyle was irreplaceable. An everlasting schism developed between my liberal father and the haughty James R. Herbert Boone, Carlyle's older, elitist brother. He looked at Estelle the way I wanted to—as though she were a bug.

Uncle Herbert had inherited Oak Hill House from my grandparents. He presided there in lordly fashion, courtesy of his fortuitous

marriage to Muriel Wurts-Dundas, heiress to the Lippincott publishing fortune. The couple also had a home on Oahu and twenty-
two rooms at 765 Park Avenue. Sweet Aunt Muriel, childlike and
overweight, served me tea on the new flagstone terrace that had
replaced Grandfather Boone's old wooden porch and ivy-covered
columns. I enjoyed scattering Uncle Herbert's peacocks from the
terrace onto the lawn and wished that I could visit more often. My
androgynous uncle—his rich taste and elegant lifestyle—awed me.
My vague desire to emulate his English cape-wearing ways began
to foment. My father sensed this and would have none of it. His
former brother-in-law was a snobbish Anglophile whom he had
not much cared for during his marriage to Carlyle. The poseur and
the dilettante were anathema to my father, who denigrated Herbert's pretensions to Estelle and to me—and, when too fueled with
alcohol, to his tight-lipped subject's face as well. My father found
particularly hilarious the legend of Aunt Camilla (who had just
departed Oak Hill's rarefied confines for what she hoped would be
the headier constraints of marriage) having stuffed her snotty
teenaged brother into the Oak Hill dumbwaiter and leaving him
between floors. A butler discovered him after some minutes and
lowered Herbert into the kitchen to set him free. My father badg-
ered the adult Herbert about everything. He saw Herbert as a
pompous, politically uncaring snob who had never done a day's
work, and a man who had never had sex with his wife. Finally, Herbert—his mournful, maidenly eyes affronted by the truth—
banished Dad from Oak Hill. There went my exposure to the
Boone grandeur throughout my formative years. All was not lost,
however; Uncle Herbert was more than kind to me on later visits
with a different stepmother.

Dad did not tell me until after the fact that Aunt Muriel had been
committed in 1944 to an asylum on her native English soil. In Dad's
opinion, the infantile Muriel was mentally impaired because she
truly adored an asexual opportunist. However, she too would welcome me again to Oak Hill in the days before her death in 1970.

• • •

Dad taught me to ride, *de rigueur* then for the establishment young Marylander. How proud he was when I unexpectedly made my first jump. My horse simply leaped over a hurdle in pursuit of his; he was patient when the process was not repeated. I did like to gallop. The fast gait was easier on my spinal column than trotting. An easy canter through the crackling woods together was a pleasure too.

We found privacy from Estelle behind the closed door of Dad's den. My father got tight and jolly while we listened to his substantial record collection. Bix Beiderbecke's "Sister Kate" featuring Louis "Satchmo" Armstrong stood out in the Dixieland racket, but I preferred two favorites that Dad sang loudly off-key while they played on his Victrola: "As Time Goes By" and "Night and Day." His resounding vocal accompaniment to "There's Gonna Be a Great Day" generated even more cacophonous emotion.

A hamstrung actor at heart, my father gazed drunk and somber into space when he listened to old recordings of John Barrymore's Shakespearean soliloquies. My Grandfather Posey had sneered down through his pince-nez at his son's theatrical hunger. My more lenient father instilled his love of the theatre in me. He took me to plays and musicals at Baltimore's Ford Theatre. He made me a disciple of Eugene O'Neill's for the duration of my adolescent years—until the slightly less mournful, more easily understood pipe dreams of Tennessee Williams superseded. I sat on the floor of his den to pore over his bulging *Playbill* collection. I store my own programs in sequence and rate them on a score of one to ten exactly the way my father did. But instead of Barrymore, I stare toward the past, stoned on Frances Gumm recordings.

Ill health can drive the final wedge into an eroding relationship. I neither knew nor cared what caused the basic conflict between Estelle and my father, but their marriage was over by the time I was eight. Save for a single incident in my early twenties, Estelle seemed to vanish from my life as abruptly as she had entered into it. For most of her last two years as Mrs. Posey, Estelle was confined to Saranac

Sanitarium in upstate New York's Adirondacks to recuperate from tuberculosis. TB, a fearful disease in those days, blessedly kept her from me for fear of contamination. The malady would continue to influence the circumstances of my boyhood. Estelle had dieted to model high fashion at Bergdorf-Goodman in New York, and her system had weakened by the time she met my father. But her health would be sufficiently robust again for her subsequent marriage — to her doctor at Saranac.

The last time I saw her was years later at St. Thomas's Church in Manhattan. I attended a Sunday service with Aunt Camilla. Mischievous Camilla was flabbergasted that Estelle and her doctor-husband were parishioners. I strained over my prayer book to glimpse her handsome profile across the aisle. She turned. I believe I smiled. My second mother spotted me with the wary eye of a jaguar and looked back at the pulpit. There was no sign of her when the congregation dispersed. I was crestfallen. Estelle's good looks were intact, and I had wanted to show off my own.

Life was less placid after my enrollment at Gilman School, one of Baltimore's more venerable and strict institutions. Daily discipline was an unendurable shock to a child accustomed to getting what he wanted by widening his eyes and looking baleful. The ploy had no effect at Gillman. I did poorly in nearly every subject. Math, like deciphering hieroglyphics, mined real fear. Without a calculator, I remained knuckleheaded on its basic intricacies. I cheated on term exams by surreptitiously copying the figures from another boy's notebook — and barely completed the course. English, history, and reading — especially aloud — were my burgeoning interests. Storytelling in any form calmed and enlarged my imagination, setting me forth on endless flights of fancy.

Instead of completing my homework, I preferred to moon over my movie-star clippings of Lux Beauty Soap ads. Constance Bennett was an early preference. I believed all the perfect ladies of the cinema were celestial beings. Estelle's ferocity and Mum's and my father's protective indulgence had produced a thin-skinned, devious, and daydreaming child.

Old films are the signposts of my growing up. Many are more vivid to me than actual happenings. My first eye-popping respite from reality was *Snow White and the Seven Dwarfs* in 1938. Frances Kefauver Grieves provided reassurance from the terror of Snow White being alone in the forest and the Wicked Queen's incarnation in Estelle. She took me and her athletic son Jimmy to see the film. Snow White's wicked stepmother prompted me to wrap a blanket around my head and under my chin to croak "Who is the fairest of them all?" to my bedroom mirror. The only laughter Jimmy and I ever shared was over Dopey's soap-bubble struggles.

Frances Grieves was a chestnut-haired widow whom my father called Fanny and began to see on a more and more regular basis. She lived in the same apartment building we had moved into in Roland Park. She was a native Baltimorean with the prettiest smile I had ever seen. Her son and her Irish setter Jerry were the objects of her devotion. Jerry was lovable. He hid under Mrs. Grieves's four-poster bed during thunderstorms. Jimmy was blond with a crew cut, one year younger and six inches shorter than me. His bankrupt father had slipped from the stern of a boat and drowned during the Depression. Mrs. Grieves's older son was confined to a home in the country; she visited him every Saturday. She explained that a nurse had dropped him as an infant. There would be times when I would wish that it had been Jimmy who had landed on his head.

Mum's abiding affection helped me keep unhappy, going-under-again feelings at bay when Mrs. Grieves became the third Mrs. Posey on July 17, 1939. They were married in a chapel in Washington, D.C. My new stepbrother and I were not invited. Mum, being the proper gentlewoman, smothered me with kisses and kept her mouth shut.

Jimmy and I were packed off to Mrs. Bennett's Summer Camp while our parents honeymooned on Lake Louise in Canada. The boys' camp was Mrs. Bennett's converted farm in the Western Mountains of Maryland's Carroll County. Mrs. Bennett was a firm, weathered woman who welcomed stoic Jimmy and anxious me with wrinkled smiles and assigned the two of us to, thankfully, separate cabins. They were built among dogwood, birch, and oak trees whose dappled shadows poured through the screened windows that had frames propped open with stakes to allow bird and nature noises to awaken us before the camp bell clanged at dawn.

I shivered as I made up my cot, performed icy ablutions in a communal facility nearby, and then tore into an abundant breakfast prepared by Mrs. Bennett herself in the central farmhouse. I nodded a remote good morning to Jimmy and began a day warmed by the sun and filled with farm chores, hiking, swimming, and boating on a nearby lake. On my after-lunch assignment, I learned to mimic the grunting of a pig. Feeding the hogs required me to dump the contents of a heavy slop bucket over a fence into their empty trough. Their oinking clamor was never louder than on the afternoon I landed bottom-sideways in their garbage-filled midst. I shot up and back over the fence, smelly and embarrassed. Some other kids had seen my Humpty Dumpty act, and their laughs were contagious. They led me to a back-porch shower to clean up. Clumsy Posey, but now at least one of the boys.

My life has been populated with cats, nine in particular—and you will meet them all. My first anguish concerning the animal I have often loved more than people—we have selfishness in common—occurred at Mrs. Bennett's. It is as upsetting in retrospect as it was sixty years ago.

Number One was a maimed, nearly lifeless mouse-colored kitten with dust-encrusted closed eyes. I retrieved it along the dirt road that led to the camp. Its fur was matted. Its nose felt as hot as a pilot light. Mrs. Bennett thought the kitten had been battered by another farm animal, or even a car. She showed me how to gently swab out its eyes with a piece of cotton warmed under the tap. Together we bathed it thoroughly with damp towels. Mrs. Bennett provided me with heated milk and a shoebox to place the creature in to take it back to my cabin. When I lined the box with a sweater, I was certain it started to purr in response to my ministrations. The milk went untouched. So I returned after dinner with an eyedropper and sat down to dribble the liquid drop by drop onto the small pink tongue. There was a bit of tired swallowing.

I went to bed that cool night lying with one hand hanging beside my cot to caress the kitten. Mum had trained me to say bedtime prayers, generally recitations to God asking Him to bless everyone I came in contact with, including myself—I still mutter them when I need a favor. That long-ago night, I prayed fervently with all the innocence that was mine as a child for the kitten to please, please get well.

I awoke with the morning's first light. I looked down and saw that the kitten lay frozen in the same position as the night before. A summer fly buzzed on the kitten's slitted lids. I touched the little body. It was marble hard and colder than any morning chill. At breakfast, my tears instilled an aggregate silence. Afterward, the other boys looked on respectfully while Mrs. Bennett helped me bury my first cat casualty in its cardboard shoebox in the ground at the edge of the woods.

CHAPTER THREE

SINNER AT ST. PAUL'S

617 WEST UNIVERSITY PARKWAY was intolerable, from the day Jimmy and I arrived at the close of Mrs. Bennett's summer camp until I finagled my escape. The first house I had ever lived in was, like the traditional others along the fence-enclosed block, ivy-covered red brick with white trim, dark green shutters, and a slate roof. A cherry tree stood in the back yard at the top of the slope that led to the garage. Japanese beetles ate the cherries before I could. Jerry, 617's one untroubled occupant, would skid and slide down the graceful stairway when Dad collared him to take him out to pee. On the second floor there was a new den for the Dixieland jazz collection, a large master bedroom for Frances Grieves's four-poster bed, and an empty, sunny room for my sister Ann, who, praise be, was on her way. Off the top landing in our very own enemy camp—the third-floor bedroom—there were two armchairs, separate desks and waste-baskets, two bureaus, and twin beds beneath dormer windows for Jimmy and me.

We shared the third-floor bathroom too. For that, I resented "Mother," which is what my father requested me to call his new wife. She allocated the second bedroom on the third floor for storage. When Jimmy was absent, I opened her storeroom door to peek, confused and questioning, at Carlyle's portrait amongst the clutter, and wished the room were mine. My rancor toward my new stepmother festered through my addled little manhood. It was much later, when I finally did think of Frances Posey with great affection as my mother, that I came to realize that her own new position could not have been easy either.

Mother drove her mismatched roommates downtown in our spiffy black 1939 Ford convertible with its running boards and rumble seat. We went to the plush Loews Century Theatre, Baltimore's finest purveyor of Metro-Goldwyn-Mayer films. There I was brain-damaged for the first of countless times by *The Wizard of Oz*.

Dorothy's desire to fly over the rainbow to a place of perfection and to escape from troubles struck an instant chord. Although relieved for Dorothy's safety back in Kansas, I felt that happiness in your own back yard was flat-out baloney—then. The easy-to-grasp lyrics and lovely music were instant enchantment, the Cowardly Lion made me quiver with laughter, and the flying monkeys scared me down into my seat like a contracting bug. I yelped in pain, then relief when the Wicked Witch finally melted and went down in an astonishing puff of smoke.

I did not want Dorothy to go home to Kansas! When she had to say goodbye to her Land of Oz companions, I felt that I would explode with sorrow. I would have climbed through the screen to comfort her for the rest of her days. I fell agonizingly in love with Dorothy that afternoon. She sang in a voice I had never imagined the likes of. There had never been a sound as lovely as her laughter. Dorothy made me want to grow up with her. I wanted to join her somehow, to put my arms around her and try to give her back some of the happiness she had given me.

And, ultimately, I did. Judy Garland gave me much more pleasure, and pain, before and after I became her friend and, yes, lover. Neither of us would be red-hot successful in the growing-up department. She remained Dorothy—sometimes in spite of herself, in the ugliest and sweetest of our moments—the very first object of my total, unswerving, absolute affection.

The late '30s and early '40s were invigorating times to arrest development in womb-like picture palaces. Neither Hollywood nor I knew that its collective output would be downhill ever after, or that the chimera of that era's celluloid would ensnare me in an ever-tightening grip. Jimmy could not comprehend the new obsession that began to play havoc with my school and home life. I was disdainful of what he enjoyed: the dreary Westerns we were sometimes sent off to sit through. My preferences, black and white or in Technicolor, were lush love stories from MGM. When I rode home on the bus with my head buried in *Modern Screen*, Jimmy got so embarrassed that he angrily changed seats to get away from me.

Mother and Dad and Mum and Colonel Dale took the two of us to the Baltimore premiere of *Gone With the Wind*. The Century again, where the usherettes, like Mum, wore crinoline and hoop skirts and all the audience dressed formally. The Civil War captured my step-brother's attention. Scarlett and Rhett fueled my own romanticism. They still do. I began to dream of being a movie star. Not an actor, mind you, but a splendid, shining movie star—with his name swept on the screen by the music and looming above the title. My favorite reading matter was *Photoplay*. My destination was MGM.

Before his tolerance for lousy report cards turned apoplectic, Dad yanked me out of Gilman and enrolled me at the less formal St. Paul's School for Boys. In the beginning, I studied with fresh determination to please my Lower School headmaster Donald Pierpont. Mr. Pierpont was that first awakening teacher remembered by every fortunate student. He taught English and history with vivid imagery and an urbane acting ability. Amongst brocaded pillows in his theatrical living quarters hung with tapestries lighted by candles, he conducted popular tutorials. He had a crinkly birthmark beside one of his vulnerable smiling eyes. When he left St. Paul's at the end of my second year for Choate, many boys, including myself, felt adrift at the loss of a mentor. He was homosexual. Not that we knew it then, but Mr. Pierpont and I kept in touch. We had warm, stimulating talks over long lunches at the Hotel Bel-Air when he visited Los Angeles in the late '50s. He was still the perceptive sage.

A lady teacher came up with the idea that those of us embroiled in the study of fourteenth-century Egypt's customs and artifacts should take part in a grand panoply of the ancient era in the St. Paul's gymnasium. Furious preparations began: the copying and cutting of costumes, the dyeing and painting of donated bed sheets and curtains to be worn or arrayed around the makeshift stage, a raised platform with a fake throne we built and painted bright red to place dead center. Roles were rehearsed, and I grew nauseous with nerves as the day to perform approached—a feathery sick feeling I knew often and never managed to conquer. Our director lathered me with eye makeup before the performance. Someone placed an elaborate cardboard headdress upon my sweating brow. I staggered forth in the dark—weighted down by my multicolored costume—to take my place upon the throne. I sat petrified, heavy lids over eyes staring straight ahead, two shaking scepters clutched, crossed over my chest, numbed by the sound of rustling parents on the other side of the bed sheets. The sheets parted, and I made my stage debut—as Queen Nefertiti.

I liked giving orders to my boy handmaidens and enjoyed my place at center stage. The rousing applause after we finished was the most amazing aphrodisiac of all. Mother, Dad, and Jimmy were out front waiting to drive me home. Dad, eager to point my way toward more substantive theatrical goals, laughed and congratulated me after I changed. Jimmy glowered. Mother commented, "My, you looked just like Merle Oberon!"

My friendship at St. Paul's with Terry Willmott was based on our mutual movie addiction. Terry wore glasses, practiced perfect print handwriting, and sketched broad-shouldered dress designs one after another, intended for Ginger Rogers. Neither of us was interested in intramurals—the afternoon sports program Jimmy took to, seconds after his enrollment in a lower class than mine at St. Paul's. Terry introduced me to his way of sitting off the demerits that one was penalized with for not being sports-minded. When the Saturday studyhall teacher wasn't looking, we sat filling black composition books with the names of movie stars, above a list of their vehicles. Terry knew many more titles and performers than I did. We had no other affinities and went our separate ways in all other areas.

My other St. Paul's friendship unveiled for me feelings that were second nature and stupefying. Handsome Brent was a cocksure senior who caught my eye and sometimes held it when he monitored the Lower School study hall. I was flustered, and aroused, by this unexpected contact. The game of his discovering my glances at him was thrilling. I watched him surreptitiously at his basketball practice too. I thought I admired his chunky legs because mine were skinny. He did look like the square-jawed Prince in Snow White—only better. He was hot-blooded and human. Sandy blond, he strode around on campus in his tight blue school sweater bearing the gold St. Paul's varsity emblem. I wore the same kind of hooded sweatshirt he wore during halftime at lacrosse games. I watched him from the sidelines and imagined my shirt against his skin. In my bed at home, I pictured him running in place in shorts to keep warm, his breath on the air like a signal.

One fall afternoon, my feet made crunchy potato chip noises in the fallen leaves on the St. Paul's driveway as I purposefully walked slowly to the bus stop. I knew to the second what time the Prince, the privileged senior, would drive his own car along the same orange-red, leafy route. I walked alone, the corner of my eye on the shadow of every passing car. Dramas rooted and spread like weeds in my head, underscored by the trademark lusciousness of MGM violins.

One car slowed in the darkening sun. It stopped as I had willed it to. I opened the door and got in. The Prince tossed my books and empty lunch box onto the back seat. We drove in silence through the

countryside. I was ramrod alert, but aloof with shyness. He turned
suddenly off the highway, into an area of remote Maryland homes
not far from the secluded acreage of Oak Hill. He veered the car
again, down an isolated dirt road familiar to him from adventurous
dates with tipsy debutantes after a few cotillions. We entered a cul-
de-sac concealed by the forest. The car coasted quietly to a stop like
a bear going into its cave. The Prince finished his cigarette and rolled
the windows down to admit a sliver of wintry air. He caressed the
back of my head with one hand and rummaged in his bulging crotch
with the other. I then had my first sexual encounter with anyone,
male or female—guiding and leisurely on the Prince's part, like a
dam bursting and heart-stopping on mine.

He helped me clean up. He stuffed the towel we used back under
the front seat. Then he drove me to within a block of 617 West University Parkway. On the way, there was banter about whether or not
St. Paul's would be the victor in an upcoming game. Was it basketball or lacrosse? Who knew? Who cared? He would play like the
Prince. He smoked some more and confided what I already knew: As
a varsity squad member, he was not supposed to indulge. He asked
me not to tell anyone. He was loose and jovial. I pretended a relaxed
goodbye when he cheerfully let me out of the car. For him, nothing
had really happened. For me, the cannonball event very slowly
receded into a small, immodest memory. After our encounter, the
Prince was pleasant—period—to the Lower School boy. He graduated that spring. Other than at the aforementioned cocktail party in
Baltimore fifty years later, I never saw Brent again.

Of course, I wanted to repeat the experience. Sometimes I tried to.
But no stranger could replace the Prince. After the Prince, the excitement of playing footsies in the marble stalls of the upstairs men's
room at the Enoch Pratt Free Library, of locker-room fumbling in the
downtown YMCA, of awkward balcony gropes during lucky forays to
the movies was offset, always, by the fear of being caught. I wondered
what the punishment would be. And the name of the crime. I pictured Dad waiting at home with a doctor, Jimmy in boxing gloves.

Being sent away would be all right. But where did they send people like me? To reform school? I misbehaved very, very cautiously. The years that would be dominated by diddling—and other stimulants—were far off.

I did have some adventures with Jimmy and other neighborhood kids playing "Tarzan." Jimmy was *always* Tarzan. He targeted me as an unsuspecting White Hunter. He sprang screaming a lousy Tarzan scream at the top of his lungs from the cherry tree branches—to wrestle me to the base of our backyard hill. To Jimmy's pawing pleasure, Marlene Hicks, a voluptuous teenaged neighbor, condescendingly became Jane—when she made herself available. Her younger brother Charlie, a skinny hellcat who hid giggling while his parents took turns shrieking for him to come home, played a pimply Boy. When he became bored with Jimmy's bossy star turn, Charlie ran off to masturbate in the bushes—sometimes with me. Marlene returned to more important pursuits indoors such as trying to decide how to wear her hair the next day. I was partial to the Hickses because their father owned a chain of movie theatres and drove a smart Lincoln Continental. Nice Mrs. Hicks tended toward flashy clothes and looked like Dorothy Lamour. Mother, more Mum-like than she knew, thought Mrs. Hicks looked "common," and "too old to wear shoulder-length hair." Mother favored an understated Duchess of Windsor approach to style, although she termed the Duchess "an ordinary woman with no real family background."

We had the occasion to assess the Windsors in person in October of 1941. Our family, agog like all of Baltimore, hung out the window overlooking Charles Street from the apartment of Mother's brother to watch the royal couple parade uptown in an open car with their police escort. "Hiya, Duchess!" my father howled. He drowned out the cheering sidewalk populace. Baltimore's own Wallis Warfield Windsor looked up smiling, right at him. Mother, mortified, vanished from the window. She regained her composure later in the day when we stood, thrilled, in a long line to greet the scandalous pair at

Baltimore Country Club. The blue-eyed, knife-like Duchess showed no sign of recognition when Dad bowed politely, the wan Duke opaque by her side.

Number Two: Snowball was my cat at 617. She looked exactly like her name, coped gracefully with canine Jerry, and sometimes caught mice in our cellar, where she was consigned overnight. She proudly deposited their remains at the top of the stairs outside the kitchen door, agitating Hazel, our day maid, and sickening Mother with her prowess. Snowball is a blur today, but blubbering on the floor of our locked garage at her sudden absence is not. My cat was gone. Vanished. By the time Dad took Mother to the hospital to have their baby, Snowball had been given away. My half-sister Ann Rutledge Posey was born on April 17, 1940. There was a fear of cats smothering infants by sitting on their faces for warmth; an old wives' tale then, and now too, in my opinion. Hence Snowball's departure and my heartbreak.

My spirits lifted one week later, the evening Dad drove up, opened the passenger door, and Ann, tiny in Mother's arms, did indeed arrive. Despite the hodgepodge of our genealogy—and the disappearance of my cat—she has been my real sister from that moment on, a felicitous constant, too, in all of our lives just when we needed one. She held our family's seething factions together far longer than they would have held without her. Jimmy and I would not be close again after uniting to welcome Ann. We had strewn the walkway, assisted by Marlene and Charlie Hicks, with green leaves, honeysuckle, and dogwood blossoms to usher her into her first home. Mother was radiant with her sleeping bundle. My father's eyes were brimming at our salutations.

He was resolute during Ann's infanthood and the first years of his third marriage to behave, to stay sober, to work hard at his new position, though he brooded over not enjoying his post as an assistant state's attorney. There were lapses, some depressing, usually on holidays. One Christmas Eve he came home drunk. Mother, Jimmy, and I, working quietly so as not to disturb Ann, had finished decorating the tree. Above our heads, my sleeping sister did not see the family Santa (Charlie Hicks had torpedoed that myth for Jimmy and me, with no disastrous results) lurch through the front door and head for the tree. Ranting with false sentimentality, Dad nearly toppled our handiwork onto the floor of the living room. Jimmy, with Mother's approval, brandished a baseball bat from the hall closet and prodded my father upstairs to bed. I found Jimmy's approach brutal but stifled my resentment like always and kept my mouth shut. Such scenes were not as unnerving as the tearful apologies that inevitably followed them.

In Mother's eyes, my father's drunken falls from grace were appalling. Sometimes, to me, they were appealing. Because when he was happy under the influence, he was theatrical, colorful, and expansive in his affection. Then his formidable intelligence heightened too much for Mother's. He became larger than life, larger than she was comfortable living with. She became less capable of granting forgiveness. I played both sides as best I could.

Back at St. Paul's, I began to sneak through a back hedge to avoid intramurals. I would take the bus to Pimlico or downtown Baltimore to lose my afternoons in the movies. My favorite destination was the Loews Valencia, built upstairs above the Century. It was ornate with Spanish grillwork. Its inky ceiling twinkled with hundreds of stars when the lights went down. The garish Hippodrome, already frayed, was another downtown hideaway. There I marveled at ancient and expert vaudeville acts between showings of less exalted films than those of MGM. *Rebecca* was a noteworthy exception. Struck by the loveliness of Joan Fontaine, I returned to see it a second time. I became possessed by the lady, a fanatic who saw her every film while amassing a collection of scrapbooks filled with any picture taken of her, cut carefully from a myriad of '40s movie magazines. Perhaps I meant it when I laid it on in a first fan letter: Her bewitching face and patrician persona were a substitute mother symbol. Yuck. Small wonder there was no reply. Later, our correspondence flourished, along with an uncertain relationship that must be interpreted further down the road. For my sake, not Joan's. She takes me in stride and is sometimes grateful for my tenacity.

The curious combination of Judy Garland and Joan Fontaine in particular, and the movie medium in general, became fetishistic. Mother dragged me away with Jimmy for the American history lesson in visits to Mount Vernon and Williamsburg. Dad tugged me off to stimulating matinees at Ford Theatre. On the scholastic front, his patient attempts — mostly, he was no whiz himself — to make sense of mathematics for me were unrewarded. Jimmy terrorized me. He tried to teach me to handle a lacrosse stick. Hollywood concoctions prevailed.

One night at dinner, my father's tolerance for my single-mindedness evaporated. We stepbrothers dressed in jacket and tie for this nightly ritual. We washed our hands before we came to the table and excused ourselves to go into the hallway if we had to blow our noses. Hazel served. Ann looked on from a highchair. We discussed one of my woeful report cards, or the war in Europe, which was no more real to me than the map of Europe stuck with colored pins in my father's den. I managed to change whatever the subject was by abruptly reciting the entire cast of *Boom Town*. My mind was on a publicity broadside I had memorized from *Photoplay*. After actress Marion Martin's name, my aggravated father snatched me from my chair. He hauled me three flights upstairs by the back of my shirt collar. My collection of *Photoplay* was stacked in monthly sequence on a low chest at the foot of my twin bed. Mint-condition Paul Hesse covers were destroyed as Dad tore apart as many magazines as possible, thrashing and cursing me at the same time, scattering the remnants of glossy falsehoods around the bedroom.

That night, miserable, I slouched over my homework. I turned in the silence to glare at Jimmy's stiff back at his own desk. His very presence quadrupled the restrictions of my punitive surroundings, made more unbearable by two wastebaskets filled with shredded *Photoplays* I had to take out to the trash. Later, in the dark, to get attention, I imitated what my father was beginning to go through every morning: an acute, ugly-sounding coughing attack. The shadow I expected of my father listening appeared, within minutes, beneath the bedroom door. The slap of his slippers grew faint going to the pantry on the first floor. He shortly returned up the stairs to sit beside me on my bed. Surely Jimmy listened, staring in contempt at the wall. My father cradled me with his arm to sit up. He offered me the shot glass half filled with oh-so-soothing bourbon. He kissed me good night and my sleep was imperturbable.

A sighting at the close of 1941 was a miracle. Jimmy and I went to Marconi's one night with Mother and Dad. Antique Marconi's, Baltimore's au courant restaurant still, was known the length of the East Coast for its impeccable food and drab decor. All parties, whether the Poseys or Mayor and Mrs. McClendon, were required to wait without reservations in its narrow hallway for the chic length of time the jammed clientele found necessary to finish its meal. We were led at last to a fine table next to the most preferable booths along a far wall. I beat the waiter to hold Mother's chair for her, the way Jimmy and I took turns doing at home. The proper young gentlemen had barely gotten seated when Dad, with controlled aplomb, stage-whispered, "Carlyle, don't stare, but look over there." I turned and dropped the napkin I was unfolding to put in my lap. My eyes popped like a hypnotized owl's. Clark Gable was holding Carole Lombard's hand in the booth beside me. The two talked quietly, eating their dinner barely four feet away. Her coloring was sunflower blond, red-lipped, and startling. She was extremely tanned, which Mother later ascribed to too much makeup. To me, with her striking features and figure set off by a simple black suit, she resembled some beautiful cartoon that had come to life. Her husband, minus his *Boom Town* stubble, dressed in gray flannel instead of ascot and velvet, was a paler, more jovial version of Rhett Butler.

I retrieved my napkin without upsetting my water glass, ordered Maryland crab cakes for dinner, and proceeded to eat without tasting them, paying no attention either to Mother and Dad's stricken-casual conversation I tried to indulge in. Only Jimmy brought off a blasé attitude by remaining silent. The Gables lingered, as intimate as columnist Louella Parsons said they were. I would have happily daw-dled, stuffing myself with more dessert, rather than leave the restau-rant before they did. But we did leave them there at Marconi's, the most wondrous establishment I had ever eaten in.

On January 16, 1942, Mother called to me from the bedroom bal-cony. She told me Carole Lombard had been killed in a plane crash returning from a war bond tour. When we saw the couple in Balti-more, Lombard had stopped off to visit Gable, who was undergoing a check-up at Johns Hopkins. Hearing of the terrible casualty smashed my youthful conviction that movie stars could not possibly die like everyone else.

Dad had to relinquish his attorney job in the spring of 1942 when he suffered his first bout with tuberculosis. Mother nursed him for the six months he was ill. Hazel prepared his dishes separately and took them to the second-floor landing. Mother carried them from there to the four-poster or out to the balcony covered with its new awning. There he spent many daytime hours pursuing inim-itability as a professional playwright, a Eugene O'Neill-induced pas-sion he longed to make more than an avocation. His best script, *The Hair of the Dog*, garnered interest from the William Morris Agency on the condition that he do some rewriting, an effort mother claimed he was incapable of completing. He wrote five plays in all. Their merit is unknown to me — damn it — because they have long been the property of his likewise unfamiliar fourth wife. He remained upstairs for four months before being allowed to join us in the evening for dinner.

Jimmy and I were left in Hazel's care while Mother and Dad took a trip to Atlantic City to celebrate his recovery in the fall of 1943. Mother was thirty-eight and still in love, but her feelings began to change when they came home. In Atlantic City he'd announced that he did not intend to return to law. He was going to be a playwright. His decision was irrevocable. Mother's doubts produced a hellish confrontation at the Marlborough Blenheim Hotel. When they returned to 617, the house was the setting for silences and sulking. In direct ratio to his getting stronger physically, my father began to drink heavily again. Under duress, he took a job he found negligible, as a publicity director at Peabody Conservatory. He worked under the auspices of autocratic conductor Reginald Stewart, whose imperial dealings reminded him of Uncle Herbert. The Peabody day allowed him time, over long liquid lunches at his club on Mount Vernon Place, to reflect on his beginning sessions in Freudian analysis. Grandfather Posey's inheritance, though insufficient in Mother's eyes, provided him further leeway for the pursuit of writing plays.

The schism between Mother and Dad was nothing compared to the friction between Jimmy and me. When our parents sought marital solace by going out to dinner on Saturday nights, Master Grieves gave me boxing lessons. Hazel, flattening the crisp pages of the *Baltimore Sun*, looked disapproving as I followed Jimmy through the pantry, out the back door, and up the back steps to the garage. I trudged behind him, intimidated by his and the world's dictum that the necessity to learn the manly art of self-defense was absolute. I did not know how to escape the bashings I received in the closed garage. Jimmy sent me flying bloodied over the concrete floor like an off-balance kangaroo. His grunting taunts took too long to unleash enough murderous rage within me to make me hit him back. When I finally did, thus earning a modicum of his respect, our fisticuffs slowed to a halt. Being Jimmy's punching bag in those boxing sessions filled me with scorn. They led me in later life to seek control in more subtle ways, and I have remained something of a physical coward.

"He'll kill you one day, Jimmy," commented Hazel one night when we returned to the house. She was an outspoken but inaccurate seer. I staggered to the third floor to clean up. I made certain my face had not been permanently mauled. My self-protective instincts and vanity were shaken for a long, self-conscious time when a front tooth cracked off at its center. The damage terminated the boxing for good and lost Jimmy a patsy. He should have paid the dental bills which continued until a California dentist capped my tooth successfully. He made my smile a budding screen star's again—after years of fearing that whatever wobbly correction had been done in Baltimore was about to fall out.

How cognizant were Mother and Dad of our Saturday night bouts? I must have been bruised and puffy on Sunday mornings. But I don't recall any battle-ceasing pronouncements until the broken-tooth incident made Jimmy hang up the gloves. Mother thought Jimmy had struck an accidental blow. Was theirs a tacit approval of my being led along an acceptable route to rugged manhood? Boy, were they wrong.

The time has come for me to make amends for my larcenous transgressions at St. Paul's. I began to support my moviegoing habit by stealing small change from wallets and pockets in the empty locker room beneath the gym. The other boys were at intramurals, where I should have been. Their exuberant noise reached me from the nearby athletic field. At the sound of the slightest creak on the gleaming wooden floor above me, I froze. But the stimulation of my furtive act was as exciting as an escape to see films. Depending on the amount I had stolen, I went on foot to Pimlico for the second-runs—and boarded the streetcar to ride downtown for new releases. I cringe anew not just at the thought of stealing. For the price of a ticket today, I would have been thrown out of St. Paul's a lot sooner. My arrival home was timed to coincide with the end of the school day—intramurals included.

My thievery was carefully calculated. It continued for a long period of stealthy afternoons. I was penalized five demerits for every intramural absence and obliged to return to St. Paul's to work off the accrued amount every Saturday. One sat emptyhanded at one's desk, staring straight ahead for thirty humdrum minutes per demerit. My demerits were posted on the St. Paul's bulletin board. Over many Chinese-torture Saturdays, I stayed on top of them. I cannot imagine what lies I told Mother and Dad about how I had accumulated them in the first place.

The accumulation got out of hand in the winter of 1945. I began to develop real or psychosomatic colds, sinus attacks, and full-blown flu that overcame me on weekends. I underwent radium treatments for my sinus troubles, listened to dire warnings regarding the future consequences of a deviated septum, and once on the back lawn lapsed into a pre-paralysis, twenty-four hour coma from symptoms of polio. I emerged ambulatory, however. I learned the nature of the power of sickness, of the worry and anxiety that my ailments provoked. They often legitimately precluded both intramural attendance and my working off my mounting demerits on Saturday.

Was I punishing myself? Yes. Did I want to be caught as a thief? No. Did I want to leave 617 West University Parkway with its now silent, drunken, or acrimonious evening meals that desperately? Absolutely. My house of detention was a dolorous residence whose occupants put on a happy face only for a little girl who ate early and went upstairs to bed.

Jimmy topped his sterling athletic exploits at St. Paul's by ratting on me at home. He announced that Carlyle was never seen at "sports practice." Students complained to headmaster George Hamilton that their wallets were being pilfered. My demerits skyrocketed toward fit-for-suspension status. The affable Mr. Hamilton and my parents began to travel in the same social orbit, which led to troubled questions and talk at clubby dinner parties about my distracted scholastic conduct, low grades, all those demerits, and my erratic absences.

The result was a gentle interrogation. Mr. Hamilton suspected that I was the culprit responsible for the stolen cash. With every ounce of large-eyed sincerity I could muster, I denied the charge in the privacy of his office. He was the wiser. Although I was never caught as a thief, his plan to take a more hard-nosed course concerning my outrageous demerit record began to take shape. He was a diplomat who had to wield his weapons wisely.

Meanwhile, Mum went into a decline following the death of Colonel Dale. The colonel, who died of a heart attack, was interred in Arlington National Cemetery with full military pomp and circumstance. Mum had looked on tearlessly. I wondered, as I studied the monuments and the countryside, whether she had been dry-eyed at Grandfather Posey's service as well. These days, she took too great pains, when Jimmy and I went to dine with her once a week, to mask the fact that her unstructured days lacked discipline. We were sent to alleviate her loneliness, and, surely, to give Mother and Dad more privacy to air their own troubles. We dutifully reported in a coat and tie to an increasingly disturbed Louise. Louise greeted us warmly at Mum's door. She led us softly toward the musty, antique-filled living room where we had to wait for longer and longer periods. Jimmy was sullen. The suspicion of what was happening made me embarrassed. Mum was my grandmother, after all. Her stately, weaving entrance with the scent of too much fragrance shrouding her long black dress did nothing to diminish my great love for her. I was more nervous than annoyed at her staring long pauses at the dinner table. Her frequent clutching grasps to hold my hand made me wary and alert, as when my father was drunk. For me, an inebriated female has been the more sorrowful ever since Mum. A strong whiff of brandy accompanied her kisses at the end of those melancholy evenings that Jimmy could not wait to get home and complain about.

My father, a fine one to talk, berated his idle mother on the telephone after such incidents. His angry voice reverberated through the house. He accused her of undoing her own good influence. She made matters worse by ridiculing his efforts to be a playwright— accusing him of jeopardizing his marriage and the welfare of his family. Conductor Reginald Stewart was a pillar of Baltimore, she said, and my father should concentrate on his job. He belittled her snobbishness and banged down the receiver.

I agonized over Mum's and Dad's quarrels and yearned for harmony between these two above all. I pondered the change in someone when robbed of companionship, whatever its merit. I vowed never to be totally dependent on another human being. How often trying to live up to that early, empty pledge would lead to exhausting ambivalence or grief!

"Carlyle, come down here at once!" My father's tone was enraged. I was heavy-footed as I obeyed. He had received the phone call I'd dreaded, from the headmaster.

"You've been going to the movies all week," Dad accused when I faced him. "Don't lie to me, goddamn it! Get in there and take your pants down." He threw me halfway across the master bedroom and shut the door. He brandished a shaving strap that hung beside his bureau while I struggled with my trousers. He had only thrashed me on two or three previous occasions—over being disrespectful to Mother. This time he lashed me harder and longer than he had ever brought himself to do before. He sent me red-assed and reeling, in less pain than hatred, back out of the room. Downstairs, I tried not to choke over Mother's breakfast, served in silence, before Dad hustled me into the Ford convertible for the drive to St. Paul's. He told me that I was on the verge of being expelled, that I was growing up to be a "congenital liar and something has to be done about this damn movie business." I moped the distance to my final Saturday in study hall, wishing that my father, like the Wicked Witch, would vanish in a puff of smoke.

My comeuppance came at a special student-body meeting called at the end of the winter semester. Mr. Hamilton, after the customary general announcements, addressed us sternly: "I do not like to single out one student, but one boy here is going to have to serve as a reminder to this student body that the rules set forth by this institution must damn well be obeyed. St. Paul's deserves its reputation for being one of the finest schools on the Eastern seaboard. I'm sorry to announce that, as of this moment, Carlyle Posey is expelled. At last count he was credited with two hundred and thirty demerits. In spite of the warnings of myself and other teachers, even of his parents—who had, until recently, been ignorant of the situation—discipline has eluded him, and so, now, are passing grades. He is one among a few of you who must learn the hard way what St. Paul's stands for. This meeting is adjourned."

I was embarrassed that every eye was on me, but the prick of abject humiliation escaped me. The first barrier on my road to freedom had been overcome. Off campus, my attitude was to hell with St. Paul's and everybody in it. I felt an overwhelming desire to quit stealing and relief that I had not been caught. To say that I was lucky is an understatement; I would have been beaten by someone other than Jimmy and for good reason. In the years that followed, I felt chagrin whenever I heard that judicious George Hamilton had proffered me his best regards.

Democratic Dad sent me to do penance and complete the school year at Roland Park Public School. The hurly-burly of mixing with all manner of colliding boys and girls in ugly corridors and tawdry classrooms made me dumber than I had been at St. Paul's. This brief, brought-to-earth episode did not come to mind again until I pitched chalk and profanities with an eclectic group of young actors testing for *Blackboard Jungle* at dear old MGM in 1955. It was not helpful to me then either. I was relieved to quit my streetcar ride to and from the Roland Park Public School hoi polloi at the beginning of summer.

Marlene and Charlie Hicks and Jimmy the Jock departed with their name-tagged clothes for their respective summer camps. I had the bedroom to myself, but my sorry state was awash in self-pity and loneliness. That lingering summer, Ann was my saving grace, but I must have driven her crazy. I lugged her down into the cellar where I had constructed a makeshift art studio—enclosed, for fancied privacy, on three sides by tall, unused shutters. Ann's periods of patience shortened each time she sat before my easel that had been a Christmas gift from Mother and Dad. I had a modest talent for capturing in oil or charcoal adult faces frozen on magazine covers. However Ann's very much alive unformed features, blue eyes, pale coloring, and incessantly silenced mouth provided trials for both of us.

She began to astonish me by forming her own opinions on everything from movie stars to life in general. She put a stop to my habit of brushing or rearranging her hair; she did not want to look like Judy Garland or Joan Fontaine and was not interested in hearing too much about them in the first place. So I tried to help her with her reading or spelling and began to know her. I became delighted with her stubbornness and relaxed some of my own. Those humid days and lightning-bug evenings of 1945 established our foundation for an enduring, no-matter-what affection.

My parents resolved that my salvation lay in boarding school. The decision to pack me off to Christchurch School for Boys in Virginia was less difficult for Mother than for my sentimental father. I wanted to burn my bridges elsewhere, and that brought him around. The Christchurch brochure featured a bell tower overlooking sailboats on the Rappahannock River, a headmaster's house that resembled Mount Vernon, and pictures of cubicles in a dormitory reminiscent of *Goodbye, Mr. Chips.*

There would be a wrench, however, before Christchurch. On September 4, I walked slowly home from a movie at the Belvedere Theatre in Roland Park. The summer heat of a cloudless day began to dribble away with a merciful evening breeze. I climbed the six concrete steps of 617 and admired the flowerbeds along our path that I had weeded and turned the day before. Jimmy would not do half so good a job when I was away at school. My father surprised me by throwing open the front door. Mother looked troubled in the hallway behind him. He crouched, controlling his tears, into a near kneeling position and threw his arms around my shoulders.

"Daddy, what's wrong?" I knew whatever it was had nothing to do with drinking. He was stone sober.

"Come and sit down, son. I have something to tell you." We guided each other to the living room and settled into a clumsy twosome on the Victorian sofa. Mother sat quietly opposite us in one of the wing chairs. There were faint noises overhead from Ann in her room. I heard Jimmy's hard lacrosse ball bouncing off the garage door in the distant dusk. I was the last one home.

"Son, Mum died today."

"Why?" For an instant, Dad looked as though he would succumb to his first laugh of the day. His news did not sink in. I had the odd feeling that a very large reaction was expected on my part.

"She had a heart attack. Louise found her in her room looking very peaceful."

"In bed?"

"No, son." A pause. "On the floor beside her bed, leaning against her chaise longue. We're certain there was no pain. Maybe only a moment."

Then it registered. The possibility of her hurting. My father and I fell against one another, our bodies racked with croaking sobs. I cried for lost comfort, for not being able to read her spidery message on another birthday card, for the end of a bountiful love through touching and holding as far back as my beginnings. I thought of the pitchfork in Rye Beach, of being treated like the luckiest little hero in existence. That afternoon, the act of holding hands lost its artlessness. The silver spoon had fallen from my mouth. I would never be so spoiled again.

CHAPTER FOUR

LETTERS TO AND FROM A WELL-KNOWN WOMAN

"THERE'S SOMETHING FOR you on the hall table," said my father, pulling himself together. He pointed to the letter.

The typewriter ink on the white envelope was pale blue. Joan Fontaine's embossed name on the back flap was the same shade. The color of her handwriting on the brief note inside matched everything else. She thanked me for my interest and assured me that an auto-graphed picture would be forthcoming.

That first of countless notes in my lifelong correspondence with Joan Fontaine momentarily put my grief over Mum on hold. I ran upstairs to my room to smudge the ink a smidgen and held it to the light to read the stationery brand. Crane's, which I bought from then on. I also began to imitate Joan's unique handwriting. Years later over dinner, I told her this story. She smiled in her Mona Lisa fashion. She remained silent, maybe in the knowledge that time had blunted such adolescent fervor. Her notes stopped when I told her I was writing this book.

A few days after the momentous letter arrived, I beheld, with ill-disguised fascination, my first corpse. Mum lay exposed in an imposing open coffin surrounded by a suffocating array of floral arrangements that took up an entire wall of her living room. Her face looked waxen. Her eyebrows were too darkly penciled, her cheeks too rouged, and her mouth a slash of bright red lipstick. My father was horrified. There was no time to soften her makeup. The family had gathered and the mourners were arriving. They were mostly elderly, wondering who among themselves would be next, eager to observe my grandmother, dead at only sixty-eight. Some sort of service was conducted in the oppressive heat. Louise wept quietly in the background. Dalcour stood perspiring with his chauffeur's hat in his hand. At one point, my father struggled to control a ripping, animal-like noise that erupted from his throat. I was worried that Mum would melt, or that I would. I was engulfed repeatedly in the well-meaning arms of strangers. Jimmy and I did not go on to Druid Ridge Cemetery for the burial. I waited in Mum's car with her memories, and Dalcour helped me toss breadcrumbs to the swans. At home after the service, Hazel was solicitous and Jimmy was subdued. I mulled over the weight of my first great grief.

In September, I packed the green-and-black footlocker Dad and I had selected. Mother had helped me shop for shirts, slacks, and other moderate necessities. Jimmy, impatient for solitary domain, looked on from time to time. The following afternoon, Dad's convertible turned onto the long Christchurch driveway. Mother sat in front and I looked ahead from the back seat. The early-morning start and drive from Baltimore through Maryland and Virginia had been lovely but tiring for my parents; their passenger was a nerve end. We parked in the shadow of the large brick dormitory building where I would be studying and living for the next five years. And eating, in the basement dining room beyond the fender of our car. The box-like building with its tall windows to our right was the edifice I could have done without on any campus, the gymnasium.

The crunch of cars being parked and new and old students shuffling their feet in the gravel driveway sounded like a giant, raspy whisper. Parents were to be dumped and gotten rid of fast—so that we might make our independent way into this divergent world. But the grownups insisted on helping to carry suitcases, unload trunks, and, worst of all, throwing their arms around their offspring to say goodbye. My father did that. The tremor through my upper torso caused him to withdraw as though electrocuted.

Mother was ever appreciative of splendid views. She took pleasure in the one broken by the graceful silhouette of the bell tower from the white-columned headmaster's house. The woods sloped to the Rappahannock River on the horizon. The tree-enshrouded teachers' quarters, the infirmary, and the dormitory made a half circle on the lawn that overlooked the Rappahannock.

Mother and Dad were on their way back to Baltimore, leaving me time to unpack before Sunday supper. I set out, feeling not a scintilla of homesickness, to make my cubicle into the haven I craved. Beyond its partitions, other trunks scraped across the wooden floor, lockers opened and closed, and iron beds were made up and shoved back into place. There were hesitant hellos across the hall and in the corridor from those of us tentatively trying to get acquainted with one another. Each cubicle was half the size of a train compartment. It had a Spartan desk beneath its window. I craned over mine against the right partition to look outside. I could see the bell tower and a bit of copper-colored Rappahannock in the sunset. A master pulled the heavy cord for the half-hour dinner bell; I picked up my toiletries and walked the length of the dorm to the communal bathroom—which would never be so quiet again. I returned to change into a coat and tie and check the results of washing up in the small mirror on the back of my wardrobe door. Forty-eight hours later, I would think nothing of making the same trek to the showers clad only in a towel. And to take a bit more time, before going downstairs to dinner, to make certain my '40s pompadour was in place.

My schizoid thinking and Baltimore insomnia are not unknown in turbulent adulthood, but at Christchurch I slept soundly in my narrow cubicle bed from healthy exhaustion. The seven o'clock wake-up bell was nerve-racking. On winter mornings, the wooden floor under bare feet was like an ice rink. We never stopped wailing that the racket beginning to rumble in the radiators produced no heat. These were negligible drawbacks, however, and I quickly turned my cubicle into a tidy retreat where all my belongings were carefully placed and as excessively cherished as my new surroundings.

For me, there is primary pleasure in a nest. I like things, my animals, my own company. More than people. I've been single-minded in surrounding myself with possessions wherever I have lived. I hope that good taste evolved along the accumulating way. True, comforts can engulf a home, and a self. Now I embrace the notion that it is more prudent to maintain than to collect. I simplify and discard. My house, like that first cubicle at Christchurch, is my castle.

I was possessive about new friends and favorite teachers too. I demanded the company of David Kippenbrock, a repressed and kindhearted preacher's son from Georgia. It meant much to be liked by Mr. and Mrs. Dexter Flint White. He was my saturnine American history and English teacher. On Saturday nights, the White home was the warmest faculty open house. I pored over their *Life* magazine collection and coveted their extensive Modern Library editions. Mazo de la Roche aficionado Mrs. White loaned me the Canadian author's Jalna books about the Whiteoaks family on their rural estate in Ontario. We discussed every fervid installment. Kippenbrock went with me to the White's—and everywhere else. Good David was an easily manipulated best friend, brighter than me by far, and, no, I never knew him biblically.

He did stand up to me, touting the merits of his favorite actress Olivia de Havilland over her sister Joan Fontaine. Our banter over these ladies would have turned off Hedda Hopper. It did the other boys. We learned to relegate such talk to our long weekend walks through the nearby woods, to strolls along earthen lanes that fronted decaying plantations, and when we hitchhiked together into nearby Urbanna. We never had to hitchhike for long. The townspeople gave Christchurch boys a ride as soon as they saw them. The closest soda fountain, movie magazine rack, and lone wooden movie theatre were in Urbanna. The student body filled the movie theatre for the Thursday night picture show.

Our movie night, whatever the third run fare, was eagerly anticipated. There were yowls and leers for Esther Williams. We nearly brought the creaky house down clapping James Cagney on in *Yankee Doodle Dandy*. Mr. White shepherded us on the bus into Urbanna with a less firm hand than the other teachers. He condoned our raucous noise and joined in our sing-alongs. On the dark and drowsy ride home, he discussed the film we had just enjoyed. He did not squelch or patronize the two experts on the movies either: Kippenbrock and myself. In return, we concentrated in his classroom.

During the Christchurch time of my life, I was a joiner. I took to the camaraderie of a group with gusto. I made charcoal sketches of students for twenty-five-cent Mother's Day gifts. A bit of savvy in regard to histrionics brought me another taste of that elusive narcotic, popularity. After lights-out, I sat up in my bed spinning horror stories for the boys who clustered in my cubicle or huddled in their beds across the hallway. I pitched my stage whisper beyond as many divider walls as possible—so as not to alert the dorm master in his room by the stairs. The night masked my glee at the attentions of stardom and my satisfaction at the collective intake of breath after one punch line: "He sat there eating the severed arm!" What yarn preceded this jolt I no longer remember. I learned to gain approval through performing and, in the dark, had no inhibitions. These strictures I began to perceive in the rudimentary drama department. My first efforts to appear at ease upon a stage—where one is, after all, seen—were to continue for a lifetime.

In my senior year, I was effective in the Christmas pageant, *Why the Chimes Rang*. I was so thrilled to receive a letter from the author,

Mrs. Jessie Chamberlain, that I still have it. She wrote from the Hill-
crest Inn in Urbanna on December 13, 1948: "You were so good in
your part, your diction so clear, and you conveyed the spirituality the
theme was meant to convey." Prior efforts in less-sensitive one-acts
were *racked* with stage fright and God knows what posing. They
included George S. Kaufman's wheeze *If Men Played Cards Like
Women Do*, that ancient high-school standby *The Valiant*, and I won
the ten-dollar first prize in the annual speaking contest when I
recited "Nightmare" from W. S. Gilbert's *Iolanthe*. I felt nauseated in
the shower before the latter, and my friend Tony Geiske got more
laughs in the Kaufman piece. The reason was not just that I have
never been particularly adept at acting gay; Tony knew how to throw
away a line, a knack I can master with a good director, after too many
rehearsals, and of course when drinking.

Geiske and I were unlikely buddies, but his friendship ran a close
second to Kippenbrock's. A Be-Bop jazz freak who idolized Dizzy
Gillespie, Tony wore horn-rimmed glasses which magnified the
small, pale blue eyes that lasered devil-like over the beak nose protruding from his long, Polish–Greek face. Words fell in effortless cas-
cades from his thin red mouth or produced incomprehensible scat
sounds to accompany the Gillespie records he blasted whenever possible from his cubicle. He sported pastel-hued cardigan jackets. My
father reluctantly gave me the cream-colored variety for Christmas —
so I could appear to be what Tony declared was hip in '40s New York.
Later, by the time we wore those jackets to see Brando in *A Streetcar
Named Desire* and to attend a mêlée given by my friend Diana Barrymore at the Warwick Hotel, the cardigans were à la mode only along
Forty-second Street.

Tony's insouciant competitiveness at Christchurch fascinated me.
Sometimes my own bluster in pursuit of whatever accomplishment
was uneasily skin-deep. He spurred me on scholastically, but trying
to eclipse his excellent grades was a lost cause. He wanted to be a
newspaper writer. On a weekend in Tony's home in Arlington, we
visited the *Washington Post*, where he had already apprenticed as a

copy boy during the summer. He does write today—the way he talks. His erudite reviews of jazz events for the *Hollywood Reporter* talk turkey to the sidemen if not the laymen. Mr. and Mrs. Geiske and I touched base a few times at my house and in their San Fernando Valley home, but our relationship never took hold. In later years I have discarded, like things, a couple of friendships; it is always, as was the case with David Kippenbrock, more difficult to renew one.

Tony moved gracefully. He tried to train me to be a Christchurch cheerleader. Bobby Simmons and I practiced in the gym basement under Geiske's guidance. I could never pick up the routines Simmons mastered immediately. My protestations that I should not have been chosen to cheerlead in the first place fell on Tony's deaf ears. He told me I looked terrific in the navy blue sweater emblazoned with the orange letter C, that the gyrations would come to me in no time, and that it was too late to replace me. My nervous state before the football game made stage fright seem picayune. The brightly lit sidelines magnified my awkwardness. I leapt about with Geiske and Simmons, exhorting cheers and team spirit from the student body, a Halloween smile plastered across my sweaty face. Frizzy-haired Mrs. White, her face doughy with supportive smiles, assured me at half-time that the crowd was intent on the game and not my ungainliness, and that I was beginning to relax. Her encouragement was to no avail. After the game I told Tony I would as soon play football—and I told him what he could do with his cheerleading.

The alternative to football that I cottoned to was sailing. Never mind that my Hampton was school property; she was mine provided I took proper care of her at Christchurch. She was a fifteen-footer with a centerboard, rudder, jib, and mainsail. Each winter found me recaulking, sanding, repainting, sanding, and repainting some more until her hull, carefully stored atop wooden trestles in the boat-house, was shipshape and shiny white for another season. No boy kept his boat in better condition and none derived more pleasure than I did when I placed her back into the water each spring and fall. There was an inch-wide red stripe that I stenciled to the tip of her ebony bow. I expertly painted the matching red letters of her name across her gleaming, refinished stern: *The Fontaine*.

Kippenbrock was my mate on *The Fontaine*. We learned to tack our course upon the Rappahannock, to fill the sails with wind. Our becalmed spells were private, still moments that allowed us to chatter about whatever we pleased as loudly as we wanted. David mastered ducking the boom. Once I turned the tiller too fast and sent him overboard, threatening the calmness of our friendship as well as of the water. We raced, anchored and swam, always on the alert for the vile and stinging jellyfish. When the five o'clock bell sounded, we docked to run up the long hill barefoot in damp bathing suits to clean ourselves up for evening chapel, dinner, and study hall—before lights-out at eleven o'clock. There was a bonus hour until midnight on Saturdays.

In the area of hanky-panky, which David did not like to discuss, my release was reserved for a chunky classmate. His thighs and his handsomeness made me desperate, and he grew less astonished as he stopped saying no. My tactile advances were clumsy and affectionate, usually in the boathouse, rarely and furtively in the dorm. We would not have cared or known how to talk about our inadequate dalliances, so we survived as friends. We stopped short of making love, which, although I did not know it then, is what I wanted most. Nothing has changed—except the desperation.

I excelled in English and American history and passed English history. Mr. White made Britain's array of royal amazements real to this Anglophile. I even memorized their names. The dates scattered like black-pepper specks throughout our tests, and term papers were an easier matter for Geiske. I concocted fanciful English compositions about visits to Arlington with Tony, sailing, or meaning my prayers when I said them fervently after seeing *The Song of Bernadette*. I reveled in being asked to read my prose aloud to my classmates. They were easily hooked on any accent that didn't sound like a hound dog's. Mine was more WASP than boondocks Baltimore—thanks to my father. I also played the clown for the boys in study hall rather than pore over my miserable math. I gave up math until the advent of calculators. I placed my tongue beneath my upper lip, pulled on my large ears, and made ape faces from my desk on the back row. Or I fashioned paper eyelashes and used spit to stick them to my upper lids. Like a deranged Betty Boop, I sat blinking until the first boy took notice. He tapped the shoulder of the boy in front of him. Grins became giggles. Rows of faces suppressed laughter—until I had everyone's attention and the whole room gave way to screeching.

My success as a clown depended on the character of the master in charge. I went into orbit only under the aegis of one or two poor souls who never managed to attain authority. Like all students, we knew who they were from their first moments in front of a classroom and instantly got the upper hand. The unfortunate few seldom lasted from one year to the next because we continued to take advantage of them.

I was the ideal boarding school student. On summer holiday or semester weekends, I was unhappy at home. I was always anxious to return to Christchurch. My family took a trip to New York during the summer of 1946. On my first visit a decade earlier, Dad recalled that, in Grand Central Station, I had said: "I didn't know New York had a roof over it." This time, for a group photograph taken amidst the din of Eddie Condon's Dixieland jazz, I smiled like a movie star at Jimmy Ryan's on Fifty-second Street. In his idea of seventh heaven, Dad looked tight, Mother forced a smile beneath quivering egret plumes, and Jimmy with his usual know-it-all demeanor perspired. On the surface we were a close-knit family taking the glitter of Manhattan in stride. We went to Sardi's—less the restaurant of my dreams than Romanoff's in Beverly Hills—and Dad pointed out John Carradine, script in hand, his hat tilted rakishly over his bony brow in imitation of Dad's idol, John Barrymore. His companion turned her head, and we saw the swollen countenance of Diana, the idol's offspring. Perhaps drawn to decay for the first time, I was impressed. I would shortly know Miss Barrymore, and, over the hill or not, would like her enormously.

Brassy Ethel Merman, starring that season in *Annie Get Your Gun*, did not impress me at all. Her bored performance struck me as unprofessional. Years later when I saw her in *Gypsy*, she convinced me that she could galvanize an audience—when she felt like it. She also galvanized me—into abject apologies. We were fond of each other then through our mutual friend Michael Rayhill—until the night after a performance of *Gypsy* when she asked me to join her at her friend Mitzi Gaynor's house. Those were my alcoholic–amphetamine days. Stumbling around the living room and into a coffee table, I told another guest, Rossano Brazzi, that he was too old to play romantic leads. Jack Bean, Miss Gaynor's kindly husband, patiently escorted me back out into the night. I telephoned Miss Merman, sent flowers and telegrams to her at the Beverly Hills Hotel, but she refused to speak to me again.

In 1946 we returned from New York to Ann and Hazel in Baltimore. I tolerated the end-of-summer lethargic afternoons, sticky in the humidity I've never missed, and looked forward to the cooling breezes off the Rappahannock River. The day came for Dad to drive me to the downtown bus terminal. I was happy during any season coasting through Maryland and Virginia in a Greyhound bus. It was good to rendezvous with other students boarding at other stops or to talk quietly with friendly strangers who were sometimes my seatmates. One such stranger was a horny sailor stationed in Norfolk. The shock of groping around under his pea coat left me weak – with pleasure. Another was an ample black lady who taught me to suck on a lemon to keep from getting carsick.

James Radcliffe became headmaster at Christchurch in 1947. He was a boyish-looking man with sandy hair and a commercial smile who brought an athletic air of authority to the school. His chic and effervescent wife, Beezy, whose bubbling smile and charm were captivating, abetted Mr. Radcliffe's new tenure. Even the faculty wives came around, like us, to this fresh combination of the airy Beezy and the handsome Mr. Radcliffe.

I liked Mr. Radcliffe almost as much as I liked Mr. White. His cipher-blue eyes were knowing; his expression the same good-humored, cocky mask for all the students. He was tolerant of my acting designs. He looked patient when his wife seemed to enjoy film and theatre talk as much as I. It amused him at our mail call before lunch when I brandished a note from Joan Fontaine. I beamed as though I had struck gold in my mail slot.

Once he admonished me for my poor work in science and math. "Carlyle," he concluded, "you can accomplish anything you really want to." He was right, when I applied myself.

He surely knew my sexual leanings. Nothing was said, of course, but I was aware of his discreet scrutiny of some of my friendships and relationships. I grew up in a time when discretion ruled the day. Would that caution, not only for fear of AIDS, was optional now. It made diddling more exciting. The skittish physical eruptions between boys in the dark of one or two cubicles were, after all, uncommon. There were mostly undefined crushes on those who were unattainable. That recurring state of perpetual anguish, passions, and disconcerting day and night dreams, although not unpleasant, long outlasted Christchurch. It is, perhaps, a life sentence.

For some, to accept homosexuality, like attempting to write selectively about it, can be difficult. Accepting my own was not. It became second nature and a given, thanks, I believe, to my father. I will try to tell the truth here, but I will draw the line at sleaze. I have, I admit, the old-fashioned yen to go happily to my grave with one foot in the closet. In one instance, Mr. Radcliffe had cause to be alarmed. I developed a rabid infatuation for a younger student. Jordan Street's company, his huge black eyes, and his imp smile and personality came to delight me in every way, save sexual. Our headmaster could not have been more taken aback by our companionship than Jordan and I were. The flattery of an older student seeking him out sparked Jordan's unabashed affection. I responded in kind to his uninhibited touching as we walked in the deep woods out of sight of the school. We laughed, held, grabbed, and never stopped talking. I can remember silences with everyone but Jordan. Were we afraid that quietness would lead to something else, an act that Jordan might not take pleasure in, a capitulation that we would both regret? I was. I contented myself with my longing. Mr. Radcliffe must have sensed that I made a wise decision.

I heard that Mr. Radcliffe grieved mightily just two years later. The vivacious Beezy Radcliffe died suddenly in Baltimore from a puncture after an inner ear infection. Horrified, I telephoned Mr. Radcliffe to offer my condolences. In a firm voice he was properly grateful, but we never spoke again. He remarried shortly and became headmaster at my former Waterloo, St. Paul's. Jimmy studied under him there. He found him copacetic because Mr. Radcliffe was a lacrosse freak. I was astonished to learn while writing this book that Mr. Radcliffe had died in Baltimore at the age of seventy-one. Astonished, that is, at the passage of time.

My theatrical bent and physical proclivities collided during my 1947 summer away from Christchurch. Don Swann, the entrepreneurial son of a renowned pen-and-ink illustrator of the Baltimore scene, opened the Hilltop Theatre on the women's college campus in Lutherville, Maryland. Lutherville was on the outskirts of my birthplace. Mr. Swann did not need to sweet-talk my parents into my becoming an apprentice. They were probably as eager for me to sign on as I was. At the Hilltop, I learned to build, size, and paint flats, clean the facilities on both sides of the proscenium, and cue the principal actors. I survived on coffee until a new set had been frantically built and dressed each and every week. Sometimes, when technical run-throughs and dress rehearsals lasted late into the night or until dawn, I slept over in the upstairs dormitory, in my own bed now and then, but more often in the leading man's. The principals, jobbed out of New York or California, had private rooms.

I was awe-struck by Douglas Henderson—and by his attentions.

Even by my father's George Jean Nathan standards, Doug made a most compelling Witch Boy in the Hilltop's production of *Dark of the Moon*. The too-gentle Mr. Henderson killed himself at his small house in Malibu a few years ago. I hope his suicide was not because of his carnal activities over the many summers since 1947. It is more likely that his boxer's body was gone, and with it his youth—that passing condition that he fervently clung to, together with dreams of stardom, even when I knew him. His death was a sad one, and I remembered him fondly at the Hilltop.

I thought more, though, of the 1947 me, who, provoked by the baiting battlefield between his parents one night, decided to toss a bombshell of his own. After dinner I knocked at the door of my father's den. He asked me in, closed the door, and we sat together on his leather sofa, his jazz playing softly in the background. Mother was downstairs helping Hazel with the dishes. The conversation between my father and me went like this:

"I have something I've got to tell you, Dad." More than the heat had distracted me that day while prop hunting for the Hilltop. "At least I think I want to."

"What is it son?"

"I think I'm homosexual." It sounded like a question. There was a long, long pause while he sipped his drink. When he looked down at me, his brimming brown eyes were as large and soft and unexpectedly compassionate as I had ever seen them.

"My dear boy. I'm shocked, but I'm not surprised."

He put his arms around me.

"I hope you'll never be overt, but the main thing, Carlyle, is that I hope that you will be happy."

He dried his eyes and talked about my mother and the consequences of her loss. He also explained what he meant by "overt." He placed no blame and asked for no details. He laughed half-heartedly and said that things could change. But he did not then or ever press or probe me about that possibility. In ensuing years, he would express delight and mild curiosity regarding every female whose company I enjoyed—including, in the case of Judy Garland, alarm. Yet he continued to accept with love what I had told him in his den so many summertimes ago. We kissed each other good night, and I went quietly upstairs to bed. Perhaps he got drunk, but the weight that I had carried on my shoulders when I went in to talk to him was never there again.

Douglas Henderson's attentions (other than as an actor) were short-lived, but I didn't care. When I read about his death, I was grateful to him again for that evening with my father.

I was elevated from apprentice to occasional juvenile status during a second Hilltop summer. In a revival of the popular *Dark of the Moon*, at Doug Henderson's urging, I was cast as Barbara Allen's brother Floyd. Floyd sang "Down in the Valley." I had a rousing time singing off-key hillbilly while someone behind the curtain accompanied me on guitar—as "Floyd" mimed strumming his on stage. In spite of Mother's earlier "Merle Oberon" comment, I lathered on the grease-paint like everybody else. I overlaid it with rouge and powder before heightening the whole effect with black mascara on my eyelashes. *Joan of Lorraine* was as heavy-laden as my makeup. The play starred an actress who belonged behind the counter at Woolworth's. She was dodo pretty, she had been sweet as Barbara Allen, but godly Joan was beyond her. I played her pretty younger brother Pierre. Our Maxwell Anderson-d'Arc family joshing lay there like the rest of the dialogue; so did our audience throughout the one-week run. But I learned, and I made friends. She was a fellow apprentice who nervously prepared to go on stage as a townswoman in *Dark of the Moon*—by clearing her throat loudly enough to be heard in the box office. It was tougher for me than Joan to return to painting scenery before the Hilltop closed.

It was easier to resume at Christchurch. I felt as secure and well adjusted during my last two years as an Old Student as I ever would in life. I wrote articles and took pictures for the school paper, *The*

Seahorse. Like a dictator, I planned the gym decorations for Christchurch dances. Southern belles from the girls' schools St. Catherine's and St. Margaret's within the Episcopalian Diocese of Virginia enlivened these dances. The visiting guests stayed out of harm's way in Urbanna, and on the third floor of the headmaster's house—where they must have been as hot as their waiting escorts. On Sunday night, before the girls departed, I impersonated Louis Jourdan kissing Joan Fontaine in *Letter from an Unknown Woman*. I pretended to be as horny with my date as the other guys necking and sneezing on our hayride. At the campfire on the beach, we roasted our marshmallows and our hot dogs. In lieu of choking down the latter, I invited my female companion to handle its anatomical counterpart.

I rushed to accept weekend invitations. They were more pleasant than pretending to be at ease in Baltimore. I swam off Nanticoke Acres in Delaware at John Rhein's home, explored the nation's capital with Tony Geiske, and excused myself from the tight-lipped Reverend Kippenbrock's table to go to the movies with David in Bethesda. The only thing I enjoyed at 617 was Ann, but there was less of her company because she was growing up. She went to Roland Park Country School. Her darker blonde bobbed hair was held back from her inquiring face by a barrette above a blue-and-white school uniform that she seemed to be active in twenty-four hours a day.

Back at school, I probed the effect of the rush that didn't last long enough from swigging rum and Coca-Cola. On Saturday nights—when heads could clear during Sunday services at Old Christchurch the next morning—some of us experimented with the combination that would make me gag today. One intrepid senior made the climb down the fire escape at the end of the dormitory building. He paid Coley, the black janitor waiting on the ground with the rum, then scurried back up again to share the bottle with each boy who had contributed a quarter. A Coke bottle cap skittering across the bathroom floor was cause for alarm as moist hands passed a shared glass from one sniggering mouth to another. Of course there wasn't enough liquor to get truly drunk. Pissing mightily and giggling our way back to our cubicles was the extent of our intemperance. Well, there were stealthy sexual games between one or two lucky enough to stay awake longer than the others. These disheveled doings, uninhibited by booze, formed no permanent patterns, to my knowledge, in anyone other than me.

I watched from my cubicle window as a Lower School boy raced across the grounds from the infirmary hollering: "Roosevelt's dead! Roosevelt died!" That April 12, 1945, cry was beyond belief. President Roosevelt was our omnipotent surrogate father. He had been for as long as most Christchurch boys could remember. That evening, we sat bonded in our distress for a special service in Scott Memorial Chapel. My stomach knotted with the same grief that I knew flooded through my real father at home.

Dad's 4-F classification after Pearl Harbor led him to volunteer as an air-raid warden. When I was at home, we walked together around the West University Parkway area where no bombs would ever fall. Nevertheless, Dad followed FDR's precautionary rules to the letter. He observed the blackout drills, and his helmet, armband, and flashlight were at the ready in the hall closet downstairs. He allotted food-rationing stamps to Mother as carefully as extra cash; before she died, he excoriated Mum for hoarding canned goods. His loyalties were catching when we walked patrol. His liberalism, his love of our land, and his respect for its Democratic leader made a dent in my youthful apathy. He had no gnawing concerns about a failing system. The current, corroding malaise of political pessimism was unknown to him. He was not, like his adult son, a disgusted patriot.

During the campus service for President Roosevelt, I hung my head. I visualized the closed den door at home. Behind it there would be Dixieland jazz, rattling ice cubes, and muffled sobs.

When Kippenbrock and I were seniors, we spearheaded a small group interested enough in the theatre to go to Richmond to watch Tallulah Bankhead make mischief in Noel Coward's *Private Lives*. On stage, she took the much-publicized piece from Mayfair to hysterical Alabamian heights of her own. The consummate Donald Cook deserved his own huzzahs for acting her distracted foil. The touring production was a sidesplitting treat. I promptly wrote to the cyclonic actress to ask her to visit Christchurch for lunch. Nothing ventured, nothing gained. Her polite regrets handwritten from her Richmond hotel appeared in my letterbox within the week. No matter, I had to wait a while for Miss Bankhead and, especially, Mr. Coward to touch my life later on.

There was another note from Joan Fontaine. She wrote, in response to my request, that she would be honored to be the long-distance sponsor of the Christchurch drama department. I was the drama club president. The page bearing Joan's incongruous glossy studio headshot was open and on display for my return visit to Christchurch. Her smile looms unexpectedly amidst other photographs of girlfriends and parents in my final *Tides* 1949 yearbook. Feeling foolish as I recently flicked through the pages, I spied the image of Joan and a younger, blonder me.

In *Tides*, I was voted "neatest" on account of my housekeeping. Kippenbrock wished me "Happy Hamlets!" I placed second in the "best looking" contest to John Rhein III, who was certainly first on that count. I also graduated, to my father's dismay, with blond hair. Over several *Fontaine* sailings, Geiske had dared me to dye my hair. Kippenbrock sniffed the salt air as though it were smelling salts. One peroxide application on this brunette had been insufficient under the Rappahannock sun. Judging from my family's collective expression when they drove in for graduation ceremonies, the muddy orange result must have been awful. Jimmy's look of disgust squelched my sister's squeal. Back in Baltimore, Dad rectified the situation within twenty-four hours, sending me for a brown dye job at Mother's beauty salon. Earlier, in Scott Memorial Chapel, however, their applause was supportive when I was awarded a medal for being the best public speaker of 1949 and boisterous as I accepted my diploma from Mr. Radcliffe.

There was no rebel yell out of me that June afternoon. The self-congratulatory hubbub merely put off our goodbyes. I had felt nostalgic at the senior prom, elated on our last hayride the night before, and, while getting packed through the shake of Mr. Radcliffe's hand, I felt kinship for my fellow graduates and every student. When my family and I drove away, the pain of my last look back at Christchurch was excruciating. As we turned onto the highway, my sadness threatened to get the better of me. Mother and Jimmy sat behind me. Jimmy's presence and Ann's tired crumple against my side in the middle of the front seat kept me from crying. For a few silent miles, my understanding father took one hand from the steering wheel and placed it on my shoulder.

CHAPTER FIVE

YOU CAN'T GO HOME AGAIN

MY CUBICLE AT Christchurch took on San Simeon proportions when I shared the 617 West University Parkway bedroom again with Jimmy. At least my stepbrother, a budding lacrosse star now, had begun to mellow. A dim and mostly silent tolerance of each other replaced our fisticuffs. His dating superseded our moviegoing together, and his athletic buddies kept him away from the house longer than the ladies did. While I enjoyed privacy on the third floor, downstairs Mother and Dad were on a glacial descent from which they would never recover.

The two tended to hit the ceiling behind closed doors after they thought I'd gone to sleep. The three-story house had its advantages, but Mother could not always conceal her red eyes in the morning, nor could my father control crashing into things in the grip of his ever more colossal hangovers. Plans for a summer lunch went awry once when he slammed the icebox door shut, thudded against it, and sent from its top into the dust the small sandwiches Mother had prepared. His reach to retrieve them was convulsive, and he only caught the tray. He stood, looking like a scoundrel-clown with the shakes, in the face of Mother's wail. Our new maid Gay—Hazel had retired—dusted off some of the sandwiches and whipped up a salad. Yes, Gay was really her name. She and I lived up to her name that day. We chuckled together in the pantry—over gathering up the lunch which was to have been eaten on the lawn.

The ennui of June 1949 lifted when Dad pulled some friendly theatrical agent's string. I was accepted as an apprentice who would be tossed some acting bones further afield by the Famous Artists Playhouse in Fayetteville, New York. The respite from Baltimore was more enticing because of the prospect of working with a new star each week. They were performers who were trying to resuscitate their film or stage careers, so the Famous Artists lineup was eclectic: Paul Lukas in *Accent on Youth*; Bela Lugosi in *Arsenic and Old Lace*; Eva Le Gallienne in *The Corn Is Green*; Diana Barrymore in *The Philadelphia Story*; Tom Drake and Haila Stoddard in *Her Cardboard Lover*; Kay Francis in *Let Us Be Gay*; Sylvia Sidney in *The Two Mrs. Carrolls*; and Peggy Ann Garner in *Peg O' My Heart*. In that time of thriving summer stock, these personalities and others like them were, in most cases, dependable and always popular.

Kay Francis had only to make her entrance wearing a black cocktail dress, turn upstage to reveal that it was backless—above a great red rose over her sheathed derriere—and lisp her first line, "How do you do, I'm Mrs. *Bwown*," to titillate the packed house of matrons training binoculars on her swaying rump. Miss Francis, whose vehicle would be retitled today, repaired with the rest of us after the show to the Fayetteville Inn. There she dropped more R's and knocked back more than a few gins to dispel her noble clothes-horse screen image. The sad and friendly Mr. Lugosi imbibed a lot as well, perhaps to dull the melancholy of being forced to play roles that frightened people. Mr. Lukas was preceded by his secretary stand-in. For an entire week, she walked through the star's blocking with an affronted cast, prior to his arrival in time for the dress rehearsal—

replete with valet, toupee, and maybe even his Oscar for *Watch on the Rhine*. His continental accent soothed the ladies in his audience. They saw only insecure actors in a silly play, not Mr. Lukas's bad stage manners.

I played the grubby miner John Owen in the first scene of *The Corn Is Green*, then went backstage to observe the rest of the proceedings. When Miss Le Gallienne accused me of lurking outside a stage window and destroying her concentration, I vanished.

The management cut corners by combining the servants in *The Philadelphia Story* into one very busy houseboy, Thomas. I was hyperkinetic as I bore cocktail and calling-card trays from every direction in the set. Miss Barrymore, bless her, took to me as though there was no star system. Her sotto-voce wisecracks made the feeling mutual. "You're too pretty to go on stage," she whispered in a gruff, whiskeyed baritone the first night. Had I been older, she would have gone for my crotch in the dark backstage. I was pleased to be flattered by a Barrymore. She proudly displayed the sandals that "Mummy sent me from Greece." She wore them as a bloated Tracy Lord, a part she played damn well, except for one performance when she became progressively drunk. She sent my champagne glasses flying. I spent a hammy time sweeping up the stage far longer than I had to. The audience tittered over what they had come to see: another Barrymore peccadillo—aided and abetted, we thought, by her pallid husband and leading man, Robert Wilcox. At each intermission, Mr. Wilcox swore the couple had no liquor in the dressing room. He was obviously not privy to all of his wife's secrets. A while after our time together in Fayetteville, Diana invited me to the aforementioned party I took Tony Geiske to in New York. Mr. and Mrs. Wilcox were about to wear out their welcome at the Warwick Hotel. The party was late, but to my mind Carol Bruce was leaving too early. I stopped her by telling her that her performance as Julie in the revival of *Showboat* had constituted one of my greatest evenings in the theatre. "It was for me too, honey," she replied, and kept going. She left in the nick of time, just before Diana hurled a high-heeled shoe at her husband. It missed Mr. Wilcox and smashed through the living room window. The other party guests were on their way out as hotel authorities were getting off the elevators.

The Fayetteville Inn, where the stars stayed and a short distance from the boarding house that I did not always sleep in, was the background for two movie-star infatuations. Tom Drake breathed heavily. He buffed his MGM caps with an emery board. He was a simple, hard-drinking man who wore a ski cap offstage. He believed it would keep his problem hair from getting thinner in the open air. I played a croupier with a fake moustache in his show *Her Cardboard Lover*. The Boy Next Door from *Meet Me in St. Louis* was not averse to being grilled about Judy Garland, which is one reason I went to his Fayetteville Inn bedroom—that, and the chance to shack up with my first movie star. Haila Stoddard walked in on us the morning after the show closed. My mortification was huge. At least I did not have to travel to the next stop with Tom's leading lady. After Tom checked out, I passed a few mooncalf evenings playing one song on the Fayetteville Inn jukebox—"I Only Have Eyes for You"—which, after about seventy-three hours, was a lie.

I was embarrassed for Tom in another way during an evening in the '50s. By then, we were acquaintances, and Hugh Martin took us to a reunion dinner of sorts at Frascati's in Hollywood. The *Meet Me in St. Louis* score was Hugh's, and now he was starting orchestral arrangements on *A Star is Born* for Miss Garland. I looked the other way when he buttered up the Boy Next Door, whose career had long since deteriorated, to campaign for the co-starring role of Norman Maine. False hopes began to make Tom higher than his martinis did. After that evening, Tom sadly hit the skids even harder, and James Mason played Norman Maine.

The only thing I didn't like about seventeen-year-old Peggy Ann Garner was her habit of calling me "Carl." I would sooner answer to "Johnny," and that's not easy. I was only ever credited as "Carlyle Posey" in *Her Cardboard Lover*. I had long favored the name "John Carlyle." John Carlyle was a great-uncle on my mother's side, and my father approved. What else could he do? Even now, an actor would think twice about Carlyle Fairfax Posey. When the formidable Sylvia Sidney closed the Famous Artists Playhouse season with *The Two Mrs. Carrolls*, I was, from then on, and to everyone, John Carlyle.

Peggy wore a red wig when she played a direct and endearing Peg O' My Heart. I'm certain she could have held a candle to Laurette Taylor, who originated the role. The people on both sides of the Famous Artists proscenium of the Fayetteville High School stage lost their hearts to her wispy presence. Peggy responded favorably to my offstage crush. It was real, like Peggy herself. She was a purposeful former child star, and she asked me during a flirtatious interval back-stage to be her escort for the Syracuse opening of her film *The Big Cat*. I smiled by her side during the hullabaloo for that mediocrity—costarring another boy-next-door who survived, Lon McCallister. "Bud," as his friends call Mr. McCallister, later tried to curb my drinking in Hollywood—can you believe it?

While Peggy and I were driven in my first star's limousine back to Fayetteville, I felt that some exploratory necking was expected of me. I must not have cut the romantic mustard, since comradeship was the order of the day when I took her to lunch and the theatre in New York later that fall. We saw the definitive *Peter Pan*, starring Jean Arthur. Along with a matinee audience composed of numerous enraptured children, the two of us sprang to our feet when Miss Arthur strode to the footlights to implore everyone—in her inimitable cracking voice—to stand and clap "if you believe in fairies!" We were still in Never-Never Land over Tinkerbell's survival when I returned Peggy to the Delmonico Hotel. She was staying there in Mr. and Mrs. Ed Sullivan's apartment. She let go of my hand and did not ask me upstairs. I was sorry she didn't. I walked through the Delmonico revolving door and down Park Avenue, wondering what I would have done if she had.

My father enrolled me at the University of North Carolina in Chapel Hill instead of Carnegie-Mellon. He said both had exemplary drama departments, but he felt my sinuses and lungs would be at risk in the soot and grime of Pittsburgh. His choice made little difference to me. What consequence was college in the life of a star? Only time seemed at stake, but Hollywood was beyond finagling. So Chapel Hill it was, for one barely perceived freshman year. The features and activities in the lovely village were peppier than anything scholastic on campus. I skipped classes. I griped about not having known before being enrolled that a student had to complete freshman year before trodding the boards of the oh-so-lofty Carolina Playmakers—in any capacity more conspicuous than a crowd scene.

Betty Smith's *A Tree Grows in Brooklyn* was still prominent in the local bookshop when I arrived. So was *Bright Leaf*, a first novel by interpretive dancer Foster Fitzsimmons. Both authors were residents of Chapel Hill. Seeing Peggy triumph in the film version of Miss Smith's book was as close as I ever came to the lady, but Mr. Fitzsimmons nearly crippled me when he tried to teach me some of the basic steps in his frenzied field of modern dance. His first semester was my last. I bolted tour jetés to take a brief stab at golf. I swiped large chunks of Tar Heel turf in all directions, concentrating on my handsome instructor instead of my swing. Such vague memories of extracurricular activities supersede the recollection of any class, lecture, or teacher within UNC's ivied walls.

I cannot even remember my first friend's name, a redheaded fellow who shared my freshman anxiety and bewilderment. He joined me in the initial book-buying and general indoctrination. The waiting lines were chaotic, the stacks of books formidable. Brook III, as I shall call him, due to his aristocratic nature, did most of the leading. I stumbled along behind him in the southern heat and strangeness of the makeshift Quonset hut area. I wondered if I would bump into Joyce Reynolds. Miss Reynolds had played the title character in Warner Brothers' *Janie* and had even portrayed Joan Fontaine's younger sister in *The Constant Nymph*. She subsequently ditched her career for the academic environs of UNC. I was dumbfounded by this move, and, since I never did see Miss Reynolds, it remained incomprehensible.

Brook III had rented an apartment off campus. He helped me find mine too, in the converted attic of a private home on Chapel Hill's main street. My room and private bath under the eaves were fearfully hot, but comfortable enough in late evenings or on cooler days to provide a refuge from the endless rituals of college life I refused to participate in. So as not to appear to be alone, I often asked Brook III to meet me there on the way to campus. I would walk with him to fewer and fewer classes and events.

Reluctantly, Brook III went with me to a freshman costume party. For some reason, dressed in black beneath a piece of cardboard framing my face, I attended as the double-faced painting by Picasso. I only like early Picasso and do not care for costume parties, but I was awarded a first-prize ribbon—to Brook III's consternation. I had toiled over my Hilltop-Famous Artists makeup kit without paying heed to the fidgety reaction of my sometimes pompous friend. Brook III and I drifted toward different circles. Our association was put on hold until 1951, when I arrived in Hollywood to claim the cover of *Photoplay*. It was a city of strangers to me, so I telephoned Brook III. I had not yet learned how to drive, and he very kindly drove me to an interview at Goldwyn Studios. He waited patiently in his car while I did not get the role of the drunken nephew in James Cagney's *Come Fill the Cup*. Rejection was new to me then—when fear and panic were deadening—so it's little wonder that my first college crony and I had almost nothing to say over an uncomfortable dinner in what was his hometown. We never crossed paths in Los Angeles again.

The University's theatrical hopefuls frequented Danziger's, the elite bohemian hangout in the center of Chapel Hill. They dreamed Broadway dreams over Hungarian goulash, lingered over tortes and coffee, and washed down their doubts with lager and ale in the basement piano bar. I got sloshed there as often as my budget would allow. I ate less frequently upstairs with Marty Jacobs. Black-eyed Marty, a squat and balding New Yorker, pointed out the reigning Carolina Playmaker stars. They gesticulated in their smoke-filled booths

as though they were in New York at Sardi's. Marty had choreo-
graphed and costumed most of them. Slumming, the flamboyant
Marty did the same for me—at the Chapel Hill Recreation Center. He
talked me into playing the tailor in a Methodist church production
of *Taming of the Shrew*, which he directed. The teenage Petruchio
who had taken his fancy was even more spectacular in the pale blue
tights Marty costumed him in. The role of the tailor surpassed my
tidbits that lowly freshman year for the Playmakers: a private in
something called *A Crystal for My Father*, one of the fathers in Paul
Green's tumid *Tread the Green Grass* (we fathers were directed to
move lugubriously in a pack by Foster Fitzsimmons), and one of the
boys of the chorus in *O, Bury Me Not*. My final role was in a musical
by Michael Casey, a delicate young playwright of whom great things
were expected.

Michael Casey introduced me to someone who would be a lifelong
friend in that 1949–50 year at UNC. Chuck Williamson was often a
member of the Danziger's crowd. Master Williamson played Nils in
their production of *I Remember Mama*. His characteristic foaming at
the mouth when he was excited marked his saucer-eyed performance, a trait that carries over offstage. Chuck also wrote a student
production based on his blue-blooded Kennet Square, Pennsylvania
upbringing. It was called *Family Heirlooms*. When we shook hands,
Chuck's open, marvelous smile invited friendship. His large brown
eyes, surrounded by the longest lashes I had ever seen, overcame
the usual college barriers. He knew how to laugh, he loved the theatre and the movies, and his curious lack of personal vanity—
despite the fact that his handsomeness verged on pretty—made his
company all the more appealing. Nor did he possess the arrogance
that often characterizes those of shorter stature. Michael Casey relied
on Chuck's unswerving belief in his writing talent, and Marty Jacobs
extolled his bubbling enthusiasm. My own ego benefited from
Chuck's flattering attention. He enabled me to mix with the mainstream creative community, a frolicsome society that I would be
among only briefly.

Chuck and I made plans to get together in New York the summer after my freshman year. I was more involved with packing off my cat Piaf—number three—than myself. During my last weeks on Tar Heel territory, I had rescued her from the street. She wailed her head off like her namesake, so she was not entirely welcomed by the family who lived below my dormer window. They put up with her so long as I strained her cat box and planned for our departure. Poor Piaf. I carefully boxed and air-holed and shipped my stray off on the bus to Manhattan the day before I left Chapel Hill. The next day I took the train via Baltimore. Our destination was Paul Phillips's apartment at 238 West Fifty-sixth Street where, with my father's mixed blessings, I planned to spend the summer making acting rounds. Dad already suspected that there would be no more tuition fees, but I saved my final decision for the telephone.

Paul Phillips was an apprentice friend from my days with the Hilltop Theatre. He had since settled in as an usher at New York's Alvin Theatre for Henry Fonda's long run in *Mr. Roberts*. Paul was prepared for me, but Piaf took him by surprise. He was disgruntled. Piaf was still hot and panting when I arrived. She rallied better than Paul did. I capitulated to much Italian hand waving—Paul's real name was Joseph Phillipello—and took her odorous litter box from the corner of his Pullman kitchen to the outside fire escape. She was neither spayed nor inoculated. I learned a lot of cat lessons from Piaf—the hard way.

My Big Apple experiences were haphazard. I was expected to help Paul with his rent and to work in order to supplement Dad's allowance. Sometimes I succeeded. I was one of Henry Aldrich's cronies—an extra—on several episodes of that early live television show. Mostly I was somnambulistic throughout a part-time stint serving pastries over an East Side bakery counter. I spent many late nights, sometimes with Chuck Williamson, in the aphrodisiac ambience of the Blue Parrot bar on Lexington. Promiscuity was the new-found norm in those lucky days, which meant that several mornings, instead of being bright-eyed and aggressive in agent and casting-director waiting rooms, I slept late. Trudging block after Manhattan block, only to be confronted by another abrasive secretary who looked through me to the next supplicant—who had more stomach for the brush-off than I did—was inhibiting. I lacked the actor's moxie (which must be ironclad) to persevere on Broadway.

The Blue Parrot clientele was a noisy, friendly mix of preppies and catamites dressed in suits and sport coats. And ties. We had a little more class then, scurrying about the bar, booth-hopping like rabbits in heat. Blurry eyes flashed and barriers tumbled as we vied for a conquest before the unwelcome "Last Call!" cry at 3:45. One of mine, to the glee of the officiating Chuck Williamson, was Tennessee Williams. I went home to his East Side apartment because I wanted to be with his gypsy-like companion, Frank Merlo. Tennessee, too sweet and too drunk to care, was shunted aside because he had a cold sore. So much for cultivating high friends in low places.

When I attended one particularly alarming cocktail party, another playwright did become a friend. Noel Coward was the guest of honor. He sang and played the piano in front of a penthouse bay window overlooking half of New York. The sophisticated setting was fitting. Mr. Coward grew more enchanting when he sang his "Mad About the Boy" directly to me. Our doddering host, the least attractive gentleman on the premises, announced after the songfest that there were bathrobes for everyone in the bedroom. Mr. Coward saw that I was petrified. He gently steered me aside to settle beside him on a chaise longue. The other guests drifted away to join in the kind of group activities I have never cared for. Mr. Coward was neither viper nor satyr, and we remained fully clothed. We talked quietly and at length of the vagaries of men and became acquainted. He was a lovely man. I was glad of my inhibitions. They led to subsequent visits with Mr. Coward when he was in residence at the Drake Hotel. He truly was The Master when, over congenial lunch or drinks downstairs, he dispensed unwavering warmth and encouraging theatrical advice to a novice who needed both.

Once—Chuck claims at my insistence—he and I ventured to the dank and infamous Everard Baths. We found them not only old but wanting. The pool was empty. The management refused a refund, and we two disgruntled WASPs were sent steaming into the night. On our most foolhardy foray, we were picked up by two mafioso types who drove us farther and farther downtown. We protested, to no avail, and ended up being acquiescent in their car, at gunpoint—in the silence of the Brooklyn Navy Yard. Fortunately the two returned us back uptown.

New York City brought me to life. The many legitimate theatres—when I could afford them, or, better still, be taken—were intimate showcases for Great Ladies and Mae West and for un-amplified musicals like *Kiss Me Kate* and *South Pacific*. The sturdy fare at the Horn and Hardart Automat nourished me with cherry pie for dessert and good coffee. Strolls across Brooklyn Bridge stargazing in the moonlight were dazzling. I never thought twice about walking home, alone or otherwise, at four A.M. after the bars closed. Mishaps were carefree, as when I clung to a friend on the jump seat of his motorcycle. We sped after midnight through the fall wind of Central Park. He swerved to avoid a squirrel; I was thrown to the street. Luckily, I skidded up onto the grassy curb, badly skinning my knee in the process but otherwise unharmed. We went to a West Side saloon. The bartender doused my knee with scotch to stem the blood. My outsize raglan-sleeved overcoat from Eddie Jacobs in Baltimore had proved protective. My father had authorized me to buy the Harris tweed for Christmas.

I left Paul Phillips's place shortly after Piaf died, and I moved into a high-ceilinged apartment off Riverside Drive on West Seventy-first Street. Aunt Camilla lived in the same block. She was a wry divorcée, living with her daughter Carlyle, who was named after my mother. I shared my new address with Malcolm McCormick, a soft-spoken ballet dancer who also worked as a super whenever the original Metropolitan Opera House needed help filling the jumbo stage. I slept in the alcoved bedroom. We painted every wall white except the side

of the living room behind Malcolm's bed. That was cobalt blue to set
off, I suppose, Malcolm's thinning blond hair. Aunt Camilla provided
welcome free dinners. I baby-sat Carlyle. Carlyle tells me I instructed
her not to sit in her dirty bath water. Well, naturally. I never knew her
father, architect Shepard Vogelgesang. His spectacular modern
house had burned to the ground in the woods of Whitefield, New
Hampshire. Aunt Camilla didn't idle among the ruins. It was comforting to confer—often about Uncle Herbert's money and getting
him to part with some of it—with Auntie Camilla. She was another
family member trying to make a new life in Manhattan.

Malcolm took his dance classes in the studios above Carnegie
Hall. One day he introduced me to an equally dedicated pupil, Butterfly McQueen. I asked her why she was not in Hollywood making
films. Her cheerful reply, in Prissy's inimitable chirp, thrilled me as
much as our meeting: "If Mr. Selznick needs me, he'll call me."

A job at Bergdorf-Goodman curbed my nocturnal roving, at least on
weeknights. The fashionable store in the glittering area of the Plaza
Hotel offered me the first non-acting job I enjoyed—before the
Palace. Inside Bergdorf's there were enough genuine names coming
and going to drop for a lifetime. I stood inside the Fifty-ninth Street
rotunda entrance, the only male stationed on the main floor, and
directed everyone from the Duchess of Windsor to Barbara Hutton
wherever they wanted to go. I wore a tie, and my affection for some
of the elegant emporium's chic salesladies became mutual. They
were a group of middle aged, no-nonsense career women, some of
whom had worked in the store for a lifetime and all of whom worked
on commission. Only Cobina, Marlene Dietrich's personal saleslady
for over twenty years, approached the star, who was adorned in a perfect navy blue suit, pearls, and a bemused expression. Cobina would
have bloodied the shins of any other counterjumper who had gone
near her Blue Angel.

Clark Gable and Sylvia Ashley, his bloodless wife after Carole
Lombard, shopped after causing a near-riot on Fifth Avenue. He

sported a velvet-edged topcoat collar and a gray homburg and threw me into more staring confusion then he had at Maxim's years earlier in Baltimore. Paulette Goddard left the store while I was outside on a cigarette break. She crossed Fifth and sashayed down the opposite sidewalk—beneath a trestle filled with workmen who gave her a chorus of clanging lunch boxes and Bronx whistles. Green-eyed Gene Tierney and a tiny, serape-clad Veronica Lake glided through the revolving doors. So did Gertrude Lawrence, then on Broadway in *The King and I*. She glared at me for recognizing her. I endeavored to be more blasé from then on—to perfect the covert glance at *most* celebrities.

I was in the basement cafeteria on my half-hour lunch break when one of the salesladies told me that Joan Fontaine was in the store. I ate like a garbage disposal and rushed upstairs to see the lady as she finished her shopping. She appeared with shortened '50s hair framing her lovely face, hunching toward the rotunda exit with a female companion. I waylaid her and blurted out my name. She was gracious without breaking stride. She could not have been otherwise. I had taken to sending her birthday cards to Miss Fontaine's home instead of a studio. On a New York weekend from Christchurch, in an anteroom off the lobby of the Hampshire House—while she was signing the scrapbook of her movie stills I had sent upstairs—I had surreptitiously memorized the California address on her luggage tags.

One day I heard *that* voice. I turned to see Judy Garland standing in the rotunda. She was plump, flushed, dressed badly in beige and red. She asked me where the dress department was. She too was with a female friend. I accompanied the two upstairs in the elevator as though I was sleepwalking. My innards fluttered at the sound of her laughter. It was disconcerting to look directly into her merry brown eyes. The merriment left them a bit later. She pushed her dressing room door shut when she caught me peeking at her in her bra and panties. I was not about to return to my post downstairs. After an interval of waiting, we continued over to the fur department. I hung around like a seeing-eye dog while the friend—maybe her secretary?—talked Judy out of charging another unbecoming item to MGM. She was offhand friendly again, and by then I was making both of us nervous. But something in her expression told me that she was pleased by my attention. I hated to see her leave the store that afternoon and found it hard to comprehend that she had ever been there in the first place. Cobina and her cohorts snapped their fingers at my vacant expression. They laughed and teased me until closing time.

My job at Bergdorf-Goodman ended when my father gave me permission to go to Europe for three months—with the inveigling Chuck Williamson. Dad agreed to finance my first trip abroad with a thousand dollars and warned me to be back in time for my upcoming draft physical, as yet unscheduled, to take place at Baltimore's Fifth Regiment Armory. I cringed at the thought of military service. I could not apply for a passport fast enough. The Bergdorf ladies gathered around me at the perfume counter in the rotunda to say goodbye. I also left my John Carlyle nameplate—identical to Miss Fontaine's—behind in the stationery department. Now the plate lies stored in a Francis Orr Stationery drawer in Beverly Hills. Some pretensions never die; they just become more expensive.

Chuck and I excitedly booked passage on the *Georgic*. She was the sister ship to the *Brentanic*. The two were the only smaller, one-class boats on the Cunard Line. Elliot McClanahan, a warm and wealthy alcoholic from our Blue Parrot circle, gave us a going-away party in our tiny stateroom. The two of us were bombarded with fruit, liquor, and affection. Our leave-taking was punctuated by wailing dock whistles, shouting stewards, loudspeaker announcements, and Elliot lurching against the wall in the happy cacophony of what wondrous events shipboard sailings used to be. Some of our guests barely got ashore before the gangplank was raised. Chuck and I raced upstairs to the top deck to prop our drinks upon the railing and wave goodbye.

CHAPTER SIX

AMERICANS ABROAD

ON MY FIRST morning at sea, I lay on my upper berth in a queasy fetal position, trying not to watch the gift apples, oranges, and grapes roll back and forth across our stateroom floor. I remembered that Dad—after summers in Europe with Mum and Grandfather Posey, and with Carlyle on his honeymoon—had said to get up and walk the deck, suck in the ocean air, and snack on crackers and cookies with tea. I followed his advice and felt fine for the rest of a perfect crossing. A frivolous crossing too, because the libidinous, leading-on crew was Italian. One of their limpid-eyed members allowed me to spend late-night hours with him while he was on watch in the crow's nest, a swaying aerie wherein it was proved that my seagoing constitution could take just about anything.

Since there was no class system on the *Georgic*, we were free to explore anywhere except the engine room or captain's quarters. We met people and made friends throughout the ship. Passengers came together in a democratic time warp, the way film and theatre

people cling together on a particular project and then seldom
cross paths again.

Jinx and Justin were an exception. They were a striking pair,
unmarried but traveling together as a couple and much in love. Jinx
was Ninalee Allen, a recent graduate of Sarah Lawrence College who
planned to study art in Italy. Her luminescence would bring her a
sort of immortality. She was photographed in Florence that summer;
she is the ogled "American Girl in Italy" in Ruth Orkin's famous photograph. I continued to enjoy the company of Jinx and Justin in various countries after I landed. The couple had bought a bright red MG
to see the sights. They picked it up in Southampton where we disembarked on June 10, 1951.

We Americans pant after shortcuts. Now, always in a hurry, we
board a jet. Today I shudder seeing the empty berths in New York
Harbor, the ghosts of their mammoth ocean liners. The *Georgic* prolonged the tranquility of being put on hold between different
worlds, something the cramped discomfort and speed of flying can
never do. Every traveler should visit Europe for the first time by
boat. Our voyage was such that there was melancholy in departing
the *Georgic*.

Our London address was 17 Chester Street, Belgravia. The stately
city was still Mrs. Miniver-like with bombed-out ruins, the dwindling
down of rationing, and a citizenry fond of Americans. Each morning,
Chuck and I came down from the honorable Mrs. Bethel's third floor
to present our food stamps to her butler in order to receive breakfast.
Over tea in Lady Bethel's sitting room, our otherwise perfect hostess
excoriated "that dreadful Windsor woman" when she learned I was from
Baltimore. She added that the beautiful Maryland countryside was
"*veddy* like England." Dame Sybil Thorndike, from a dais in her tent at
that season's Theatrical Garden Party, told me that the loveliest girls she
had seen when she was appearing in America were from Baltimore.
Already I was an Anglophile—now with a new respect for Baltimore.

In the midst of London's Festival of Britain, Chuck and I attended
the Oliviers in their stunning productions of Shakespeare's *Antony*

and Cleopatra and Shaw's *Caesar and Cleopatra.* The beauty of Vivien Leigh, stilled by the asp at center stage, is an ineradicable memory. She too appeared at the Theatrical Garden Party, madly peddling flowers off a cart—being steadied in an English drizzle by her solicitous husband. Teen-idol Dirk Bogarde hawked something from a makeshift stage. In cabaret each hour in his own sold-out tent, there was Noel Coward. Earlier in the week, in the downstairs lobby during the matinee intermission of *Waters of the Moon* with Wendy Hiller, Mr. Coward had waved Chuck and me toward him with his cigarette holder. I introduced him to my traveling companion. In turn we were presented to Noel's lifelong companion, Graham Payne. The reunion was head-turning. I was the indulged American; Chuck pretended nonchalance until, back upstairs in our seats, he began to salivate.

Before I left for the boat train that carried me across the channel to France, pretty, pink-skinned Princess Elizabeth and her sister Margaret Rose gave the white-gloved royal wave to the throngs of tourists from their silver Bentley. It passed in front of us through the gates of war-weary, gray Buckingham Palace under guess-what-colored skies. Chuck, after a sojourn with friends in Rome, would join me later in Paris.

I took a tiny room in the heart of Saint-Germain des Prés at the Hôtel Chambiges.

It was more agreeable to linger, people-watching, over a café au lait or un cinzano at the Café de Flore or Les Deux Magots than to take the more taxing hour or two to scamper through the Louvre in a hasty attempt to absorb culture. I experienced Paris though, through the quizzical brown eyes of my exuberant friend Coco. He was an immensely popular Parisian I met immediately at one of those snug café tables in the bustling student quarter. Expansive Coco's friends became my friends. The doe-eyed Anabelle was among them, a beauty who would marry Bernard Buffet, French artist extraordinaire— and commercial. Anabelle encouraged me to wear all black except for a silver belt buckle or medallion at my waist. This affectation

earned me the soubriquet "Black Star." Coco refused to use the nickname, but he did take me home to meet his sister in Neuilly. They
shared—with me for a time—an apartment in the fashionable
arrondissement. I moved from my atmospheric Hôtel Chambiges
fleabag to satisfy Coco's proprietorship—and to save money. I
returned nightly to the Left Bank bistros to forge a wider swath
among the expatriates and would-be intellectuals. When Coco grew
exhausted trailing me about, he went home on the Metro. I crossed
a bridge over the Seine as the sun was coming up, walked up the
Champs-Elysées, circled the étoile around the Arc de Triomphe, and,
when I reached the courtyard of the Neuilly apartment building,
rang the bell to call the infuriated concierge.

Mad Louis ran Le Fiacre, a popular dance bar (catering to any
gender) on a Left Bank side street. One night, a pair of carelessly
crossed, extraordinary legs on Le Fiacre's spectator balcony caught
my attention. Louis's frenzy turned avuncular in their vicinity. Their
black high heels kept time to the music beneath a tight black dress
topped by a rouged and ravaged face. The lady's spirited, childlike
blue eyes ignored the attentions of Louis and concentrated on the
dancers. Her white fan hands fluffed out her too-blonde '30s flapper
hair. They pawed at the real pearls around her corded neck. Coco
proudly told me who she was before he tugged at me to go home. I
got a crick in my neck continuing to check out Mistinguette, the
fabled musical comedy star of France. A star's aging is even more sorrowful to me than my own.

In early July, Coco went with me to northern Spain for the Feria
de San Fermin in Pamplona. Mr. Hemingway had me in his macho
spell. His sparse prose had convinced me that the bullfight, Spain's
great spectacle, was supreme theatre, and that the matador, dressed
to be courageous in his suit of many colors, was mystic and god-like.
How could I have overlooked the cruelty in its execution, not only for
the bulls, but also for the poor horses? The latter were at least
padded, but the bulls were at the mercy of the picador, whose lance
today is mercifully tipped. Bullfighting should be outlawed, but in

Pamplona I led the pack for the bedlam eight days of the festival's duration. I reveled in each day's heightened chaos. I slept only when I passed out from squirting too much red wine down my gullet from my hoisted goatskin flask that stained my sweat-soaked white shirt, red neckerchief, and requisite red sash.

Jinx and Justin joined us in Pamplona. The four of us snake-danced through the city squares, primed like every other tourist and native for the last day's climactic running before the bulls, along the main street, into the narrowed entrance of the corrida. That final day, there was a silence that stunned our disorder like a whiplash. The crowds along the pebble-stoned dirt road listened. Everyone strained to hear, to actually feel the sound and vibrations on the earth under our feet of freed hooves approaching—from the opened corrals a quarter mile away. Jinx sensibly flattened herself against a wall. Justin, Coco, and I staggered then ran as the reverberation grew and as howling fools were scattered in all directions, overwhelming us as the bulls bore closer. The three of us made it through the entrance into the bullring. The snorting creatures behind us charged straight across to the opposite side. They were slammed into gated paddocks to await their next entrance, this time one by one, to serve our disbelieving, hysterical pleasure. The jackals in the rickety, sun-baked stands screamed as each new animal broke from its barrier, squinted, and zigzagged its powerful path through our taunting, routed lot. Fortified by vino and the force of a Spanish audience, I bolted head on into the path of one bull—before swerving for cover to the sidelines upon feeling the brush of its glistening body against my side, seeing its lowered head and the glint of one horn tilted toward the space I had fled. That action made me a hero to our foursome. The afternoon's applause was of blockbuster variety.

When Madame Victoria Akbar Kadjar visited Paris, she stopped at Le Château Frontenac on rue Pierre Charron. A tiny, hawk-nosed woman, she was a genuine Iranian princess from one of Tehran's wealthiest, most privileged families. She was great fun too, and extremely generous to her friends and escorts. Coco and I enjoyed both categories; we saw Vicky frequently. We helped her select her gowns in the house of couturier Jacques Fath, left the lavish tip that she slipped to us when she took us to lunch in the Bois de Boulogne, and dissolved with laughter when we discovered her squatted over her Château Frontenac toilet seat like a black-eyed bird. She screeched us out of her bathroom in her high-pitched voice, then joined us in our fits of laughter over what, to Coco and me, seemed gymnastic Persian toilet training.

Vicky took me on excursions to Geneva to escape the Paris heat. We stayed on the cool lakefront at the Hôtel Élite. Sharing the same king-sized bed was a small price to pay for my privacy. I can count on one hand the women — two sparrows and a secretarial squab — I have slept with. One of the sparrows, Judy, snored. Not so Vicky, the sparrow with no interest in sex.

Vicky allowed me to try to drive her new red Jaguar from Paris to Deauville — for a gala being given by the old Aga Khan; Princess Kadjar was a cousin of the portly potentate's mother. After her shrieked instructions led me off the shoulder into one ditch too many, she reclaimed the wheel. She could not teach me to drive. The French motorist's habit of grazing your car if you do not speed fast enough was no help either. For the sake of propriety, we checked into separate suites in Deauville, numbers 94 and 95 at the dignified Hôtel Normandy. It was August, the height of the stylish French resort's social season.

That night I sat resplendent in the evening clothes Vicky had rented for me. She was opposite me, bejeweled and bedecked by Monsieur Fath, at the far end of the long main table. Our hosts at dinner, the Aga and his stunning Begum, headed the table facing one another in the center, European fashion, over candlelight. The Aga had received us beforehand. From his throne-like chair upon a solitary dais, he proffered a kindly smile and an inconsequential comment before he was helped by his aides to settle down to dine. Aly Khan's horse trainer sat beside me at dinner. He decried his employer's breakup with Rita Hayworth. He confirmed that another actress was on the scene. Joan Fontaine and the Aga's playboy son did not join us, damn it. The multi-coursed repast—with more accoutrements than anyone would know the use of—finally climaxed outside the casino's floor-to-ceiling windows with one of the few fireworks displays that have ever taken my breath away. Afterward, Vicky and I curtsied and bowed to murmur our thanks to the Aga and his statuesque, sari-clad Begum. We left to finish the evening in Deauville's most popular nightclub, a dim, grotto-like affair, where we found the bedroom-eyed Aly Khan upon the tiny dance floor. The unknown beauty in his arms, alas not Joan Fontaine, was obviously done for. We returned to the Normandy to telephone Coco at home in Neuilly—to crow about the glamour of it all.

When I was preparing to return to Europe twenty years later, in 1971, Mother sent me "this letter from your Princess. Maybe you can discover her all over again." It was addressed to Mrs. C. Rowland Posey at 617 West University Parkway in Baltimore:

Dear Mrs. Posey—

Perhaps you will be surprised to receive this letter from Paris, coming from an unknown person. Excuse me disturbing you, taking your time and also for my bad English but I hope you can understand me.

I want to write to you about your son, whom I have met in Paris with lots of pleasure. He is very popular over here and I am crazy about him.

If you ask from me, I am from a country very far away but living in Paris. I am a Persian (Iraniene) Princess who pass eight month of the year in Europe, Paris, south of France, Switzerland, etc. Everything about your son is mysterious to me. His real name, his age, especially because people give him from twenty to twenty-nine, and he never tells the truth. It is very important for me because I am borned at September 1922 and I can't marry someone much younger than myself. We shall go next week to south of France in my car, a Jaguar Sport, which I bought two months ago in Swiss.

*Please, Madame Posey do write me soon to my hotel address in
Paris and let me know all about your son John, and also if you will
ever agree to our marriage. If so I shall soon come to America to
visit you.*

Affectionately,
Vicky Kadjar

The fact that I unearthed this letter while writing this book is not
half so startling as its contents were to my family when they received
it. Coco and I, on one rainy Château Frontenac day when Paris
offered no other instant divertissement, helped Vicky with its message, but not its grammar. Jimmy's reaction is unrecorded, but my
father smelled a lark. Ann and Mother envisioned foreign dignitaries
bearing wedding presents to the front door. Very shortly I had to pla-
cate all three via overseas phone. Our intentions were not entirely in
jest; as a married man, I could escape the draft. Vicky, as my wife,
could legally emigrate to establish residence in the United States.
Time, fortunately, diffused our chatter into an unrealized prank,
dashed Coco's hopes of playing the role of my best man in America,
and vetoed, too, any future possibility of the late Ayatollah Khomeni
holding up my own head on a plate. Does Vicky still live in Iran, less
wealthy by far, with her extensive land holdings long since confis-
cated? It would be a hoot to discover her again, but not in her own
country.

When I discovered the communiqué sent by my Persian princess,
I found someone else's note. From the Neuilly apartment I wrote,
inexplicably and prematurely, to Noel Coward to obtain seats for
South Pacific in London. His August 17, 1951 reply from his house on
Gerald Road was not untypical but was more than I deserved:

Dear John—
*I could possibly have managed to get you seats for South Pacific but
for one insurmountable obstacle, which is that it does not open until
November.*

Mary Martin does not arrive here until the middle of September.
Anyway, call me when you get here—I shall be in the throes of
rehearsing my new play.

Yours,
Noel Coward

Chuck Williamson had returned to Paris just before I departed the
Hôtel Chambiges, at the beginning of my Left Bank time with Coco.
He left me a note to arrange a meeting with his new friend. While
Tucker Fleming ambled off to the Café de Flore men's room, I asked
Chuck where he had found "that marked-down Gary Cooper." In
Cannes, he informed me. Tucker was a tall, attractive native Cali-
fornian, a graduate of the Thacher School in Ojai, and had served as
a medic in the Army. He and Chuck announced that they were planning to continue to travel abroad together. They did, to my vexation.
The kicker is that they are still living together today, to our mutual
satisfaction. Tucker became a dear friend, but when the two first
joined forces, I was unhappy and timid at the prospect of being
without my European traveling companion. I felt abandoned, like I
do today when my companion John Paul goes up in smoke in a shopping mall or in an airport crowd. In Paris, I did not go ballistic
because first Coco, then Vicky, and finally M. François Reichenbach
replaced Chuck to allay my fears.

"Squirrelish" could best describe thin-lipped François, a sweaty
and skittish documentary filmmaker who could be large-hearted to
achieve his own ends. Coco and a good many other Frenchmen disliked him. His art-dealer father was a suspected collaborationist in
occupied Paris. François himself openly preferred the company of
handsome young Americans. Coco stood by helplessly as François
took pains to add me to his collection. M. Reichenbach twitched
delightedly over my fascinated curiosity when he and one of his few
French friends, the singer Charles Trenét, led me down into the tun-
neled sewers of Paris on le Quatorze Juillet. Coco lagged behind us,
sulky and anxious to celebrate the French holiday above ground and

alone with me. I saw François intermittently, then more frequently, and eventually without Coco—who moped at Café de Flore with Vicky and a legion of St. Germain allies, all of whom were rightfully on his side. But François was cultured, amusing at times—and rich. He lived in the posh Paris apartment complex at 17 Place des États Unis he had inherited from his father. One day he asked me if he could take me to the South of France. Despite Coco's baleful demeanor and the contempt of his friends, I accepted the invitation.

We drove with the top down from Paris to the French Riviera in my host's late-model Cadillac convertible. We rounded a curve to see the Mediterranean stretched before me for the first time. I was as stunned by the most beautiful area of the world as Joan Fontaine had seemed as "Rebecca" in Hitchcock's film when she saw the same cliffs. By nightfall, we were checked into Cannes's esteemed Carlton Hôtel where the balcony of our rococo suite overlooked the sea.

The excursion was all down hill from there. François allotted me chips to play the roulette tables at the ornate Casino de Monte Carlo, a gilded yawn before the Monaco Grimaldis were blessed with Grace Kelly to liven things up. I feigned sophistication over cocktails on the terrace of the Hôtel du Cap, before an endless M. Reichenbach business dinner at the nearby Eden Roc. I was bought lunch in Provence and dinner at Le Carousel in Cannes. Fine wines stupefied me over dinner in Aix en Provence. My pampered senses were numb. My first exposure to the magic of the Côte d'Azur was a dud.

François's endomorphic company was not the only problem. It bothers me to be beholden. I came to resent him because he was paying my bills. He meant to be a kind man when his interest was new. It was not his fault that God made him physically repellent. More often than not, I rebuffed him. Yet, because this beggar was choosy, I returned with him temporarily to live in the elegant yellow and white guest suite in his handsome apartment on Place des États Unis. François had no desire to throw me into the street—he still found me a charming beggar—and he understood that I could hardly revisit Coco in Neuilly.

The three-month time limit on my European trip was up. My angry father had wired me an additional five hundred dollars in care of American Express in Paris. I squandered it as though it were fifty. I asked him for more—for new clothes to keep up appearances, and new theatrical photographs to obtain continental acting jobs—to no avail. Dad condemned me for taking advantage of his largess. He wrote, in the letter alluded to at the start of this book, observing that I was "hypersensitive to criticism," that I was to report back to Baltimore, as agreed, for my Army physical. That prospect was so terrifying that it was tantamount to guaranteeing my stay in Paris indefinitely. The City of Lights had become my home base. I no longer had the funds to explore further European reaches even if I wanted to. The miracle was that François Reichenbach kept me—tethered to a flimsier financial leash.

One night, François took me to the lavish Lido de Paris nightclub. While Les Blue Belles, actually hard-working English girls, were exposing their pearly breasts, he pointed out the gold-coin handsome film star Jean Marais. He was seated at the adjacent postage-stamp–size table, and François, who knew everyone, catered to show folk. Some hours later found us floating on the river Seine aboard Jean Cocteau's houseboat—at Monsieur Marais's invitation. All of us rocked gently, doing some heavy necking amongst art nouveau patterned, oversized floor cushions, more than a little relaxed from sniffing M. Cocteau's cocaine—long before the habit became fashionable, at least in America.

There was a more formal salon in François's high-ceilinged, antique-laden drawing room. He presented the first showing of a Jean Genet pornographic film for a select audience. The black-and-white film depicted two handsome fellows falling in love with one another through prison walls. Their means of communication, while playing with their own cocks and writhing on their separate cots, was blowing cigarette smoke into each other's mouth through secretly bored holes. Michele Morgan, with her husband Henri Vidal, was one of François's guests. The sight of the actress gazing at the flickering screen, green-eyed and impassive, was almost, but not quite, as exciting as what was on the screen. The two protagonists were hirsute and swarthy and, as my late friend the actor Murray Matheson used to put it, "my tasse du thé." Ordinarily, as in life, after lovemaking, I am bored by pornography almost before I climax—too quickly. In this case, though, I could hardly ejaculate in François's drawing room—not with Michele Morgan looking on.

François and I took tea or an aperitif on occasion *chez* Raymond Duncan. That was an eye-opener. One had to strain to see through the scrim of haze collected from our host's cigarillos. He chain-smoked them in an airless chamber whose heavy draperies were always drawn against the sun. Isadora could not have been any flakier than her surviving brother. He was a pale, spidery man who wore sandals. Ageless Ray spoke in a reedy voice while his hands fluttered—usually in my direction—from the folds of a white kimono. He wore rimless spectacles tucked into long white hair and affected a studied vagueness on all topics until he launched into long monologues to summon up the minutiae of his departed sister, at which point he sprang to life in flawless and beautiful French according to François, so no one minded listening to his stories. François's respect surprised me until I saw his unspoken pride in his native language.

With fall dappling the boulevard trees, it was too late, not only to improve my French but also to sustain François's interest. He exiled me to a bleak, whitewashed room in the top-floor servant quarters. When I requested so much as the fare for a taxi, he made me feel as guilty as my father's letters from home.

Vicky had returned to Iran at the approach of cold weather, but Coco began to come around again on a more realistic basis. He was newly objective about my foibles, and he proffered his friendship as well as his affection. I gratefully accepted both. I was shorn of my summer's arrogance. I wore warmer winter clothes in place of my dramatchka black. The radiator in my attic room hissed into action at its master's whim. Coco climbed the back stairs to chuckle over the impecunious ways in which François ran his household.

• • •

My gloom and ego lifted temporarily when the men's fashion magazine *Adam, la Revue de l'Homme*, hired me for a modeling job. I posed in French topcoats and spectacular sweaters in their Octobre–Novembre 1951 issue. That was my one European working experience and, judging from some of the peculiar but admiring letters that the prestigious magazine forwarded to me, I was certain that there would be more. Nonetheless, moths were soon escaping again from my wallet, and Dad did not give a damn. My trip wound down toward chillier Paris days. My spirits were sustained by a few good friends and, yes, more than a few generous strangers. I had lost track of Jinx and Justin. I still wonder what became of Justin. I dreaded a return to America. I grew less confident regarding any possible employment, or a new and fortuitous liaison. I thought perhaps I would go home in time for Christmas—a season for forgiveness.

One nippy night, Coco and I were hailed by Noel Coward. He sat close by a glowing brazier with a silver-haired stranger in a Left Bank café. I was delighted that he asked us to join him. He introduced us to Edward Molyneux, whose celebrated *maison de couture* I had passed often in the rue Royale. Mr. Coward was warm and outgoing. He was on weekend holiday from work on the play *Stardust*, which would star Maria Montez. This was the play he had mentioned in his note about not being able to get me any *South Pacific* tickets. His talk whetted my nebulous acting appetites. But our surprise encounter seemed an inappropriate time to attempt to induce beneficence in that department. Mr. Molyneux said little; he seemed sad rather than remote. I remarked upon his gentle eyes: "You have eyes just like a James Thurber dog," I said, trying to be clever, meaning it kindly. The silence was broken by faster chatter on Mr. Coward's part, and the weariest of thank-you noises on the troubled, barely smiling face of M. Molyneux. The four of us soon left the café. We crossed avenue St. Germain to hail a taxi for the two older gentlemen.

"You ninny," said Noel Coward, grabbing my arm in the middle of the boulevard, "Edward is very nearly blind, and it's made life sheer hell for him. You've simply got to learn, dear John, to be more fucking tactful. Call me if you come to London." All of us said good night. Coco restrained me from shamed hysterics in a nearby pissoir.

Not long after my faux pas, I mustered the gumption to write the Master for a job anyhow. He replied on 9 November 1951, shortly after Maria Montez fainted and drowned in her tub. She was weakened from too-strenuous dieting for her London stage debut. Mr. Coward wrote:

> *Dear John—Nothing at all is happening about that play yet as it was being done for Maria Montez and is now shelved till we can think of someone else to play the part which will not be yet awhile. I do advise you to go back to America and do some television particularly as a labour permit for this country would be very difficult to get.*
>
> *If you are in London be sure to let me know but I shall be in New York in January so hope we may meet then.*
>
> *Yours Sincerely,*
> *Noel*

A feasible reason to return to London was out. I had worn out my welcome in Paris. Nearly groveling before François for another handout, my financial position had become an embarrassment. Coco was busy laying the groundwork to become a decorator. Vicky was in Iran to help launch Coco's stylish taste among her wealthy friends, some of whom have since fled to bigger and more nouveaux digs in Beverly Hills—where the beleaguered Coco, himself displaced after the fall of the Shah, still obliges their flamboyant preferences. He has assisted me in buying some of my own upholstery fabric—with his decorator's discount. Now we pass on the street and we sometimes hug. His intact charm has always made up for his incomprehensible English.

I had no choice, before the fickle Parisians put me into an expatriate's pasture, but to heed Mr. Coward's advice to return to America. New York was again the answer. There I would zealously seek work—in my native tongue. I told myself that my French had not been fluent enough to obtain an acting job. Besides, Chuck was on his way back to New York with Tucker, and in January I hoped Noel Coward would give me a Big Apple leg-up. And there was one other incentive to propel me home to New York. The French edition of the *Herald-Tribune* had bannered the rave, Piaf-like reviews for someone already in New York I had to see: Judy Garland had opened at the Palace Theatre on October 16, 1951.

Coco and I bade each other a mournful adieu at Gare St. Lazare. Two friends rode the train with me to Cannes. Portly Lester Judson and undernourished Elliot—whose last name I have forgotten—were songwriting partners. They were ecstatic at completing their engagement under the aegis of virago Madame Spivy at her Mars Club in Paris. They longed to write songs for an original Broadway score or for a calm performer who would headline at the Blue Angel. The three of us would await the arrival in Cannes of the *Olympic*, a small Greek liner on its way from Piraeus and Genoa.

The Cannes that we arrived in was a far windy cry from the boisterous carousel of a resort that François had introduced me to. Shutters were bolted, and bundled-up senior citizens promenaded the almost deserted streets. The colorful awnings were rolled up to admit a grayer light from the clouded sun into what few shops remained open out of season. On my last night, the seaside gusts pushed me out to the distant end of the quay. I sat down in tears, frightened to be going home, scared of facing my father, overcome with depression at the thought of leaving Europe, and especially my beloved Paris.

My first passport is stamped "Sortie de Cannes December 14, 1951." The longest voyage of my life seems largely lost in fog banks upon pitching, stormy seas. I do remember many Canadians layered against the cold creating a happy furor when they neared their native shores. The ship assumed an eerie emptiness when they disembarked. I recall dead-drunk Elliot falling down the stairs to the lower salon—into a blond and black-tied heap on Christmas Day. Lester huffed and puffed as we tried to help him up. Our mirthless holiday laughter was more forced than the captain's cheer.

Young Elliot died from cirrhosis of the liver too soon after our voyage. Lester lasted longer, despite cigarettes and emphysema, but the dawn of December 26, 1951 saw the three of us ascend to the top deck when our excited fellow passengers sighted the Statue of Liberty in the New York Harbor. The tiny sea-green symbol grew larger as we approached New York, cheering with hung-over, mixed emotions.

CHAPTER SEVEN

YOUNG LEADING MAN
IN THE HINTERLANDS

AFTER MAKING MY amends in Baltimore for staying abroad too long, I returned to my ushering job at the Palace by mid-April for what my brownstone neighbors Benny and Harry considered the Greatest Show on Earth. Not Judy Garland, but their favorite, Betty Hutton, who was a galvanized sell-out. Watching fifty minutes of her desperate energy grew tiresome well before the end of her four-week engagement. After she closed, the Palace sadly reverted back to its pre-Garland policy of eight acts of declining vaudeville, with a movie. The Garland stalwarts who remained said goodbye to our boss Mr. Bonus and applied for unemployment.

I do not recall collecting an unemployment check in New York. In Hollywood, yes, where the inglorious weekly ritual is impossible to forget. Eight twenty A.M. was my ungodly time to report. Those mornings when I feared oversleeping from impromptu partying or buggery were hair-raising. I gave Western Union a couple of hours' notice for a wake-up call. On near-bended knees for alms at the building I reported to on Santa Monica Boulevard, I took fearful intakes of air to keep from breathing upon the interrogating clerk. Those monsters seemed unrelenting in their harshness. One halting fib about how hard I had searched for a job could send me reeling to the end of another line, to fill out yet another form, before re-emerging, dazed, into the California sun. By then it might be noon.

The sequence of jobs that took me to Los Angeles, my imagined destiny since reading my first movie magazine, is clear indeed. I made my way across the United States as a bona fide actor, playing juvenile leads in two wildly different theatre companies. No, today the "juvenile" label is antiquated unless pertaining to a child, so let's say that I became a Young Leading Man in the hinterlands—where an actor always sank and had to swim. That experience was invaluable.

Ben and Harry wired me on June 16, 1952 in Brainerd, Minnesota. They were "hip that everyone will dig you the most. Kill 'em." They had the key to my room at Harmony Mansion. They had agreed to watch over my brownstone belongings during the ten weeks that some undistinguished agent had arranged to get me out of New York.

I was opening the Pine Beach Playhouse season in Ruth Gordon's World War II comedy *Over Twenty-One*. Initially the local critic was kind to the new boy in a barely professional company. He wrote that John Carlyle was "a top-notch new 90-day wonder worrying about protocol and a new wife, a role played with cracked-voiced naïveté that was genuinely charming and abundant with humor." Wow! An acceptable start in the bucolic state of Minnesota. The grand lakes and pastoral countryside failed, however, to calm the ensuing discord within a resident group of New York jobbers interspersed with locals. All parties came to respect and respond to only two directors within our ranks. Our producer was a mean-spirited tightwad we loathed for the duration of the season. He even made us clean the toilets. We suspected that he was the local critic. Actors can receive raves, but they memorize their pans. My two brickbats that summer are indelible: "John Carlyle (in *John Loves Mary*) is less happy, despite the fact that he got his share of the laughs. We wish that he would stand up and not perpetually bend over while delivering a line." And, in *Claudia*, "John Carlyle appeared and was quite decorative as usual." I was little else in the latter. I tried to correct the stooping forthwith—which resulted in some of the stiffest performances ever seen west of the Mississippi.

I grimaced and wore spectacles as the soda jerk in *My Sister Eileen*. No actor should be required to play Dr. Sanderson, straight man to Elwood P. Dowd in *Harvey*. My friend Bob Snook brought the house down as Elwood while I, with mechanized rote, threw him laugh cues. Rotund Robert was a fine and versatile actor; his company on visits to Minneapolis for dinner and a movie took the curse off the summer. So did our production of *The Hasty Heart*. Minnesota native Leo Hartig directed and splendidly played Lachie, the doomed Scot. Even our mystery critic without a by-line praised the production. He wrote that as Digger, the Australian boxer in *The Hasty Heart*, I distinguished myself with my finest performance of the season. The comfortable Digger wore pajamas for three acts in his hospital bed. My pugilistic stepbrother Jimmy would have gasped at the casting. The handsome people of Minnesota's Gull Lake area—they looked so *healthy*— were like sedate chamber music audiences compared to the trial-by-fire crowds that I was about to be exposed to.

I gave up my room on Thirty-eighth Street because of another job offer. Arrangements were made by phone for Mrs. Harmony to allow Ben and Harry to store my things in her basement until I returned to the city. I took a bus to Montana to sign up with the Virginia City Players. Their theatre was on Wallace Street in Virginia City, a one-storied, ramshackle town that was like a Western movie set. The place in September was dusty and barren until night fell. Then the saloons opened. The entertainment-starved townspeople transformed the area into a raucous beehive of outback hedonism, Montana-style.

Crowds of locals stormed the wooden sets of the Old Stone Barn Playhouse to cheer, applaud, and hiss our production of *Rustle Your Bustle*. That was our executive director's revision—and title—of the

1875 melodrama *The Almighty Dollar*. He played the villainous judge.
He cast me as bashful Charlie Brood. Each night, the impetuous
Libby proposed to Mr. Brood. Her amatory efforts only increased Mr.
Brood's befuddlement, which brought moans and groans of impatience from the foot-stomping audience. The jeers and boos for the
judge provided the company mini-rest periods, pauses in which we
learned and honed our melodramatic craft—for the tour that was to
take us on one-night stands throughout Montana, west into Idaho,
south into Wyoming and Colorado, and down to Phoenix, where we
closed in November. This was early regional theatre. Its public,
apoplectic in its fervor, demanded laughter, sniffed out phoniness,
and could produce, during an unwarranted silence, pulse-stopping
flop sweat.

At the end of each *Rustle Your Bustle* performance, my burgeoning
theatrical savvy dissolved into old cheerleader clumsiness. I was
required to sing and dance in Olios, to such songs as "I Never Cried
So Hard in all My Life," or "Clem, the Coal Miner's Daughter." The
director rehearsed me diligently in these proceedings, but my St. Vitus
dancing ability and tone-deaf vocal prowess made me his least favorite
pupil. These musical climaxes were meant to stampede the ticket-
holders home on a high note. They found me vamping ineptly in anxious anticipation of the final thud of the garish, brightly painted
curtain. Miss Elmarie Wendel, the saucy ingénue who played Libby,
did her best to coach and cover for me during this cacophonous mish-
mash. That made us fast friends, and, afterward, we set off from the
Old Stone Barn Playhouse as giggling seatmates when the Virginia
City Players' bus door creaked shut and its tired engine coughed into
gear to bump us toward another town. There were dwarfing western
vistas and homespun sights to see at unadorned stops like Great Falls,
Chinook, Rawlins, and Rifle. But ultimately a bus tour is stultifying.
The friendliest of passengers lapse now and then into stupefaction.
Dissension can only be relieved, briefly, by privacy, sleep—or sex.

I make the not-so-facetious observation that had I not directed
such formidable energy into my sex life, I would have—before both

became badges of baloney—earned an Oscar and graced the cover of *Time*. For years, a sexual partner took less effort to come by than a job in the acting profession, so the scale of my ambition tipped to favor the libido. The early-to-bed, family-oriented atmosphere of a little town in the West did not always repress my consuming horniness. For instance, the sensual glazed eyes of a young American Indian grew larger one night when I fell into step beside him on some nameless thoroughfare. Lucky for me, his mystification gave way to pleasure under a whirring ceiling fan in a nearby hotel. Sometimes I searched the deserted streets after *Rustle Your Bustle* like a fevered adolescent. My cruising was not new. It was to be endlessly repeated, later on more cosmopolitan avenues.

Charlie Brood bordered on moronic by the time the Virginia City Players completed their tour in Phoenix. I was so antsy to experience the wonders of Los Angeles that I hugged Elmarie goodbye and hitch-hiked to California. That seems youthfully nervy in retrospect, but I had never been so close to Hollywood, and I did not think twice.

There might have been an Erich Wolfgang Korngold orchestral outburst in my expectant head when some sharing soul drove me across the California state line. I plotted no clear course. My most valuable possession was exuberance. The countryside that I had so often imagined seemed unduly lush. The fragrant orange groves were more profuse and highly colored than on the tinted postcards that I had tucked into my mirror at Christchurch. The odor from the largest lemons anywhere was pungent, and the vivid, multicolored bougainvillea that was new to me looked jungle-like in its onslaught.

The ubiquitous Los Angeles palms were triumphant. Their towering crowns that fascinated me upon my arrival and evoked memories of the South of France still sway greetings to the hapless tourist. My memories of the Riviera evaporated when I was deposited on Hollywood Boulevard. According to Joan Fontaine, the street was already blighted in the supposed glory days of transfiguring premieres in the '30s. My aspiring gaze passed over the tackiness that was country-village clean compared to the squalor of today. I studied the sites that I knew from the pages of *Photoplay*. Their scale seemed reduced in the same way that Oak Hill became less majestic when I roamed there as an adult. Some famous façades, in a city whose buildings beneath pristine skies struck me as being low and close to the ground, were imposing nonetheless. The rococo Pantages Theatre was my first pilgrimage, at the mystifyingly famous intersection of Hollywood and Vine. From there I thought nothing of walking the length of the boulevard, carrying my one suitcase, to see the DeMille -like Egyptian Theatre with its long stone courtyard lined with fake sarcophagi, before crossing the street to trudge further west to gawk at the one and only Grauman's Chinese Theatre, encrusted with more ornamental chinoiserie than Nathanael West could have described. I saw where Judy Garland and Miss Fontaine had been immortalized in cement. I stood in thrall with the other tourists murmuring over all the famous signatures and handprints preserved in the theatre's forecourt and wondering too at the smallness of their shrunken footprints.

I asked for directions to the Hollywood YMCA but passed it by when I saw the Wilcox Hotel further south at the corner of Wilcox and Selma. I'd had enough togetherness for a while. The appealing rooms at the Wilcox were not only private, but also clean and moderately priced. They had no kitchens, but the small residential hotel, one block below Hollywood Boulevard, was located in a working-class neighborhood abundant with coffee shops, family restaurants, and, as it turned out, bars. Floyd, the tall, doughy night clerk at the Wilcox, chain-smoked through his shift and never missed a thing. He was "camp" before the term was coined. The art deco *Hollywood Citizen-News* building was just around the corner on Wilcox; I read Sidney Skolsky's gossip column each morning in a nearby coffee shop. Then I scanned the Help Wanted ads, where possible positions in the motion picture industry were naturally never listed.

I was quickly welcomed into Hollywood not only by Floyd, but by everyone from my waitresses to a talkative movie extra I recognized from the group of gentlemen gathered around Rhett Butler at Twelve Oaks in *Gone With the Wind*. He was cadaverous from sustaining himself on coffee and crossword puzzles while doing slave labor on various movie sets. He was still at it in 1952. He and others like him gave me my first paltry inklings of the periphery of the moviemaking fraternity I had traveled west to be a part of. I had neither a car nor the money to buy one. The truth was that, even had I known how to drive, I had neither the contacts nor the least notion of where to go to penetrate the industry that sprawled around me. This holding pattern lulled me into a pleasure-seeking limbo for my first weeks at the Wilcox. Behind the front desk, Floyd was my night nurse when Hollywood got too kinky.

I did have to work. What little salary I had saved from the Virginia City Players, even combined with my father's diminishing donations, could hardly sustain my living in a hotel indefinitely, even at ten dollars a night. My first job was at the nether end of Hollywood Boulevard beyond Pierce Brothers Mortuary. I was an assistant night manager at the Paris Theatre. Since demolished, sparsely attended even then, its screen offered grainy revival prints of French films. I worked on my French and became overly familiar with Raimu in *The Baker's Wife* and brassy Vivian Romance in *Carmen*. The dilapidated theatre seats sometimes supported young Marines. They were impervious to culture, but I passed the good-looking ones in anyway, to doze through the hours until their preferred hangouts grew festive later in the evening. They were all over Hollywood, lonely and eager, on leave from Camp Pendleton, loath to serve in Korea in a now-forgotten war. The forlorn box office lady watched her prostitute daughter work the boulevard for these Marines. She remained oblivious to everything else — except making certain that the cash was added up correctly when we closed the theatre.

I was in my own favorite hangout within minutes after closing down the Paris. The Comet Bar on Cahuenga was the liveliest of wartime Meccas for the Marines I met — and befriended. The Comet and its civilian clientele buffered the Marines' fears and restlessness with countless beers and a neon-lit turntable jukebox that played the pre-Beatles, still rhythmic hit songs of the early '50s. The harder stuff was also theirs for the asking, together with a place to stay, frequently offered by generous character actors such as Peter Brocco and Raymond Burr. One of the era's popular leading men, Dana Andrews, once found it necessary to crawl on hands and knees to the Comet entrance, from where his cab dropped him on Cahuenga. This spectacle called forth the cheers and laughter of those for whom he had bought round after round of drinks, matching each with another shot for himself.

Now and then, everyone but the bartender enjoyed a good fight. The bloodier the better, and best enjoyed from the safe vantage point of standing on top of the seats of the orange-red Naugahyde-covered booths—where those in both uniform and civvies urged their buddies on. When patrolling Military Police, often more youthful and wary than the combatants, sometimes broke up these battles, the dim Comet lights quickly grew dimmer—to soften and disguise the pulp and bruises wrought in the havoc. After a reluctant shake of hands, a compress of ice cubes within a bar towel was a soothing antidote to being hauled off to the brig in Camp Pendleton down the coast.

On the sidelines of one such mêlée, I met my permanently AWOL friend Paul Kennedy. Despite his pugnacious Boston nature, Paul dared not become involved. He had experienced enough sadistic punishment in the brig, so he vowed never to return to the Marine Corps. He was in hiding in Hollywood for good. So long as he did not get caught, he gave the finger to the ignominy of remaining a military fugitive. That status apparently meant nothing to anybody in the Comet, save the MPs. Rebellious Paul retained close-mouthed friends in the Corps, but he had been unable to buckle down under its rigid boot-camp discipline. He regretted his rash decision to enlist at sixteen to escape the dreary life he had in Massachusetts. He rejoiced at being in California, under whatever cloud. He too had escaped from quarreling parents and the cold that he hated back home by hibernating in movie houses. Film and its luminaries were the fascination that we found we had in common. Above all, Paul's cocky certainty that I could become a movie star solidified our friendship.

Raymond Burr became Paul's benefactor. He took Paul to dinner, gave him cash, and hired him later to be a personal assistant on *Perry Mason*. Mr. Burr paid for Paul's funeral, when Paul died of bone cancer at thirty. Long before the pain in his legs began, and when he was in my corner, he gained access to roam the sound stages on the Twentieth Century Fox lot. This privilege, through his rapport with an assistant casting director, enabled him to pant after Marilyn Monroe, whom he adored. It also made him the envy of the uniformed Marines. Soon Paul and I would ogle Miss Monroe together.

When the Paris Theatre shut down for good, Paul took to sacking out in my room at the Wilcox—to replenish his energy so that he could attack the Comet pool table to win free beers or to hustle another dinner. He had no interest in sex with me, unlike the other Marines who shacked up with me after the Comet closed. The morning after, they showered and pretended that nothing had happened. After so many such visitors, Floyd informed me that the hotel manager was threatening to double my room rate. When I realized he wasn't kidding, I put a time limit on my traffic.

I experienced a walloping blow with one daytime encounter. I have fancied myself "in love" countless times, but the memory of my hours with a gray-green–eyed, tow-headed corporal still persists. His build and looks personified a poster ad to entice young men to join the Marines. He swore that our experience was new to him, and I believed him. It was overpowering for both of us, and when he had to return to Camp Pendleton before being shipped out, no leave-taking was more poignant. I never saw him again and I only have this letter—and a snapshot—that he sent me from Korea:

Dear John,

I received your books and letter on the same day, both of which were evidently lost in the shuffle between here and Hollywood. Thanks for them John, both the letter and the books.

I'm most happy to hear that you're doing well in Hollywood & hope you continue doing so from here on out. Perhaps if I come back from this dying land, we'll go on together. Alone, each of us is lacking in something, but together we have everything. I believe this with all my heart John. It's something I never knew until I thought over the few hours we had together. The most enjoyable ones since I was a child. So stick around kid.

In order to attend college I may be forced to stay in the service for three or possibly four years. But most of the time will be on the west coast and we'll be together & I sincerely believe that this is all that counts. I'm sorry I can't express myself too well by writing a letter!

Good night, John, I'll try to be more cheerful next time. Rex

He expressed himself—in his loopy, aggressive scrawl—commendably, and I have treasured his words. Could we have lived up to them, I wonder? Perhaps not, but oh, to have tried! In the enclosed tiny snapshot, he is nude, looking quizzical in the sunshine, as powerful as the Korean rock that he sits upon. I treasure the picture too. Is he only nineteen? What did he want to study in college, and where? Was Rex killed in his Korea? His letter bears the Navy postmark March 18, 1953, the day before I attended the first Academy Awards ceremony ever televised, at the Pantages Theatre, over half a century ago.

I next worked as a soda jerk at Will Wright's ice cream parlor on Vine Street. I was fired after about ten days. Ozzie, Harriet, David, and Ricky Nelson—that quintessential American family—had been a pleasure to wait on. The cool setting with its miniature tables, delicate wire chairs, and pink-and-white decor was almost as picturesque as the Nelsons. I was unable to whip up twenty-four ice cream cones in as many seconds for an irate customer in a hurry to take them to a football game. I told him where to take them. My supervisor told me to turn in my apron.

Shortly afterward, I was hired to be an information clerk at the Hollywood-Roosevelt Hotel. I smiled a lot behind the luggage desk in the ornate old Spanish lobby and relied heavily on maps of Hollywood and Beverly Hills and Greyhound bus schedules for the tourists. I wore a coat and tie like I had at Bergdorf-Goodman, and my eight-hour evening shifts passed quickly enough. George Liberace and his band played in the hotel's Cinegrill, which I never set foot in, and wispy, malevolent character actress Elizabeth Patterson lived upstairs. It distressed me that she was the first among many that I have met in my profession who are not what they seem. She gave the lie to all of those agreeable movie characterizations. She never smiled, and she always complained. Her sour countenance made bellmen vanish and room-service waiters want to overturn her tray. Avuncular Mack Sennett, on the other hand, never asked for anything. He crossed the boulevard from the Garden Court Apartments, where he lived, to sit for vacant hours on one of the lumpy sofas in our foyer to dream of days gone by.

Montgomery Clift stayed at the hotel while he filmed *From Here to Eternity*. On drunken evenings, his friend Jack Larson assisted him through the side entrance and helped him upstairs to bed. Jack played Jimmy Olson on the early *Superman* television series that starred George Reeves. My curiosity regarding Mr. Clift's less-than-routine behavior and my sworn silence at having witnessed it prompted Jack's friendship. Sweet and erudite Jack had become bored with playing the *Daily Planet*'s boy reporter. He delivered many a one-man commentary on everything from acting to Charlie Chaplin to Virgil Thompson to this would-be movie star loose in Lotusland.

One afternoon, I accompanied Jack on a reconnoitering mission to his agent's office on the Sunset Strip. I waited in Jack Pomeroy's anteroom reading old copies of the *Hollywood Reporter* and *Daily Variety*, vicariously soaking up the atmosphere that I wanted to gain entrance to. When Jack made his exit, Mr. Pomeroy stared at me through his open office door. He asked Jack to introduce us. After we talked for a while, he said, to my everlasting gratitude, that I had contract potential. He became the first of my many "artist's representatives," ladies and gentlemen some, charlatans all.

Soft-spoken Mr. Pomeroy fit the last two categories in a far less offensive fashion than those on the higher rungs of his regurgitative profession. He had a smallish office in that quaint time before the power breakfast, e-mail and the fax, videotape, and blizzards of script breakdowns, when agent and client could drive all day from studio to studio, drop in on casting directors and sometimes producers, and lunch in whatever commissary offered the more contacts to garner.

Jack Pomeroy's tenacity paid off at Paul Kennedy's playpen, Twentieth Century Fox. The studio, on my looks alone, placed me under contract. The standard six-month option clause set an ominous timeframe for a newcomer edgy enough to require sixteen months to relax just walking onto the lot. I continued working in the evenings at the Hollywood-Roosevelt. I began to commute by bus during the day to classes required at Fox.

The two ladies who taught them had somehow been deemed acting coaches by the studio. Natasha Lytess was a twitchy, white-haired ferret who only wanted to be the mentor of Marilyn Monroe, which she was for a time. She liked to cast against type. Me as *Golden Boy*? She had me read the role of Joe Bonaparte for a scene presentation in class! Marilyn, her willing Galatea, whispered moist enticements into my ear as a highly provocative Miss Lorna Moon. I had barely been introduced to the gossamer Miss Monroe; our twenty-minute rehearsal time in Miss Lytess's outer office was frantic rather than familiar. Marilyn's subsequent performance as Lorna was less full-blown than her figure, and my Joe a clammy caricature of Clifford Odets's New Yorkese. This unlikely pairing, unfortunately never to be repeated, sent me across the hall to be shaped by Miss Helena Sorell, a pale, patient lady with crimson lips and matching hair. She tried, while my lips widened and froze over bared teeth, to teach me the inflaming power of smiling—*slowwwly*—on the silver screen. She seldom believed me when she commanded me to say "I love you" time after plastic time to Darryl Zanuck's mistress, Bella Darvi. With Bella, during awkward scene rehearsals on Helena's office couch, it was like making love to an ironing board.

Paul Kennedy was more spirited on studio property than I was. He propelled me from set to set, dispensing his dead-end kid charm for both of us—to the grips in the catwalks and the stars on the floor. We lounged against a portable phone table in the dark area beyond a living room set for *How to Marry a Millionaire*, watching Lauren Bacall and Betty Grable smoke and pace while they waited for Marilyn Monroe to finish her makeup and report for a scene. She smiled hello to us when she did appear, nearly tripping over Paul as she undulated into the light. The fretful assistant director—aren't they all?—shooed the two of us from the set as the three strained ladies finally took their positions.

We had better luck when we next came across Miss Monroe taking the sun between publicity photo sessions for *Gentlemen Prefer Blondes*. Dressed in black scanties, her meshed white legs alluringly crossed, false lashes fluttering against her peach cheeks, her shiny red mouth parted upward toward the sky, she looked like an ice cream cone. She sat tilted backward on the porch outside the still department, awaiting her turn for setups inside with Charles Coburn and Jane Russell. She was sweet to Paul, the idolatrous puppy who sniffed her out anywhere on the lot. He swore that he could go straight for her, and I understood. She asked me in a timorous breath, one contract player being helpful to another, if I wanted to have my picture taken with her. Her name was being called. No, I replied, she was too busy. She waved and walked into the still gallery. Paul's glare was more murderous than Jack Pomeroy's would have been.

Hollywood *is* a small town. Pamela Robinson was a fellow pupil who suffered and snickered under the admonitions of Madame

Sorell's near-silent screen technique. It turned out that Pamela's mother Audrey was Colonel Dale's daughter. Thus, until her screenwriter father Casey Robinson divorced Audrey to marry ballerina Tamara Toumanova, Pamela was my late grandmother Mum's step-granddaughter. Yes, I know. That's hard for me to unscramble. Pamela and I talked of securing roles in *The Robe*, a first Cinemascope production of mammoth, hopefully majestic proportions to arrest the burgeoning television foolishness and repopulate Fox's movie palaces.

Through her father, Pamela obtained top-dog orchestra seats in the Pantages for the 1953 Academy Awards. For the event, I rented—while Rex was writing to me in Korea?—evening clothes. Paul excitedly attended me as I nervously put them on in my room at the Wilcox. He fastened my cummerbund, adjusted my vest, and yelped that the tuxedo transformed me into a star! Floyd seconded this notion in Aunt Pitty Pat fashion in the lobby. Paul, on his feet in the bleachers when I alighted from Mr. Robinson's limousine, led a momentarily bewildered mob of fans in wild cheers.

Everyone, from Joan Crawford to Charlie McCarthy, in a staid parade of icons, was still in evidence during the 1953 shenanigans. Joan Fontaine wore a Spanish shawl to make a presentation, but I was never able to get near her. Jean Peters, wearing too much makeup, stood in line with us when the show was over, waiting for our cars. Gloria Grahame made a tongue-wagging entrance into the celebratory party at Romanoff's. She tripped on the step leading into the main room and sent her Best Supporting Actress Oscar rolling across the floor. Her tipsy joie de vivre helped Pamela and me to relax in the midst of the town's most posh après-Oscar soirée. What entrée we had for being there, other than the presence of Casey Robinson, escapes me.

The Robe was the downfall of all but a few bona fide stars who did not have long to remain under contract either. We fledgling mortals and many other Fox workers, because of the enormous costs incurred in the studio's frantic conversion to the numbing ratio of Cinemascope, were dropped then and there. Pamela departed after some handmaiden moments in *The Robe*; I returned to freelancing. My regret was that I hadn't learned how to create my own luck at Fox in the first place. As is the wont of all agents when their enthusiasm begins to wane, Jack Pomeroy turned his attention to newer clients. I would shortly begin a new relationship with Henry Willson, the town's champion in the business of yo-yoing new and appealing toys—in Henry's case, primarily *male* personalities.

Floyd was more aflutter by his switchboard than usual one work night when I walked back to the Wilcox from the Roosevelt. Doubtless in response to my hundred-and-first letter, note, or card, Joan Fontaine had telephoned! An invitation for cocktails found me in a cab a few evenings later, being driven to Mr. and Mrs. Collier Young's hillside address on Fordyce Drive. I was deposited wearing my gray flannel suit in front of the sequestered and wood-shingle-roofed house that would be a total loss less than a decade later in the 1961 Bel-Air fire—fortunately *after* Miss Fontaine had relocated to New York City. Mr. Young, dapper, pleasant, and an eventual employer— he produced *One Step Beyond*—greeted me at the front door. He showed me to the light wood-paneled bar area and left me to await his wife.

I had no time for nerves because Joan is never late. There she was, with scant makeup, blonde hair drawn severely back, wearing a black cocktail dress, her hand outstretched in a no-nonsense manner. I do not remember what drink she went behind the bar to fix for both of us. One did not mull over a choice with this petite but formidable lady of the manor. And I had not yet formed the nightly ritual of having either bullshots, vodka Gibsons, or Cape Cods before dinner. There was not a trace of her trademark wistfulness in her lynx-eyed gaze, nor did I detect the heightened Mayfair accent in her throaty voice. Her forthright persona brooked no fan murmuring and never has. We discussed the difficulties in the pursuit of an acting career and the inherent artifice in her sister Olivia de Havilland's current vehicle, *My Cousin Rachel*. Joan dispatched another role that she

herself had recently played as being "too straight up and down." I
found that a dead-on phrase and a minor conversational highlight in
a friendly but otherwise mostly impersonal cocktail hour. Her beauty
had grown more remarkable than her talent, and Joan has never
divulged to me the extent of her regard for either. She has chalked
the former up to good genes. She has dismissed my taste for the
latter as being a case of "arrested development." Did she whip up
Stingers behind that bar?

Mr. Young reappeared to say that they had best be on their way to
a dinner engagement. Mrs. Young solved the problem of my not
driving by announcing that their houseman would take me down the
hill to a Sunset Boulevard bus stop. Joan's adopted daughter from
Peru, Martita, accompanied us into the fragrant Brentwood night.
She snuggled warmly for the ride into the middle of the convertible's
front seat. I thanked my hostess, who was going off in the family car
with her husband. Young Martita's outgoing chatter went unheeded
as I was driven down the winding road out of a dream. Back at the
Wilcox, I could only describe, in minute detail for Floyd, a complex
woman's appearance—from her earrings to her shoes. Joan Fontaine
herself remained a tantalizing enigma. After only one meeting, that
was natural enough. But in fact, after opening and closing doors for
over forty years, she grew ever more elusive.

For financial reasons, I moved to a cheaper room beside an elevator
shaft in the Wilcox. The noise through the wall behind my bed
became as bothersome as my weekly bill, so I said goodbye to dear
Floyd and moved to a bare-bones apartment on Orchid Avenue.
Orchid, across the street from the Hollywood-Roosevelt, intersected
Hollywood Boulevard where the ghostly and decrepit Hollywood
Hotel was still standing. Its long wooden porch looked forlorn
because no one sat or rocked on it anymore. It has long since been
torn down—like the two-story Raymond Chandler–esque dwelling
that I moved into. My ground-floor apartment, the last door at the
end of a long, old-smelling hallway, had high ceilings and two double

beds. The Murphy bed that I slept in crashed down out of the bed-room wall. The other, hidden beneath deep wooden shelves that I painted tomato red, was a ten-ton affair that squealed its way on rollers into the living room. In the bathroom, beneath a circular shower curtain that had a life of its own any time there was a breeze, there sat an old tub with iron claw legs. The tub perched upon a small diamond-patterned tile floor that always needed scrubbing. The kitchen was ancient too, but adequate. The rent was seventy-five dollars a month. The pullout bed would prove to be a bonus, and I could walk to the Roosevelt at the end of the block.

Michael Rayhill was a friend who was trying to work as a singer - actor. He was going to visit his mother in New York. He agreed to contact Mrs. Harmony to arrange, with the help of Benny and Harry, to ship my few Thirty-eighth Street belongings back to me on Orchid Avenue. He found, when he arrived, that Benny and Harry had vanished. Mrs. Harmony had sold the brownstone to be demol-ished. All that remained of me was my green footlocker, locked and stored in the cellar. He managed to retrieve it before the wrecking ball arrived, and he dutifully sent it to me on the West Coast. Other than some linens and shirts, and my diploma from Christchurch, the contents were irrelevant to what I had lost: whatever winter wardrobe I had left behind, books, my LP record collection, ten scrapbooks devoted to Miss Fontaine, and a handsome leather pho-tograph album chronicling my trip to Europe. My loss was hardly the equivalent of one's house burning down, but it seemed so to me then. I was glad that I had traveled with one sporty link to the past, my raglan-sleeved Harris Tweed overcoat from Baltimore. Now the footlocker is stored on a shelf in my garage. I keep saying that I shall take it down to examine the contents of later years. My senior-year 1949 *Tide* yearbook is still inside. So is a stack of worldwide news-paper accounts of the death of Judy Garland. And, of all things, the film reel of Joan's Technicolor wardrobe test for The *Emperor Waltz*.

CHAPTER EIGHT

HENRY AND HIS BOYS

JEANETTE MACDONALD WAS the only singer that agent Henry Willson would represent. That association, since Mr. Willson liked neither musicals nor women, was inexplicable. Therefore, struggling Michael Rayhill, more singer than actor, became a friend instead of a client. Henry's legend was exhilarating for young men about town, which Michael certainly was. After Michael returned from New York carrying the paltry remains of my previous life, he took me to visit this man who could make stars out of handsome young men.

We turned off Sunset Boulevard and drove past the Bel-Air Hotel along one of the loveliest streets in the city to 1936 Stone Canyon Road. The house, like the street itself, looked serene, the kind of understated country place where Greer Garson might be found wearing a picture hat pruning roses. A uniformed black maid answered the door. Michael introduced her as Truie Delight. Truie led us through the chintz-covered sofas and New England bric-a-brac out the French doors of the rear patio to the back yard.

Mr. Willson sat shirt-sleeved in the sunny Sunday afternoon, making one feverish phone call after another. He made points by snapping, like a snake that slithered at his command along the grass, the long extension cord that he had dragged out beside his pool. His one good feature, dark brown eyes that missed nothing, including me, did not offset a small pouting mouth, a pale, flaccid body shaped like a honey pot, and a jowly, chinless head topped with thinning brown hair. The overall impression was that of a predatory bird whose head is always in motion. We stood watching, waiting, and listening to his small outbursts of hysterical laughter and malicious humor until he beckoned us to sit down. I was to learn that his high-pitched giggles were usually at the expense of others. Our host, pulling my lawn chair closer, zeroed in on me.

To cap what verges on a thumbnail assassination, I must state that from that first Sunday afternoon when he began to make me laugh, through his rages and machinations when he was still powerful, and even in the paranoid days before he died, I liked Henry Willson. At the end, his suspicions and fears—those of loneliness and death that can visit the ill-favored homosexual—became pathetic. He liked me too, and that has always been enough for me.

He had hustled new talent for David O. Selznick and represented Lana Turner early on. Miss MacDonald was his temperamental diva. The teenaged Natalie Wood was a current client. But Henry Willson's success and infamy had crystallized through discovering, renaming, and not *always* bedding down his male clients before he often made them stars. Guy Madison, Rory Calhoun, Rock Hudson, Tab Hunter, and a score of less well-known others contributed to Henry's meteoric track record. He believed that the man who set his loins afire— whether lifeguard, sailor, gas station attendant, or truck driver—could produce the same effect upon the screen for the female audience. Henry's long winning streak with this credo continued until pretty boys with flippant names no longer generated box office salvos.

A few prestigious doors were just beginning to close on Mr. Willson when he bade me leave Mr. Pomeroy and sign with him. The exposé magazine *Confidential* was sniffing out a piece on him. Both the IRS and his man Rock Hudson were growing restless. Rock was testy under the confines of the new Universal contract Henry had renegotiated. The taxmen suspected that the gigantic Willson deductions were unwarranted by Henry's claimed expenses. They were wrong; he refinanced his house more than once to entertain too lavishly. He was frequently cash-poor and borrowing because he wined and dined his clients in an exorbitant fashion that few of them, including me, deserved. His gifts were bountiful when one was in favor. In the beginning, after I could not sign fast enough with this Merlin who would finally do my dirty work, he outfitted me in an impeccable suit, pinstriped gray and single-breasted, from Carroll's Clothier for Men on Rodeo Drive. For Christmas of 1953, one of his presents was the largest bottle of Aramis cologne that I had ever seen, and which I never used.

He did not need to teach me—as was his custom with other clients—table manners or the correct wine—well, sometimes—to order with a particular entrée. I already knew what accessories to wear with my new Carroll's suit. So Henry groused and grimaced and snorted about other shortcomings. At an overwhelmingly star-studded gathering, or when I was under casting cross-examination, he tempered my nervous laugh. He supervised my haircut by Barney Sheeler at The Comb and Shears in Beverly Hills. When Barney retired after twenty years, it was like changing doctors for me. Henry nagged me to hold my shoulders back. He ordered me not to wear black trousers on interviews. They made me look too thin, he said, in that far-off time when I was. Upon departing Stone Canyon or his hangout, Frascati's, I could count on a telephone call to make certain that I had gotten home sober—and alone. Then, depending on the hour and my stamina, I hit the street or went to the Comet. What Henry did not know couldn't hurt him or me.

Henry urged his clients to study with a former "new talent" coach from Universal, Estelle Harmon, who taught screen technique in florid fashion at her home. My best benefit from doing scenes in Mrs. Harmon's makeshift dining room stage area, with mostly Henry's

beautiful young people, was my enduring friendship with Barbara
Rush—and her sainted sister Ramona. Barbara and Ramona and
their mother asked me to dinner once a week in their Byrd-designed
house on a hill off Laurel Canyon in the San Fernando Valley. The
evening was my fondest outing away from Orchid Avenue. Now, after
the requisite deaths and divorces, the Rush rapport remains intact.
Barbara and I recall, among other things, a rather lachrymose *A Place
in the Sun* piece that we trotted out for the studios, which we originated in Estelle Harmon's dining room.

There were sustained and unnerving titters during another scene
at Estelle's. I grew wild eyed-mystified at the beauties giggling; I
thought I was going great guns opposite Susan Cabot in a grandiose
bit from *The Lady's Not for Burning*. I was, but my fly was open.

Henry took me for the first time to the Mocambo on Sunset Strip.
One of his few starlet clients was my date. The three of us were
joined by Natalie Wood, chaperoned by her watchful Russian
mother and Natalie's escort, Tom Irish. Tom, a favorite Willson
client, was chipper and collegiate and the pretty spokesman for
Paper Mate pens. The Mocambo's Mexican motif sported huge
baroque tin flowers, flaming candy-cane columns encircled with
oversized ball fringe, and a raft of servicemen for Henry to stare at
as they circulated among the movie stars. The sardine-can pastiche
of nightclubs has taken on the allure of nostalgia. They were still
crowded to their noisy rafters in the '50s. Competing Ciro's across
the strip was as de rigueur to be animated, drunk, or uncomfortable
in as the Mocambo. We were jostled on a dance floor the size of an
elevator. We wondered while shouting at one another where and
how to brandish our cigarettes over the minuscule table. Even
Natalie envied the powerhouse celebrities their attendant hullabaloo and flashbulbs. She was in that moping, uncertain period
between child-star status and grownup stardom in *Rebel Without a
Cause*. Perky Tom resigned himself to taking her home early with her
equally moody mother.

Their exit left Henry to grow mottled and excited from Pink

Ladies and the bodies in the crowd. He insisted, without having to twist my arm, that we send my starlet home in a cab and go sit at the bar. We perched on the tall stools to charm two sailors Henry had taken stock of. He used me and his standard "you could be in pictures" ploy as bait to engineer a foursome for nightcaps of his own making. I was careful on Stone Canyon Road not to show too much feeling for the sailor Henry was right about. The evening is otherwise vague, save for the sight of a nude sailor careering away from Henry and landing on the carpeted floor, between the wall and my agent's king-size bed. Late, late night arrangements were made—when one risked tricks turning into thugs—for a taxi to show the sailors more of Bel-Air after dark. The two left with Henry's business card and cash to pay the cab fare to get them home. I, damn it, had to spend the night. I had not yet learned to drive in a city where a getaway car is imperative.

One day, Henry drove me to his former employer's studio in Culver City, housed in the graceful, columned building that prefaced the main titles for *Gone With the Wind* and every other stylish film assembled and controlled by Mr. Selznick in his legendary heyday. We parked in the circular driveway and crossed the long front porch. Henry announced himself at the inner reception desk. Within minutes, we were ushered into Mr. Selznick's small, cluttered office on the ground floor. The room—crowded with stacked books, packing cartons, and crates—was all that he had left, silent testimony to the imminent moving day for its occupant. Due to recent failed films, and the settlement with Irene in their divorce proceedings, the homely giant who rose to greet us was near bankrupt, relegated to the equivalent of a broom closet within the Selznick International Studio that had once been his empire.

Henry, who had brought Mr. Selznick Guy Madison and Rhonda Fleming in better days, was now proffering me. My agent did most of the talking, and I did not need to be jumpy. Mr. Selznick's handshake was a bear hug, his smile his dentist's Christmas card.

"Well, the eyes have it, Henry." The eyes appraising my own were vulnerable, which seemed ironic in a motion picture wheeler-dealer, who typically fancy themselves all-powerful before, during, and after their salad days.

"Montgomery Clift. Maybe better." Henry was peddling softly and with charm.

"God help us. Bobbie Walker."

I thanked him for the compliment (Judy made the same comparison fifteen years later), addressed him as "sir," and told him Baltimore when he asked me where I was from in the East. He put me totally at ease. I had no knowledge that I was a witness to the toppling of this particular giant. Henry did, and it is to his credit that he sang my praises and possibilities with all the eager fervor of an agent still certain that miracle deals were workable. Mr. Selznick listened, he made enthusiastic comments, and of course he demurred. He had to. He stated delicately that at that particular time he was in no position to place anyone under personal contract. But, he said kindly, who knew what the future, perhaps in independent production, might bring?

I certainly didn't. I left the office in a haze of fondness for a man who ten years earlier could have made me a household name. Timing is all, and Henry, who remained behind to gossip for a few minutes, never did admit that ours was lousy. Even though I knew that I had been privileged to meet David O. Selznick, as I walked past the tall white columns of his once-magisterial kingdom to return to Henry's car, I merely accepted it as my due.

Henry monitored the activities of his clients from his home and from his office at 1046 Carol Drive. He tried to be the arbiter of their public and private dating habits as well as their careers. He made it his business to approve or disapprove of who slept with whom—regardless of gender. That made for some furtive subterfuge on our part. Overnight trips were contrived, answering-service operators cajoled, autos parked a block away from assignations, curtains drawn and lights turned off for fear that our omnipresent agent would search us out in the middle of the night. Woe, too, and implied ruination, to a Willson client reported being seen in a gay bar. Henry, ever afraid of black-mail, avoided such bars like the plague; he insisted that we do the same. Whenever I exited to the Comet, I darted in and out like a chicken hawk—which, for those wondering along such lines, I was not. No one wanted to be dropped from Henry Willson's good graces. He alone controlled our professional destinies—a maxim so pounded into his clients' heads that we believed it. An invitation to be stuffed and coddled at dinner by Truie Delight on Stone Canyon Road was not to be turned down either, although stalwarts like Race Gentry, John Saxon, and John Smith got out before coffee was served. Broad daylight was stud time. Truie brought them bath towels by the pool while Henry looked lascivious wielding the telephone.

Frequently, vocal lessons were required for Henry's boys. Corpu-lent Lester Luther taught them, who was another coach largely sus-tained, in Lester's case justifiably, by Henry sending him his brood. In my case I specify vocal as opposed to singing lessons; jolly Lester knew that warbling was beyond the ken of tone-deaf me. Jammed into his overstuffed chair, the former opera singer gave me rigorous scale exercises that I always practiced in traffic on my way to inter-views. They strengthen the larynx, clear the throat to lower and place the voice, and divert other drivers. Rock Hudson owed his baritone to Lester; his voice had been high-pitched and nasal until he visited Lester. Lester's exercises while Rock had a cold froze Rock's lower tones into permanence. Lester's booming laughter was contagious; his mountainous belly shook, his brown eyes watered, and he sent many a pupil into paroxysms of giggles until he lifted a pudgy hand to signal us back on serious track again. I often saw Rock going to and from our coach's studio. The sound of their combined laughter shook the floors of Lester's shabby building on Selma Avenue in Hollywood.

Another Willson client, and a close friend of Rock's, came and went as well. We smiled at one another because Lester's thin walls disclosed

that he couldn't sing any better than I could. He was a handsome
bobbysox idol whose real name was Cragill Fowler. Henry named him
Craig Hill, a Willson moniker closer to the truth than most.

The vast back lot of Twentieth Century Fox was still full of sur-
prises when I made a return visit there with Henry. It is Century City
today, barren despite its density. Skyscraper condominiums, offices,
and hotels have replaced old sound stages and rolling hills. Stone
bridges and entire villages from *The Song of Bernadette* and *How
Green Was My Valley* have given way to airless parking acres under
shopping centers, junkfood stalls, and erector-set movie theatres.

Did I tell you that at Fox I pushed shy professor Fred Astaire onto
the gymnasium floor to dance the "Slue Foot" in *Daddy Long Legs*? I
was Cornelius, a dashing over-hill-and-dale Australian tour guide, in
Untamed with Tyrone Power. Except that's not me in the long shots
on the videocassette. For close-ups, after brushing up on my riding
for two weeks at a stable in Burbank, I mounted a movie horse that
knew its marks, indoors, in front of a process screen.

Henry took me to the outdoor set of a Fox western co-starring Craig
Hill. On that particular day, Mr. Hill was to be penetrated from
behind by an Indian arrow. He rode on horseback over a grassy knoll
onto the set. His pale blue eyes were a prowl to charm, like they
always were at Lester Luther's. He dismounted, and our mutual
agent officially introduced the two of us. Craig stripped to the waist
while we talked, and prop men affixed a thick strip of balsa wood and
a pouch of fake blood to his back. He put his tailored western shirt
back on the torso that was as sexy in person as it was on the screen.
Henry suggested, as Mr. Hill climbed back upon his horse, that the
three of us meet for a drink after shooting. Craig agreed, and rode to
his position some distance away for take after take of being pierced
unaware by a lethal-looking arrow rigged on a wire. A difficult feat
for the actor, but boring to watch in its repetition, especially for
Henry, whose concentration span was short unless it was focused on
agency business or a new male physiognomy. We left the set with

Henry chattering about how unusual it was for Craig Hill to agree to socialize, with another gentleman client present. Having reciprocated the glint in Mr. Hill's eyes, I was *not* surprised.

The three of us met for drinks at a dive on Pico Boulevard favored by the folk from Fox, across the street from the studio's back gate. The place, which due to its location was less likely to be under the scrutiny of members of the press or the wives of the grips, was lively and festive. Before heading home to change, Craig Hill accepted the invitation to join Henry and me later for dinner at Frascati's. At the restaurant, the mischievous Henry, trying to bait a trap, offered us his matinee tickets for *John Brown's Body* later that week at the new Huntington-Hartford Theatre on Vine Street. Henry claimed he had too much work to do.

Craig's *heterosexual* affairs were well known in town, including a recent one with Marlene Dietrich, who had aroused Craig by moonlight, bending over him wearing only her diamonds, in their room at the Sands in Las Vegas. She nursed him when he had the flu and taught him about the good German food she cooked for him where she was staying in Billy Wilder's guest house. Then she dumped Craig in favor of the older, more cosmopolitan actor Michael Wilding.

At Frascati's, Henry looked Machiavellian. When we accepted the theatre tickets, his puckered mouth got even tighter around his Brandy Alexander straw.

John Brown's Body starred Tyrone Power, Judith Anderson, and Raymond Massey. Most of it was as lost on Craig and me as it would have been on Henry. Our distraction was more carnal than intellectual. Being so delighted in the pressure of each other's thighs, we were barely audible when we talked together during intermission. We reluctantly went back to our seats and sat, light-headed, awaiting the finish of the final curtain calls. Then we escaped to Craig's apartment above a garage high up on Sunset Plaza Drive. There was a view that overlooked the city, which I paid no attention to until well after the lights of Los Angeles had flickered on.

When Craig drove me back to Orchid Avenue, my answering service told me that Mr. Willson had called four times. Craig's phone also rang half the night.

Henry was perplexed but seldom the wiser at the start of my involvement with Craig. The day of its beginning—at a matinee, mind you—marked the only time that the two of us went alone together to the theatre. Or nearly anywhere else, for that matter. Double dating was the demanded norm in the film world, at dinner in a restaurant, going to a movie, and certainly at any gathering labeled a "Hollywood Party." *Confidential* affected primarily the high and mighty, but any talk could be ruinous for the up-and-coming. Craig once asked me to lower myself to the floor of his convertible when he spotted his friend Peter Lawford driving up beside him on the Sunset Strip. I did as I was requested. We were fooling no one, of course. Certainly not Peter Lawford, or, as it turned out, Henry. Yet having an affair was wild and exciting under those closet circumstances, when discretion was still the order of the day.

Craig had been a lifeguard on the beach in La Jolla. He had no formulated ambition until one of Henry's minions photographed him and seeded the lure of the movies. Henry was impressed. Craig joined five others to test for the role of a lifeguard in a film being planned at Fox. The female secretaries on the lot gathered in a screening room to judge the contenders, and they chose Craig hands-down. When Craig's debut was released, there were squeals across the land in support of Henry's newest bit of beefcake. Craig's two or three subsequent films with his clothes on were less well received. He was the first to admit that he was slow to learn to act. His unique charm had more impact in a drawing room than on screen. Hollywood socialites seized upon him. His genuine warmth and goodness made him more relaxed in their circles than in the competitive camaraderie of a movie company. When we met, Craig was dating a ball-breaking daughter of a studio head, and Peter Lawford was providing an abortionist to help him disentangle from another relationship. Henry was beginning to tout Robert Wagner for the roles that should have been assigned to Craig, and our falling upon one another did not help matters.

Craig wanted to come and share my apartment on Orchid Avenue. There were two beds for the sake of appearances, and there was the bonus that we could share expenses. It is time to let it slip, without guilt, and with a great deal of ground kissing, that not long after I turned twenty-one, I became a trust-fund baby—courtesy of a great-aunt on my mother's side. The dole that one so quickly gets used to was minor in the beginning, but it permitted me to quit my part-time job at the Hollywood-Roosevelt and not be empty-handed with Craig.

When Henry was confronted with the folly of our joining forces, he flew into a flabbergasted rage and flew me to Las Vegas. We would attend Jeanette MacDonald's opening at the Sands. During the short flight, Henry denigrated Craig as, among other things, a playboy. Throughout our time in Vegas, Henry railed at our plans to live together. He said that Craig's option would probably not be picked up—which meant that he would see to it that it was not. He called his client an ambivalent, ungrateful prick-teaser who would one day opt for the company of a rich female. At the time of my first at-sixes-and-sevens trip to the mecca of neon lights and bad taste, the phrase "bad career move" had not yet been coined, but Henry could have introduced it in his incessant attempt to keep me from cohabiting with a well-known male roommate.

We scuttled away from the distraught Miss MacDonald's dress rehearsal, her shrill screams at our backs. The kitchen help and the waiters were making too much noise setting up for the opening, the tinny orchestra was playing her arrangements improperly, and her lights had to be reset because the nervous, color-blind coloratura had chosen the wrong gown. That night she made the usual fantastic, harridan-to-gracious star transition, and she warbled gaily enough to be inordinately well received by her thrilled, middle-aged audience.

Such was not the case with Miss Shelley Winters. Her lugubrious debut at the Flamingo just fell flat. For the finish of her off-key, miscalculated efforts, she boo-hooed her way through a monologue from *A Place in the Sun*, her face framed in a baby spot. She noticed Henry in the audience, and we reluctantly joined her for drinks between shows. Her vocal level, sitting in the crowded showroom, was almost as unnerving as her act. I would have been flattered to be told that I resembled the Italian star Vittorio Gassman, had Shelley not bellowed the comparison to her ex-husband so repeatedly, and with more tears.

Henry and I fled the Flamingo for the gaudier, grittier, equally popular Silver Dollar, located in a seedier section of the garish Las Vegas strip. Within seconds of checking the jammed casino, my agent moved like a streak of lightning to introduce me to a shy, brown-eyed man standing by himself on the edge of the crowd. He wore an open white shirt with a navy blazer, gray slacks, and, yes, the startled Howard Hughes was wearing tennis shoes. No, I did not look to see if he was wearing socks. He was handsome, I thought, and those eyes were something. He nodded, spoke in a warm, deep voice, but he did not shake hands. I had to repeat my name because he was hard of hearing. Henry yelled something about the Silver Dollar being his favorite casino, and that this was my first trip to Las Vegas. The bedroom-eyed Mr. Hughes pulled some chips from his pocket. He dropped them into my hand and grinned for me to go and have a good time. The smile faded as he reached for more chips to get rid of magpie Henry. When we turned to wave goodbye as we walked away, the uneasy owner of the Silver Dollar had disappeared.

The maxim that Henry had imbued in me to concentrate solely on my career evaporated in feelings of affection and relief to see Craig— waiting for us at the airport back in Los Angeles. When Craig actually moved into my apartment on Orchid, Henry did an about-face. He was seemingly acquiescent, grumbling only about the terrible location when he stopped by to take us to dinner out of "crummy" Hollywood. He still received, after all, ten percent of Craig's weekly paycheck. He continued, half-heartedly I suspected, my promotion when he submitted me for work. In reality he was badmouthing

Craig in studio offices. He implied that Craig was irresponsible, lacked ambition, and was not particularly talented. Slowly, Mr. Hill was being left to battle for parts on his own.

A visit to another back lot, this time at Warner Brothers, proved fortuitous. Henry, in conversation with George Cukor, signaled me over to meet the director, who was framing future shots with his hands. He held forth with his location manager and Henry at the same time. In one breath, the charming Mr. Cukor wished me well and went on conferring with his aide. Walking away, Henry told me in matter-of-fact fashion that I would be in *A Star Is Born*. My pulse and heartbeat did nip-ups. Instead of driving Henry crazy, my outpourings of desire to be in Judy Garland's film had paid off.

Too many weeks of doubt and disappointment followed. No contract was forthcoming. I ranted to Craig that I'd not even been given an inkling of what part I would be playing. He was placating and tender, stating that uncertainty and delay—especially in a venture with Miss Garland—was the way of the business. He said shortly he would label me his little movie star.

Alas, that was not to be. But just as I became convinced that Mr. Cukor had forgotten me, four script pages of *A Star Is Born* were messengered to me on Orchid Avenue. The role of "Assistant Director" was marked upon my four pages. He had as many lines of dialogue—in a sequence that showed the drunken star Norman Maine attempting to shoot a swashbuckling scene in the movie-within-the-movie. Seeing that Vicky Lester's services were not required, I told myself that that was just as well—Miss Garland's presence would have reduced me to pulp.

The late Ronald Haver, to speak ill of the dead, wrote incorrectly, as film historians sometimes do, of the making of *A Star Is Born*. Being left out of the index smarted more than his mistakes. He also omitted, from the index and the text, my friend Vern Alves—the film's associate producer! Ah well, at least I can reconstruct the making of my scene because I was there.

A Chinese junk, surrounded by seventy-five extras squatting and smoking in the very early morning, loomed up on the back lot at Warners. Its tall black hull seemed threatening enough—without feisty Charles Bickford appearing at my side to play the head of the studio. Gradually, as we rehearsed a long traveling shot of the studio head (Charles) and the assistant director (yours truly) walking onto the set of the movie-within-the-movie to cope with Norman Maine's drunkenness, Mr. Cukor's savoir-faire and cheer eased my nerves and Mr. Bickford's gruffness. James Mason, as the inebriated Norman, cavorted in pirate costume on the decks above us. Our goal was to talk him down, subdue him gently, and take him off to his dressing room. The extras did not always look alert or put out their cigarettes. I missed my marks a couple of times. But Mr. Cukor took every mistake in stride with patience and firm control. Under his perfectionist's guidance through many takes, no one's head ended up on a plate. Mine ended, eventually, on the cutting-room floor. But that was later, and it had nothing to do with Mr. Cukor. That day's thunderbolt occurred when, standing and waiting, and waiting, between Cinemascope camera setups, I turned to exhale the smoke from my Spud cigarette and saw Judy Garland watching me.

She was perched on her tall, name-embossed canvas chair, dressed in a white Jax slack suit with matching slippers, and she was smoking like everybody else. She smiled, and Mecca Graham, the actual assistant director, called out: "Judy, this is John Carlyle."

"Hi, darling."

Mecca looked pleased that his star was pleased, and I walked over to her. That Voice was like a magnet.

"I ushered for you at the Palace, Miss Garland. You had pink ribbons in your hair at the closing night party." Talk about out of thin air; the ribbons had barely registered at the party.

"Oh, my god," she laughed, "I knew I'd seen you before. Welcome to Warner Brothers, darling."

Judy was always a charming liar, and her friendliness relaxed me immediately. She was warm and adorable as we talked about the picture, the Palace, and Spud cigarettes. We both liked menthol, and they were her brand too. I offered her one of mine and lit it for her. We had something in common and I intended to make the most of it. Vern Alves appeared by her side, and Judy introduced us. She proclaimed my Palace position to him, a link that delighted her. Vern was the gofer extraordinaire on *A Star Is Born*, primarily for Sid Luft. Everyone wanted to keep Judy happy, so, noting that Judy liked me, Vern said that after I completed my own small role, he could arrange for me to visit the set. That was akin to being given free rein in the Pentagon. I wrote down Vern's office number as Mecca called me back to the set.

"I wish I had a scene with you, Miss Garland."

"Oh, darling, so do I."

I went back to work. Actors and civilians grow bored waiting around on movie sets. That, unfortunately, was the case with Miss Garland as filming went on, and on. Sometimes she did not bother to wait around. I spent my first afternoon as a visitor to the set watching the infinitely patient James Mason reacting for his close-ups—to the dancing stand-in mimicking Judy's turn in the number "Someone at Last." In the absence of the star, Vern took me to the most sumptuous office that producer Sid Luft would ever occupy. I sank into a designer sofa while Vern played the freshly minted soundtrack for this *A Star Is Born* remake. The new score was original. The stereophonic blast of Judy's voice through the open windows of Sid's office in the Warner Brothers administration building almost made up for her not being on the set. I was among the first to be blown away by "The Man That Got Away."

The lady was present, and then some, on my next visit, to perform one of the finest dramatic scenes ever put on film—the scene in which Vicky Lester collapses in front of Mr. Bickford in freckles makeup and newsboy costume between takes of singing "Lose That Long Face." There was one inaudible rehearsal. Mr. Cukor demanded silence. Then her heartbreaking monologue poured forth in one perfect take. Judy did not know that she was addressing her own corrosion and not Norman Maine's, and neither did we. The riveted silence when she finished was broken by the applause of the hard-boiled grips, juicers, and the rest of the crew. It was taken up by Mr. Cukor, Mr. Bickford, and all the rest of us clustered on the sidelines with tears in our eyes. Judy was spent, slumped in her tiny mock dressing room on the verge of real hysteria. I dared not go near her.

Craig advised me not to wear out my welcome on the tense set of an already over-budget film that was going further and further over schedule. But I was drawn back weeks later, when Judy's nerves and too few others' were being soothed by night shooting, to watch portions being filmed of the mammoth "Born in a Trunk" number. It was a musical albatross decreed by Jack Warner and is better left as a short subject.

There was a surreal quality in going from the studio's dark streets onto a brightly lit soundstage bustling with dancers, technicians, and a star in plumper but finer fettle. I was still careful to address her as Miss Garland when I offered her one of my Spuds. She bummed them frequently when she saw me. My gaze, when I looked into that face of my dreams and lit the smokes for her, became more direct. The knowledge that a cautious flirtatiousness was surfacing in our pleasantries delighted and terrified me. On those evenings after she sat smiling at me with melting eyes, her husband hovering in the immediate vicinity, I drove shaken over Cahuenga Pass to Hollywood — where Craig pronounced me crazy and overly imaginative, just as my old friend Hugh Martin did later when I really was. Hugh also told me to be careful, to not get involved. Needless to say, their admonitions — Craig's mock jealous, Hugh's a real warning — fell on deaf ears.

The last night I was on the set, Judy rested on my lap, cozy in a fluffy white robe between takes. I remember the scent of her White Shoulders perfume. She held my hand when I said more than one good night. Judy seldom wanted to let go of anyone. Neither of us knew that our transient emotions would manifest themselves for real nearly fourteen years later. I was ready for her then, back at Warner Brothers, or so I thought.

• • •

I also thought I was ready to learn to drive, and Craig calmly and painstakingly taught me, mostly on the secluded offshoot streets and hills of Bel-Air and Brentwood. Soon I was free to terrorize the busier lanes of Los Angeles in my first car. I bought his 1951 Oldsmobile on an easy installment plan, and Craig purchased a newer model. Either he or Rock Hudson drove us out of the city on weekends. Sometimes Rock went with us to a friend's cabin in Palm Springs or J. Watson Webb's house at Lake Arrowhead. In good humor, Rock was high camp, a laughing lunatic, but he was a glowering bore when he wasn't. Already fame kept his closet door closed, which he said was hell. His towering melancholy and inherent unhappiness could empty a room, and his buck-toothed haw-haw could convulse the same. Both moods were fueled by gigantic amounts of alcohol. The lighter usually prevailed, fortunately for his friends, which included, for a time, me. During my time with Craig, I became close to Rock, and it was a joy to make him laugh. I can also be a campy maniac.

Rock was a compulsively generous man if he liked you. On my birthday in 1955, I went to the grocery store, leaving Craig and Rock in the living room on Orchid to bitch about Henry Willson's monkey business. I looked forward to being taken out to dinner, but I was verging on my own gloom because there had thus far been no gifts. I walked back from the store a block away on Highland. My two friends sat smirking in a fog of cigarette smoke. The sliding doors leading to the bedroom were closed. I shoved them open. There, with no room for the pulldown bed, sat a shop window display. Rock presented me with the sturdiest easel made, a dozen empty canvases, and a fine wooden box of oils, with all their accoutrements. They included an elaborate variety of brushes that I had no idea how to use. Rock's guffaws surpassed my surprised yelps of gratitude. He knew of my old interest in painting, which he wanted to revive, and he was eager for me to show him a thing or two as well.

Afterward, three Sunday painters relaxed through many evenings.

We sprawled, our drinks by our side, daubing on Orchid, or upon the floor of Rock's Shoreham Drive apartment. For Craig, the libation was more stimulating than the painting. Rock, who had bought some paints of his own, painstakingly copied a portrait of the Pope off the cover of *Life* magazine. He zealously tried to learn what little technique I could teach him. I managed a striking copy of Marlon Brando as Julius Caesar from the same magazine. The result was too purple and photographic, but satisfying. It's reprehensible that I have not developed my gift for capturing at least the human face; anything else seemed beyond me.

J. Watson Webb, Jr.'s luxurious house of rustic stone and timber overlooked the north shore of Lake Arrowhead in isolated magnificence. The independently wealthy Watson reminded me of the American eagles he displayed at Arrowhead and around his elegant home in Brentwood. He was a retired Fox film editor who collected celebrities—whom he thrived on gossiping about. Craig arranged for me to be included among his famous weekend guests. The groups that fended for themselves at ample mealtimes sans servants were select and ever-changing assemblages. They didn't set out to intimidate as the acerbic Watson could with his savage tongue. Our freeloading was too good to bite the hand that fed us. On my first visit, hyper Debbie Reynolds held her own at the top of her lungs. Her betrothed, the reticent Eddie Fisher, seldom got a word in edgewise. The matador Luis Miguel Dominguin acted gracious when asked to display his bull-fighting scars. The ageless Annabella feigned amusement at Watson's venomous stream of studio gossip. I listened, bright-eyed, afraid to go to the bathroom, the same way I would in coming years in the presence of a neighbor—the sometimes vicious Dorothy Parker.

Craig taught me to water ski off Watson's dock. Before I managed to hoist my skimming rump out of the water, I swallowed half of Lake Arrowhead. Craig glided on one ski off the top of the dock in enviable fashion. He gave pointers to the petrified Eddie Fisher and, when he was amongst the pines, the determined but clumsy Rock, who was top heavy. Luis Miguel mastered water skiing and became almost as graceful a sight to behold as my roommate. After watersports and hours of conversational one-upmanship during three days intended for relaxation, Craig and I drove down the twisting mountain road in quiet, relieved exhaustion.

We sometimes dined at actor George Nader's house. On one occasion, his lover Mark Miller showed us a cluster of newborn kittens burrowed in bath towels in a half-open bureau drawer. No one rested until I picked my two—females—out of the litter. Cats number four and five went home with us in a cardboard box. Craig's protestations subsided and our landlords, an elderly couple who lived behind their Orchid building, came around too. I shredded newspaper into a box in the corner of the bedroom and set out to be a California cat owner. The newspaper was replaced with sand when one kitten preferred peeing on the floor. I named my house cats Maggie and Judy, the former after a friend, dancer Maggie Banks, and the latter after you-know-who. Judy, perhaps because she was taken too soon from her mother, tried to suckle on my neck in bed each night for eighteen years. When I was not alone, she chewed holes in the sheets or in tricks' socks and underwear. Maggie was neurotic, only affectionate when she felt like it—she took after me—and she was to remain by my side for an astonishing twenty-three years.

Craig doted on his parakeet Jo-Jo. He kissed its beak when he took it out of its cage in the living room. Not comprehending such an attraction, I was as oblivious to Jo-Jo as the kittens appeared to be. A few weeks after our black, golden-eyed innocents became acclimated, we returned home after an evening out. The only evidence left of Jo-Jo was two tiny legs on the living room floor. The beginning of the end, perhaps, of Craig and me? He suspected that I had deliberately left the door open to Jo-Jo's wire cage. I charged that it was more likely that he hadn't closed it properly. Maggie and Judy feigned obliviousness.

The other two constants in our social life were the astrologer Carroll Righter and social dowager Virginia Burroughs. Carroll gave a group of us dinner every Monday night. Virginia gathered Craig

and me into her elite Sunday-afternoon salons at the venerable
Château Marmont on the Sunset Strip. Astrologer to the Stars—
Marlene Dietrich would not go to the bathroom without his
advice—Carroll goosed and poked his twenty or so dinner guests.
He pulled on the men's ties, thwacked the ladies' bottoms, and
hailed everyone by their birth signs. He was kind and frisky and his
meat course was sometimes horsemeat, with no one the wiser until
after they had eaten. Carroll's nickname was "Pappy." He frowned
on a second cocktail, and the guest who got soused was never
asked back, which put all of us on good behavior. The same
decorum prevailed at Pappy's monthly parties, when, depending on
what sign was being celebrated, a Capricorn goat might be found
tethered on the front lawn. Once, we came upon Nancy and Ronald
Reagan on the side porch, gazing into each other's eyes through a
bowl of Pisces fish.

I believe in fairies but not the zodiac. The day's scattershot Capricorn nugget could come true if it sinks in, so I always turn the page.
Pappy's ferociousness on the subject put me off, but I only admitted
that to Craig. In fact, Craig was paying less heed to the galaxy than
the exploration of another area of belief that I was too insecure to be
patient with. My position as number one was usurped by a doughy,
pale version of Aunt Jemima, Craig's Christian Science practitioner.
She advised him to leave Henry, which he did, and Henry saw to it
that Craig was dropped at Fox. Craig found another agent, and for a
time the practitioner's syrupy sagacity bore fruit. He freelanced successfully in small films and on television. Meanwhile, I began to
understand Mother's feelings of being abandoned when my father's
psychiatrist became the mainstay of their marriage. I blamed Craig's
increasing remoteness on the tenets of Mary Baker Eddy. I imagined
Aunt Jemima bumping around her kitchen for her best china
teacups, exhorting Craig to live alone.

Most of the six to twelve actors and writers in Virginia Burroughs's
fashionable living room forsook tea for cocktails, and sometimes
plenty of them. Our patrician hostess was a striking sight, with her

upswept carrot-colored hair and green eyes. She lived with her ancient mother, whom we seldom saw. Virginia's eager listening made for good conversation while she presided over whoever surrounded her on Sunday afternoons as the sun went down. To everyone's consternation, her great friend Greta Garbo—"G-G" to Virginia—always fled upstairs to her own Château Marmont retreat before Virginia's guests arrived. We looked in vain for the retiring Swede in the elevator and hallways of the landmark apartment-hotel.

Frank Tack, a convivial musicologist and my friend until he put a bag over his head at age seventy-seven to go off to the races, was Virginia's co-host and, as they used to say in the columns, her frequent escort. He was not, as they also used to say, the marrying kind. He made the drinks, refilled the ice bucket, lit Virginia's cigarettes, answered the door, and, in one instance, acted as referee. Actor Kurt Kasznar leaped in red-faced rage for the neck of his wife Leora Dana, upsetting Virginia's coffee table in the process. Frank managed to keep the couple apart, and he volunteered to drive the growling Kasznar home. Another evening ended when Frank and Craig and I carried sodden screenwriter Mel Dinelli down to the vaulted, sepulchral lobby and sent him home in a cab. On the whole, however, overindulgence, before abstinence became the rage, was rare. It was a decorous group that broke up long after Craig and I did, when Virginia died of lung cancer.

CHAPTER NINE

THERE ARE NO SMALL PARTS

I LOST MY agent when he lost his secretary. Phyllis Gates and Rock Hudson began to be companionable, and not, so help me, solely for the sake of appearances. Craig and I accompanied the couple on one trip to Palm Springs. We slept on the outsize sofa in the living room of their hotel bungalow. We could overhear their laughter and giggles that, in time, in the bedroom, in restaurants, and everywhere else, by day or by night, became nonstop and constant enough to make their friends feel excluded. Come to think of it, to toss off a thought and unravel it later, when our time of palpable togetherness came, sometimes Judy and I did the same. But we did not get married, so I am still here.

Pert and perky Phyllis seemed to look askance at Craig's and my middle-class digs on Orchid Avenue. As she threw more and more weight around in Henry's office, she did the same, I suspect, regarding Rock's friends. Her growing influence seemed insignificant in the face of her unremitting sunny personality. Craig and I were glad for the couple's happiness, which, for Rock, seemed to be escalating. Their appearance in public was a Louella Parsons orgasm. Craig's and my feelings were decidedly mixed when Henry announced to *Photoplay*, and thereby to the world, that they were to be married. We wished them well. What else could we do? It turned out that we were losing Rock, not only to Phyllis, but also to *Giant*, the most touted opportunity in his blooming career. Rock returned home to new, mixed friends after he and Phyllis honeymooned and went off on location for *Giant*, and Henry pared his client list. I was on the chopping block because I still lived with Craig. Only Henry's contract players, some promising studs, and a new secretary remained with his office. Rock was temporarily the pick of the pack. But not for long. Corporate vultures who could offer more perks than Henry were beginning to circle. When Rock finally left the best agent any of us ever had, Henry's clout was finished.

I must tell one vignette of Rock the bachelor. He nursed many a hangover in a Hollywood bathhouse. He chose Craig and me to be his confidants when he had crabs, that niggling hazard of promiscuity — before the penalty became life-threatening. We spread newspaper on the living room floor while he used our bathroom to douse himself with Cuprex, the smelly, greasy, stinking ointment used as a cure for crabs. While Craig and I laughed for the twenty minutes required before he could take a shower, Rock just sat there, nude, large and writhing in discomfort upon the *Los Angeles Times*. Later, when I romped with more people than I knew what to do with, oblivious and insatiable on uppers in the "tubs," and also before AIDS, Cuprex was obsolete. Now, so are the bathhouses. I wonder where everybody goes.

Craig and I saw two other gay friends regularly. I have mourned the loss of one of them. They lived in our friend William's splendidly simple bachelor home designed by architect Richard Neutra on Avondale Road in Brentwood. It was constructed of old brick with double fireplaces, beamed ceilings, floors of large Spanish tiles, and immense sliding glass doors that opened along the one-level length of the vast living and dining room area. Rock and I wore bath towels pantomiming "Diamonds Are a Girl's Best Friend" in front of those doors, and I danced there—fully clothed—with Judy. Get the picture? A lot of elbow bending and partying went on at Avondale.

Jack Owen lived in William's compact guest quarters beyond the kitchen at the end of a Williamsburg wall. Thomas Jefferson's serpentine design of single-layered brick enclosed the entire lush property with its hidden circles of fish ponds, jungle-like gardens, lovely pool, and the skirmishing occupants inside the striking house.

Sweet, staunchly, guiltily Catholic William was a mild-mannered Los Angeles transplant from Grosse Point who happened to know Aunt Camilla. For a time, after serving in the Navy, he had been an architectural apprentice to her husband Shepard Vogelgesang in Whitefield, New Hampshire, where William's family had a home. He liked to recall making himself scarce so that Camilla could entertain Archduke Franz Joseph for lunch. He was very fond of her. William's personality was muted until, on the dot of six each evening, he began to drink. Then, as he tossed back his "marts," he became a loquacious, mirthful lover of his schooner anchored in Newport Harbor, his hidebound family, his two dachshunds, the younger man Jack Owen, and his friends—in that order.

Jack, an agnostic, would-be Faulkner–Carson McCullers character, was from somewhere in Mississippi. He had tried without success to bed down Craig in Laguna. He did bring him home to meet William, who had struck it rich—richer—in oil. Jack never took it in stride when Craig brought me onto the scene. I had succeeded where he had failed. The saying should be "Hell hath no fury like a *faggot* scorned." Jack liked to entertain with a vengeance at Avondale because, as he constantly snarled over his own double-gin martinis, William had bored him since day one. He did not like to spend the evenings alone with the man who unaccountably cared for him. Maids, gardeners, and cooks came and fled because of Jack's drunken demands for perfection. The results were delicious but tense dinners where Craig and I, when Craig was not working, could best be described as being on the dole.

William was a consistent, giving friend, but he ruined Jack Owen. It became a tradition for Craig and me to spend Christmas Eve at Avondale. We greedily received our lavish gifts and didn't care—much—that we were too strapped to reciprocate. William already had everything and Jack could not be satisfied. He was not averse to yanking down his favorite gift, a money tree, and throwing it across the room if William had not hung enough bills of large denominations among its branches. Jack resented William for supporting him. He toiled in spasms to be a successful writer; he remained neglected. He quite rightfully blamed his failure on his cushy situation at Avondale. He tried to break the mold—but could not—by decorating an apartment William rented for him at the beach. One Sunday, his muse blunted by the sound of the waves and alcohol, Jack unexpectedly returned to Avondale.

Craig and I were happily babysitting Coco and Poulder, William's beloved dachshunds. Their master was on his boat. We were very much at home watching *What's My Line?* on television in the den. Jack refused to retire to the guest house, and, when we would not depart the premises, began an inebriated argument. I went to telephone William on board his boat. Jack tore the phone out of my hands and hurled it at my head. The heavy white instrument missed, but I did not when I slugged Jack. My fist hurt, and I had opened a vein on the side of his nose. The freak blow caused blood to splash down Jack's face and slosh over everything nearby. Craig and I were terrified. We tried to sop it up with every available towel in William's bathroom. The cut, when it stopped gushing, turned out to be superficial, but Craig had to use fire tongs to subdue Jack in order to prevent him from exacerbating the situation.

A new, bloodless slipcover was made to protect the sofa from Coco and Poulder, and some time passed before Mr. Owen would welcome us—me—back to Avondale. But, finally, he had to. Jack's maniacal behavior was emptying the house of everyone but William. In time,

Jack's features thickened, his belly softened and distended, and there was no real shock when he died in the early seventies from acute alcoholism. William, passive and uncomprehending, mourned him terribly. I did not, but I dutifully attended his funeral in the chapel of the small Westwood Mortuary Cemetery. I thought of Marilyn Monroe lying in her green chiffon in a wall nearby, and I was not surprised at the sparse turnout for Jack. His ashes were scattered around a rose bush in the garden outside the chapel. Surely it died instantly.

William left us before his friend Aunt Camilla. She was holding her own with Alzheimer's, speaking words of charm but little else in her Century Apartments aerie on Central Park West. I had no idea on the day that John Paul took me, trying to kick, and growling, to Cedars-Sinai for my second arthroscopic knee surgery, that William was checking out with pneumonia at St. John's Hospital in Santa Monica. Six weeks later, when I telephoned to suggest dinner, William's departing houseman gave me the news.

I never said goodbye. His family—did the word "homosexual" ever pass their lips?—did not call me, even about the Roman Catholic funeral. That is why I call them hidebound, and why I do not use William's last name. Nine out of ten hang-ups on my answering machine were William's. He was shy about leaving a message, or even his name. I would have been at St. John's in a heartbeat—on crutches.

There were already 162 names in my lists of the dead when I added William's in 1991. Yes, I write them down—in an old appointment book; God knows how many there are now. Will someone conclude them with my own? I shall ask Robert Osborne to report the cause of my demise as "consumption," à la Garbo's in *Camille*. Yes, death is a huge preoccupation in one's less-than-blooming early seventies. Did Judy, I wonder, sitting on the toilet in London, recognize and welcome death's sting? She was more perceptive and cannier about herself than anyone else was. Will my own eyes open wide like hers, I wonder?

• • •

The only audience to see me in *A Star Is Born* was at the preview in Huntington Park and did not include me. I wish to hell I'd been there. Not long after that preview, Vern Alves telephoned the blow. My scene was among those cut soon after that first showing because of the film's excessive running time. Vern commiserated, expressing his sincere regrets, which were nothing compared to my own—his news remains the saddest single disappointment that I have experienced in my profession. Sadly, my scene is not among the lost bits and pieces restored to the re-release. For the skeptical, and the few lucky Garland freaks who enter my house, I resort to the original cast list that does include me. It hangs in my bathroom. Better Warners should scissor "Born in a Trunk" and go on searching.

I was less upset at testing unsuccessfully for *Rebel Without a Cause* and *The Blackboard Jungle*. I felt like the ingénue who once told me, in all seriousness, "I don't do ensemble." For *The Blackboard Jungle*, we were required to throw chalk, erasers, and epithets at one another in a Bronx classroom set at MGM. All day, teacher Glenn Ford threw us lines of dialogue while the director, Richard Brooks, panned the camera over our improvised mayhem. When Mr. Brooks did not linger on me, I knew that my refined puss stuck out like a WASP beacon in a sea of more street-smart and ethnic aspirants.

My friend Stewart Stern, who wrote the screenplay for *Rebel*, arranged for me to meet its director, Nicholas Ray. Mr. Ray, a white-haired chain smoker with a film noir following, seemed genial enough interviewing me in his office at Warner Brothers. That changed when he turned downright sadistic on the familiar back lot. He put his selected contenders through their grueling paces for days—in my case, three. We had to stage knife and bottle fights, both on foot and from open convertibles being driven in dusty circles. Not all of our props were fake. To introduce ourselves into the maw of the camera, he had us leap, one by one, from a six-foot trestle shouting, Brando-like, "Stellaaaa," as we landed. Day three featured partnered scenes shot late into the bitter cold evening. It was well past dark when my turn came. I was to drive along a studio street hosed down to make it photograph better, park beside a sound stage, then leap from the car to huddle beside a sheltering wall in order to confer with my waiting girlfriend, played by Kathryn Grant, who sensibly went on to marry Bing Crosby. Our scene went well enough when we scurried around rehearsing, warming our trembling hands with Dixie cups of bad coffee. Driving into place before exchanging the actual dialogue was another matter. I tried without success to drive the stick-shift car assigned to me. Finally, Dennis Hopper crouched down over the gears and out of camera range and helped me lurch and hop the car into position. When I bolted from the driver's seat, I was not only frozen, but mortified. I flubbed my lines with Kathy during each of the three chances that Mr. Ray allowed me, before being dismissed for the night and, of course, for good. I was a shivering, sorry-for-myself wreck when I got home. With Craig's blessings, I found comfort and warmth in a bottle of Scotch.

Albert McCleery was the unsung producer–director who devised the use of minimalist settings on live television. A trellised archway, a ticking clock upon a single table, tree branches that reflected upon his actors' faces; the shows were photographed in front of black backdrop curtains with various bare essentials to heighten the foreground reality and lower the budget. Craig and I knew bisexual, married Al socially, which did not preclude our auditioning for him from time to time. One seldom obtained acting jobs through friends, especially gay friends, or at a party, but Albert proved the exception to the rule by throwing me much more than a bone.

I was summoned to his office at NBC on a Monday morning. He had me stand before his desk to read a script page of verse. He stopped me and told me to take more time and not listen to the words that I barely understood. I did. He told me I would be playing the young Edgar Allan Poe on *Hallmark Hall of Fame* the following Sunday. He said Farley Granger's agent had turned down the role, that Warners would not loan out Dennis Hopper, and he was confident I would vindicate his third—and surely less costly—choice for Mr. Poe. I went reeling into a wardrobe fitting before beginning rehearsals that afternoon.

Script read-throughs, revisions, Craig's cueing my lines, blocking scenes upon a maze of taped floors in NBC rehearsal halls, and more revisions filled the frenetic madness before Sunday came. Driving at dawn toward my first camera blocking in the actual studio was like approaching the gas chamber; that afternoon the great American public would yank down the lever by turning on their television sets.

Inside NBC, my hair was curled, I was dressed in a West Point military uniform beneath a high-collared period jacket, a cravat, a greatcoat and a top hat, layers of costumes to be taken off and thrown on again as I darted dazedly from sequence to sequence in a minimal to bottom-line set. The teleplay told of the scribbling Mr. Poe being sent by his enraged guardian to shape up at West Point. He was subsequently unfairly expelled for poor grades and cheating. The equally terrified veteran actor Ian Keith played Poe's guardian. Mr. Keith managed to transpose all of his lines with no one save me the wiser. Fortunately, he left the scene long before Cadet Poe closed the show by bidding goodbye—in rhyme—to his classmates upon the West Point landing dock. Crates, barrels, and the reflection of shimmering water upon my exhausted face simulated the landing dock.

In the interim, the young Poe vowed to make good to the girl Poe's father caused to be left behind. While rehearsing the love scenes, martinet McCleery chided me through the overhead microphones: "John, you are not at Universal Studios! There is no need for you to keep sticking your tongue down the young lady's throat." All day, during breaks in my dressing room and at the makeup table on the floor of the studio, he counseled me mercilessly on the cadence of the poetry and the probity of my line readings. After he wished me well at the end of the final run-through, I was glad to see the back of him. I was also hell-bent not to disappoint him when he re-entered his control booth. The rich tones of the Hallmark Card announcer filled the soundstage. Airtime was at hand.

Mr. McCleery was pleased and relieved by the result; a journeyman performance, I felt, by a more handsome than accomplished me, a young Edgar Allan Poe driven more by the expeditiousness of live television than by subtext. Afterward, I was like an amnesia victim, accepting congratulations for not having been caught fainting by the occupants of the nation's living rooms. Someone at NBC made me a gift of the *Cadet Poe* kinescope. Years later, I had it transferred to videocassette. Only then was I finally proud of the best effort that I was capable of making in 1955.

Mother wired me: "We have rarely been more pleased and proud. So many friends saw you and are raving. Your voice splendid. Hope this is a real beginning. Love from all of us." And from my father: "Performance terrific. If offers don't start arriving tonight I will volunteer as your agent." I still wonder why offers didn't materialize. Was my new agent, whom I do not even remember, retarded? Was there a national catastrophe, or a championship playoff opposite *Cadet Poe*? I would not have known. I do know that there is not an agent alive who sustains the fervor of a parent.

Albert McCleery went on to produce *Matinee Theatre*, another live venture presented each weekday for too brief a time in the face of television's ever-enlarging economics. I acted in four of those for him, treading carefully among more sparse props in barely suggested sets. It was Albert McCleery who first paid me real professional attention. His prestige in the industry declined as the television medium became an expanding and more expensive garbage disposal. He suffered a fatal heart attack in the early '70s while attending the theatre in New York. I know I thanked you, Albert, for the start of my career.

I can only blame myself for the demise of my relationship with Craig.

Boredom—who am I kidding—*horniness* led me down Hollywood Boulevard one night. I picked up a Marine outside the Comet. Later, when I got home, the apartment on Orchid was dark—save for the orange glow of Craig's cigarette from the sofa in the living room. It was not the first time that he'd followed me in his car. He told me calmly that he was moving out. He said that my cruising was not the reason; it was the culmination. In the gradual dearth of our close- ness, there had come a worse deadening, of our companionship. I implored him, my stomach knotting, to please, please stay. I did not get hysterical or blame his meddlesome, hateful Christian Science practitioner. I did love him, I said so, and I believe that I still did. He held his ground, smoking there in the dark, with the attitude of pas- sive resistance that he tried to live by, and that he tried unsuccess- fully to instill in me.

Craig had been the one who was capable of settling down. We both knew, despite my paying lip service to monogamy, that I was not. Craig's loss was not brought home to me until after he was gone. He was a decent, caring partner in a relationship that has not been bettered. Now, with celibacy thrust upon me, together with the luck of an enduring relationship, my rutting instinct remains the same. I am a male animal and a puritanical tramp. But today, with the omnipresent shudder of AIDS, and aging, I do not have the energy. I subjugate the desire to act upon those impulses that drove Craig out of my life. Well, eighty-five percent of the time, anyway. It *is* like get- ting back on a bicycle.

I did work some after my success in *Cadet Poe*. The role of Morgan Evans in Emlyn Williams's *The Corn Is Green* is the one I wanted most of all. The auditions were so extensive and down to the wire that I felt director Ray Verity was mounting a show for Broadway instead of the Pacific Palisades Playhouse. When he chose me, I rel- ished bringing the young Welsh coal miner to life. The colorless actress who played my schoolmistress Miss Moffat was a hurdle I cleared by mopping up the stage with her. The otherwise capable cast was led—no, dominated—by Ellen Wallace as a whining, bitchy Bessie Watty. Ellen, a fellow former Baltimorean, became a friend. She was the most distinctive ingénue I have ever had to be on my toes with. She forsook competing for roles to remain a married lady who derived more succor from a gentle husband and a menagerie of animals than she did the acting profession. A few years ago, I called her for help acquiring new cats, numbers eight and nine, who have not yet made their entrance here. To my horror, her grieving husband told me that Ellen had died of a heart condition. He was off to bury her ashes under a mountain rock. I had to look elsewhere for Leap and Pinto.

James Powers, the influential critic for the *Hollywood Reporter*, maintained an interest in new faces. I thought nothing of reminding him of mine in my bombarding requests to come and see *The Corn Is Green*. I cannot resist reprinting the happy result of his making the "thirty-mile round trip to the Pacific Palisades in a prickly mood and pouring rain" to cover the show: "As for Carlyle, his belief in himself as an actor, the most necessary single quality an actor can have, is fully justified. He is an intense, sensitive and handsome young man with great natural gifts and the technical powers to utilize them. He deserves to be seen and he was correct to insist on this right."

I had thus embarked on my most active years in television and on local stages. On camera in the mid- and late '50s, from *Matinee Theatre* to *Navy Log*, I played refined, sensitive young men who were most often lovers and were frequently rich, but an occasional aristocratic villain, out to seize the heroine or else the loot, was thrown in. Those were the years when I expected and received starring roles and took for granted the luck of brief prestige. The less fruitful times of being grateful for smaller assignments—or even any—were still to come.

Briefly, here are some scattershot experiences, a soupçon of my salad-day highlights.

Feathertop, an adaptation of the fable by Nathaniel Hawthorne, was televised live on December 2, 1955 on *General Electric Theatre*. Carleton Carpenter played the scarecrow-brought-to-life title role, the temporary mortal who almost wins the affections of my betrothed, played by Natalie Wood. Carp won my affections as a playmate and a neighbor before and after *Feathertop*. Natalie, pre-blockbuster stardom, was at that point just a melancholy hellion who had been bewitched for real by James Dean on and off the set of *Rebel*. She wore too much street makeup trying to look full-blown and womanly. Among her myriad musings lounging in her dressing room at CBS Television City was the question of whether or not men liked women to go down on their toes. My reply was doubtless non-committal, but Natalie's bulging, mascara-laden brown eyes put the kibosh on mere titillation; she was serious in seeking the sexual erudition that she never got from me.

I must have discounted my *Feathertop* role as Natalie's fiancé. I had the nerve to party with a ribald Hollywood group at Mel Dinelli's house late into the Saturday night before the show. The most sedate guest, Estelle Harmon, kept telling me to go home and get my rest. Lord knows what Natalie had been up to before airtime. On Sunday, we came at each other with such nervous force and energy that my tri-cornered hat was sent flying off my head in the off-camera direction of Ronald Reagan who, no doubt having been in bed for days, was preparing to extol during the commercial breaks the progress General Electric afforded.

Lisa Gaye left me with a snappy facial scar inflicted by her riding crop when I tried to rein in her horse on *Northwest Passage*. Our real riding was augmented for close-ups by swaying about on stepladders on the back lot at MGM. I lost more touch with reality wandering about my favorite lot when not needed than I did when I was acting. I experienced realism in spades when I was flown to Moab, Utah, to play the Sundance Kid in *Wells Fargo*. On my first morning, the crusty cast and cowpoke crew fell on the ground laughing when I came on the set wearing my cocky Stetson backward. I redeemed myself by holding my own with scene-stealing Edgar Buchanan and riding my butt off across the stubbled Utah ground alongside star Dale Robertson.

I murdered my wealthy grandparents by throwing them down the stairs on *Bourbon Street Beat*. The ethereal Celia Lovsky played my lovely grandmother. The first wife of Peter Lorre had me to tea in her bygone Hollywood house and forgave me when the script wouldn't. I jumped ship in a foreign port to celebrate something with a ship-mate's relative on *Men of Annapolis*. The sight of my scrawny shirtless self descending from my upper bunk sent me to the gym for twenty years. I tried to kill my father Lorne Greene for his money on *Mickey Spillane's Mike Hammer*. I insisted that a stunt double jump from my life raft into the Long Beach harbor filming of *Navy Log*. However, I did my own jump through a breakaway glass window to escape someone on *The June Allyson Show*.

When Paul Henried directed me on an episode of *Alfred Hitchcock Presents*, he accused me in his continental snarl of not being able to act—meaning his way. I disliked him because he was humorless and autocratic, and he gave me line readings. He cut one of my key scenes as Barbara Cook's playboy lover in *A Little Sleep*. The show was Miss Cook's one and only fretful foray into dramatic television. She was Marilyn Monroe-like and convincingly brassy. In grudging fairness to Mr. Henried, he was more adept at approximating charm than I was at playing it, then.

William Shakespeare intimidated me a good deal more than Mr. Henried. I drove from my new West Hollywood digs on Hilldale— more on that to come—to the non-union Morgan Theatre in Pacific Palisades to play Orsino in *Twelfth Night*. During rehearsals, I launched umpteen times into "If music be the food of love . . ." and could not stop listening to myself, much to the consternation of the baroque director. He was also concerned with my thin legs in robin's-egg blue tights. Did he too reside in that asylum for perfect specimens, West Hollywood? I was dispatched to Men's Wardrobe at Western Costume for sexy symmetricals in the form of Tyrone Power's calves and thighs.

Opening night galvanized me into forgetting the renown of *Twelfth Night's* opening soliloquy. Making my entrance leading mooncalf Orsino's beribboned, mandolin-strumming court down the center aisle, I meant the words. Fellow actor Oren Curtis proclaimed that I had never said them as truthfully or as well. Oren played Malvolio. For years, Oren continued to judge my performances both on stage and in the living room. *Twelfth Night* was the start of our long, arduous friendship, the one John Paul took over during a seven-year estrangement. Acting is Oren's favorite topic. But in the Morgan Theatre dressing room where Oren, bearded and lemur-like, accused me of applying too much eye makeup, our chatter about the merits of everyone from John Gielgud to Bette Davis was temporarily put on hold for more serious pursuits.

In a registered letter, Actors' Equity ordered me to withdraw from the non-union *Twelfth Night* or to face charges for conduct unbecoming a member whose parent union was the Screen Actors Guild. Unions! Was acting not my life? No, unfortunately, it wasn't. I did, however, want to continue working—legally. So I left, after performing for the critics, in my one and only non-union show— that I should not have appeared in in the first place. I told Oren I was bereft that my replacement, who went on with Orsino's lines written upon his palms, was too late to benefit from my generous personal notices.

By way of a footnote to *Twelfth Night*: Jeryl Josephs was a mopish plain girl who rode with Oren and me when I drove us home from the Morgan Theatre. Neither of them drove. Jeryl was Carroll Righter's secretary. She had joined the cast as a rather heavy-footed lady-in-waiting because she thought she was in love with me. Her penchant for falling for the wrong man was consistent. Her dilemma sprang from her doldrums, which would prematurely curtail her life. She could be good, clever company around a shared card table at many a Righter Monday dinner. Her lusty humor could too often be self-deprecating when it was coaxed to the surface. She was a wonderful cook and an even better drinker. Her fare—deviled crab casserole and too many cocktails—stopped short of finding its way to my heart. But she did lull me twice into staying the night in her disheveled Hollywood apartment. I closed my eyes and stroked and petted her as though she was a longhaired, outsized cat, and I fell asleep. She made a jolting Bloody Mary in the morning, purring because I had slept over. Our long, trying-to-be-lighthearted companionship waned when I would not repeat the process. She no longer thrived on my humorous rebuffs as they became more and more callous. When she gave up on me, her pattern continued with other fellows. It escalated into suicide attempts because of unrequited love and alcoholism. As time went on, my phone rang at ungodly hours. After periods of not hearing from me, or from some other lost love, she began to hate me for not giving in to her sobbing self-pity. Still, the last time she telephoned, she begged for my company because she had been abandoned yet again. I increased my distance. When she was found dead one morning by a married lover preparing to leave her bed, I told myself, not yet certain that people never change, that I wished I had gone to her. Unfortunate Jerry—I seek her out from time to time in the Westwood Cemetery to wish her love.

Perhaps I failed another friend from that era, Peter Hartshorne. No, I closed and bolted the door, something John Paul says I am good at. He also says that I have no guilt about anything. He does not know the half of it. I am digressing. Questioning? Whatever. I would prefer to be disliked rather than ignored like Jeryl and Peter. The only certainty is that the disintegration of both of my friends was due to alcohol, that mass mutilator in my blithe years before AIDS.

I first met the always-impoverished Peter in William's den on Avondale. He had a schoolteacher face and a mind as learned as anyone in that profession. At that time, his encyclopedic knowledge, which he never put to practical use, was espoused with ineffable charm, fueled or not by booze. He was a native New Yorker who shared William's and my preppy attitudes. My Baltimore background further served our Ivy League, WASP companionship.

William's, Peter's, and my seemingly snotty talk and upbringing sent Southern drunk Jack Owen snarling to the guest house to stare at his posters of Herb Alpert, snarkier by the minute in his determination to live like an aging California beach bum. We were relieved to be rid of him. We settled deeper into the sofa cushions beside one of William's fireplaces to natter on about Aunt Camilla, William's boat, Peter's scholarship time at Yale, the best books and handsomest men. Coco and Poulder lay in our laps, hypnotized by the orange flames and blue smoke that floated up the double chimney. We toasted coincidence and the irony of meeting.

Between acting jobs and trust checks, Peter taught me to refinish furniture. He and an over-the-hill male model were partners in an on-the-brink-of-thriving establishment, until Peter's lunch hours in a nearby tavern began to last too long. Another part-time apprentice in the fine art of paint-stripping, gold-leafing, and varnishing was my friend and future traveling companion Peter de Merritt, whose eventual suicide, which I shall come to later, still enrages me.

For a time, Peter Hartshorne managed—just barely—to maintain his keep and pay his bar tabs. Friends, some in high places, kept him in demand as an astute bridge player and fed him before and after the game. Sometimes he cooked the meals himself, beautifully, and he was not averse to whipping up donated groceries in his own low-rent apartment in West Los Angeles. Mr. and Mrs. Charles Brackett had Peter for evening bridge, or at their Sunday luncheons at their English manor home in Bel-Air.

The Sabbath invitations were prized and flaunted by the crème de la crème of high motion picture society. La crème ranged from Clifton Webb and his mother Maybelle to Mr. Brackett's former writing partner Billy Wilder. When I was a luncheon guest through Peter's auspices, the teatime conversation and less rarefied atmosphere were abetted by Virginia Burroughs with Frank Tack and, once, Olivia de Havilland.

Peter admired my work. He made the effort to see each role that I played, on television or in the theatre. He praised my performance as John Proctor in *The Crucible* at the Horseshoe Theatre in Hollywood—on the night that I almost succumbed to apoplectic hysteria. Actress Ruth Philips, her eyes glinting more maniacally than usual, handed me the supposed witch's rag doll. Pointedly she lifted its little skirt. The words EAT ME were inked large and clear upon the limp cloth belly. There is nothing more terrifying on stage than losing control. Peter was diplomatic. He claimed not to have noticed the spasms I directed upstage that evening. The rest of the cast struggled with me for what seemed an eon, against their own tears of mirth at my dilemma, before Arthur Miller's script got me back on the righteous track.

Peter and the rest of the audience wept, when I dared not, in Pasadena in 1958 when I performed there in Eugene O'Neill's *The Iceman Cometh*. I was the gloomy young man who jumps to his death after recounting his betrayal of his mother. The director, Ralph Senensky, insisted that I inhabit the doomed Don Parritt without giving in to tears. There were nights after I left the stage when, like Mr. Parritt, I felt like leaping from a fire escape. The extraordinary play and our ensemble cast constituted the best production I was involved with in the theatre — a fact I state with some melancholy. Dabbs Greer and Onslow Stevens led the superb character players as Hickey and Larry. The script called for me to play primarily off Onslow. He was my table partner, scorching and infinitesimally askew in a different way with each performance, to rivet my concentration in Harry Hope's bar. Much of the Hollywood theatrical community got the word, and we were filled to capacity throughout the too-short run. Or was it? Mr. O'Neill, as my father knew, can play hell with the psyche. Our dedicated, on-stage melancholy was neck-and-neck with reality when we were forced to close. Mr. Gilmor Brown, the founder of the Pasadena Playhouse, had to have his prestigious Playbox Theatre back for another production. He was relieved. He had decreed that our rehearsals and then our actual playing time be over by ten o'clock — for fear that our sedate Pasadena neighbors would close us down for our boozy ranting and noisy O'Neill profanity.

Peter was becoming less and less a stranger to the quirks Eugene O'Neill explored. I slowly turned away from his boundless, out-of-control drunkenness. While I was no slouch with my own capacity in

those days, I could not afford to pay for his drinks. Persuading Peter
to call it a night and come down from his barstool grew increasingly
difficult. His expertise as a moocher began to be as repellent as his
breath. Even William, who was tolerant of anything and damn near
everyone, was exhausted by gunnysack Peter's night-after-night,
long-after-midnight demand from the depths of the sofa for "one
more," this after another gratis dinner that Peter was disinclined to
eat. Jack Owen was driven to enjoy new heights of distraction until
Peter, finally, staggered into the night for me to drive him home. By
then my friend was a reeking heap. Our slurred, strained conversations petered out into disgusted silences on my part that ended our
doomed-to-be-repeated evenings. Everyone, including the Bracketts,
scolded and pleaded with Peter to cut down on his consumption—if
he could not quit completely.

He could not manage either until the end of his life. The irony
then, in the mid-'60s, was that he was a stone-sober passenger asleep
in the back seat of a car being driven home from Santa Barbara by a
tired and tipsy lady friend. They had been to visit an aunt of Peter's.
He was killed instantly when his friend careened her car off the
darkened highway. Peter was hurled into an adjacent field. The lady
was not injured. Peter was in his midforties.

When William telephoned with the news, I squelched a macabre
notion: Peter might have survived had he still been drinking. His
body might have been more resilient. God protects drunks. I should
know: once, I bounced and fell down the stairs, tight, on Norma
Place, and got right back up again—no bones broken. I thought too
that Peter's humor could be as dark as my own, but it was too late to
weep. I learned a lot about cooking, literature, and good living from
Peter. But by the time of his death, I had long since gone on to other
friends. I had also relocated to Norma Place in the heart of what's
now West Hollywood.

CHAPTER TEN

AT HOME ON NORMA TRIANGLE

ONE TOO MANY evenings learning to live alone in the gloomy empty space of my Orchid Avenue apartment took on tortuous, tipsy overtones. Carefree company did not make for a brighter next day. Maggie, Judy, and I made what Alcoholics Anonymous calls a "geographic"—we moved west to start afresh in an appealing garage apartment at the end of a short driveway off Hilldale Avenue in West Hollywood. We were in the block below the then still civilized Sunset Strip. My large, screened bedroom window faced masses of banana trees. Their enormous leaves provided clusters of green fans to look upon when I awoke solo—which was most of the time. I preferred the company of my cats in my new, light-filled nest. They raced with dilated golden pupils from sill to sill, making clicking sounds at the more-plentiful birds now tauntingly on eye level. There was a compact kitchen made unique with fitted, natural wood cabinets designed by my creative landlords, two middle-aged gentlemen who lived in the front house facing Hilldale. Their compound was Cape

Cod–like, with gray wood siding and white trim on both ground-level houses, one behind the other with matching garages in the rear. My next-door neighbor was Lee J. Cobb, a ferocious actor but a hesitant neighbor who had been becalmed, naturally enough, by his divorce and two heart attacks. His apartment over the two-car garage was larger than mine. His entrance, which befitted a man who usually seemed on his way into hiding, was on the opposite side from my own, up another private stairway behind a gate and thick foliage.

An impressive crate was delivered up my Hilldale stairs. I opened it with great care and with as much excitement as I'd experienced over any gift that I have ever received. My father shipped me the magnificent portrait of my mother Carlyle that I have described in this book. The renowned artist Trafford Klots of Baltimore painted it. The Maryland Historical Society will inherit it from me. I hung it where it would dominate my Hilldale living room with class and continuity; it has continued to do so in each new place that I have lived. I recently had it restored and cleansed of old cigarette smoke. I managed to quit smoking in 1987. Hard? Don't ask. Pills and, for seven years, booze were easier to forgo. I took the latter up again, as you will see.

In 1958, my then-agent Robert Raison, one of the first in a line of lesser-than-Henry-Willson successors, dropped me off in front of my apartment after one of Cole Porter's summer luncheons. The composer lived on Bristol Circle in Brentwood. Robert was his friend and prudent pimp. Mr. Porter looked like a strained elf holding court, propped atop a raised dais by his pool. He informed his all-male company that Joan Crawford was his next-door neighbor. He pressed buttons beside him to cue the sounds of his dreamy songs to waft from within his pink palazzo house. The group of twelve, to whom only daiquiris were served, intimidated me. Each muscleman guest appeared more striking than the one beside him. After two rounds of daiquiris, Mr. Porter's butler lowered the dais to carry his crippled master to the long outdoor table—where an elegant lunch was served to the slightly woozy collection of Adonises. I wondered which of them knew who Miss Crawford was. To avoid the competition I was certain to lose over who would stay for dinner, I chose not to linger for an afternoon swim. Robert had no choice but to begrudgingly drive me home. There, beneath my screen door at the top of the stairs, was a note from my landlords asking me to telephone them.

They announced, to one who has never, ever suffered change gladly, that they had sold their rentals on Hilldale. They wanted to retire to live in Laguna. Developers were waiting in the wings to tear down my compound! The shock of having to find a new place to live set me to walking the streets of West Hollywood — for non-nefarious reasons, for a change — the very next day. I spent a week or so looking at vacancies. The cats were not a problem, but there was nothing decent available for a hundred dollars or less a month. Because I had broadcast my plight to anyone who would listen, my friends also kept an eye open. One night at a party, I was introduced to Paul Millard, who told me that he owned Norma Talmadge's old converted dressing room building. There was one empty apartment there that he said I was welcome to look at.

In the person of a once-cherubic chorus boy from the line at the Roxy Theatre in old New York, Paul was an independent real estate broker. His straw-hat-and-tap-shoe aura still prevailed. He now kicked up his heels to collect pretty possessions and to attend as many glamorous parties as possible. He had large china-blue eyes and a shock of not-entirely-natural bouncy blond hair. When I first met him, he sported a Colonel Blimp moustache. He should not have shaved it off. It flattered a too-thin mouth and strengthened a fey, girlish smile. He too drank, and how, to cloak reality. He also went to tight-fisted lengths not to part with a dollar, in part because he had grown up with very little money. He fled both rural Ohio and his given name, Fink. When the two of us became fast friends his revelation of that detail elicited howls of laughter between Fink and Posey — and, eventually, Gumm.

We greeted each other in front of his graceful, white clapboard building on Norma Place. Paul said that the front balcony had been salvaged from the Twelve Oaks plantation set of *Gone With the Wind*.

He unlocked the door to number $8954\frac{1}{2}$. We went upstairs to the apartment under the slanted eaves that constituted the peak-roofed upper story. The white-walled living room fronted a long, quirky kitchen that overlooked the trees outside the rear of the building. The large sunny bedroom's French doors opened onto the *Gone With the Wind* balcony. There were built-in bookshelves, random kitchen wall openings that gave more light to the living room, and unexpected closets and storage spaces set into imaginative nooks and crannies. The bathroom shelves and shower enclosure were surfaced with bits of beige, brown, and black marble. I wanted the one-of-a-kind, cat-perfect aerie the moment I saw it. A couple of window screens had to be replaced, the ceilings were low, the utilities were the tenant's responsibility. Paul stood firm at one hundred a month, but I had to live there. Charm and aesthetics within West Hollywood—and my budget—were in short supply and rapidly disappearing. Paul, who had an eye for both, gave me twenty-four hours to return with my check for the first and last months' rent.

Before we left, he took me back into the kitchen with its black-and-white floor to point out, through the foliage, baroque designer Tony Duquette's studio in the next block. He divulged that it had been Norma Talmadge's studio in the silent era. Now that Paul, another goner to alcohol, is sand-dancing on a cloud somewhere, I can tell you that Mr. Duquette's rococo building had in fact been a car barn—until the Southern Pacific Railroad stopped coming from downtown Los Angeles to the end of its line in the village of Sherman, before it became the city of West Hollywood. Throughout the eighteen years that I washed dishes and a zillion drink glasses in the sink in front of my new landlord, I happily settled for picturing Norma crossing a country path below me, trailed by her retinue, on her way to her private dressing room and apartments.

Two friends and their pickup truck helped me to move down the hill to $8954\frac{1}{2}$ Norma Place. My last trip back to Hilldale was to fetch Maggie and Judy in my Oldsmobile. They bounced against the sides of their carrier, berserk, until they were deposited in their new surroundings. When the three of us calmed down, I began to relish the singular ambience of the neighborhood that was to be my most utopian since Christchurch. The harum-scarum occupants of the nests just outside my door were conducive to new heights of mischief in a liberal and not overwhelmingly gay enclave, where productivity often took a back seat to party time. Most of my neighbors were hell-bent on enjoying what they could not perceive were their halcyon days, and without a care that those days would ever end. I quickly joined the pack, and sometimes even led it.

Our playground was bordered on the west by Doheny Drive, the street that marks the eastern end of Beverly Hills, and by Sunset and Santa Monica Boulevards to the north and south. Norma Place stretches one long block from Doheny to Hilldale Avenue. Lloyd Place intersects Norma and forms what is known as the Norma Triangle in a neighborhood of maze-like streets that still confuses outsiders and the West Hollywood Police trying to chase down swerving junkies, car thieves, and gay-bashers in the area. Some of the Pacific Railroad workers' original wooden railroad-flat homes were proud survivors on Norma Place and on streets throughout West Hollywood. Others had been given French Regency, Spanish, Madame Butterfly–Oriental, and other eclectic façades. The small interiors, unless the California termite had forced one to start from scratch, were frequently similar—despite archways and walls being ripped out to make larger rooms. The shallow back yards precluded Olympic pools à la adjacent Beverly Hills, but there were a few choice '50s-style pools around. Every variety of palm, bougainvillea, and night-blooming jasmine was profuse. Hedges of Ficus and Eugenia, instead of window bars and gated walls, afforded privacy. Tall and taller buildings and condominiums had not encroached. The Hollywood Hills and even the snowcaps in the distance toward San Bernardino were visible through mostly smogless skies.

My grab-bag collection of neighbors left their doors open late into the night after cocktail-hour drop-ins. *Feathertop's* Carleton Carpenter, in his house across the street from my apartment, sang and played the piano for his guests. Carp was no longer under contract to MGM, but I looked for Judy Garland in his living room anyway. I had to settle for Carp taking me to the Shrine to see her perform. Carp's carpenter father visited from New England to convert his son's garage into a guest house. Wyatt Cooper, a would-be author and a Southern charmer, was Carp's first tenant. When Wyatt left to marry Gloria Vanderbilt, the event was astounding enough to give the neighborhood another cause for joyful imbibing. Carp was the host for one night-long Halloween party. Stewart Stern failed to recognize Troy Donahue dressed as a nun. At one point, Sister Troy rapped a scantily clad young man's head with her low-heeled shoe to protest an obscene proposition, but Mr. Donahue never blew his habit. Stripper Faith Dane from the *Gypsy* touring company wore nothing except her high heels, though she did carry her trumpet.

The next morning, I awoke sharing my bed with one of Carp's guests, the short, sinewy Timmy Everett. Black-olive-eyed Timmy was fresh from his Broadway success in *The Dark at the Top of the Stairs*. He announced, while we rallied from our hangovers, that he was certain to win an Oscar for his first screen role in *Exodus*. His cockiness was no match for the arrogance of his director, Otto Preminger, who replaced Timmy with Sal Mineo. Timmy's feverish yearning for stardom and a successful transition from stage to screen went unrealized. He died of cancer not long after our one-night stand. Well, that's probably a misnomer, since Timmy and I could barely stand.

Screenwriter Hagar Wilde lived next door to Carp, across from my balcony. She was a tough and lusty lady resigned, when not in her cups, to the fact that her *Bringing Up Baby* and *I Was a Male War Bride* heyday had passed. Hagar was fitfully concentrated. We smiled at the summer-morning sound of her typewriter keys, clitter-clattering away in a valiant attempt to forge a new script in a changing market. All was lost when, as William used to say, the "sun was over the yardarm" and Hagar headed for the liquor cabinet.

Squad cars and sirens converged at Hagar's curbside one dead of night. She claimed to the cops that a six-foot UCLA student had molested her. Lucky Hagar. Or was it delirium tremens? He had, she said, climbed through an open window. Hagar made no bones about wanting a man, but she was in the wrong neighborhood. We gathered around, pretending to believe her, calm her down, and be watchdogs in case of a repeat performance. I kept an eager eye out, but no such lout was ever apprehended.

The actor John Dall lived just off the Lloyd Place intersection, on my side of Norma Place. John's prolonged shooting on the endless *Spartacus* had enabled him to buy his desirable house. It stretched through the block to Lloyd and consisted of two separate quarters. One housed his aunt and mother, whom one seldom saw; the other, himself and his priggish roommate, Clem. Clem sulked and snapped if he was called Clement. I ignored his request because he cold-shouldered John's drunken conviviality by shuffling lugubriously off to bed. I spent many evenings with other friends from the neighborhood in John's spectacular living room with its beamed ceiling and large fireplace, discussing everything from the Olympics to every movie ever made.

John was the only actor I have known who kept his sour grapes to himself as his career went into decline. He was insouciant on the surface and unfailingly supportive of the ambition in others, despite his unspoken torment. John's self-assurance would be renewed by technology. Today, he could dine out on videocassettes of *Rope* and his fine performance in the forerunner to *Bonnie and Clyde*, *Gun Crazy*. Then there is his Morgan Evans with Bette Davis in *The Corn Is Green*, but I will not, being an actor, go into that. In the end, John, a closet homosexual—to the motion picture business—with the wrong partner, out of work and favor, overdosed. By then, he had sold the house on Norma Place, but he may as well have been alone in the hilltop home that he bequeathed to his roommate.

John and I took Dorothy Parker's presence among us in stride. Clem, who had never gotten over appearing in her one New York play, the short-lived *Ladies of the Corridor*, was the unctuous sycophant when she returned from New York to live with her writer-husband Alan Campbell, in his house at 8983 Norma Place. Dottie the fragile harridan put Alan down behind his back the way she did everyone else. Her round brown eyes glinted, moist, as she savaged people and the world around her in her sad, smoky voice. We held our bladders while gathered for cocktails at the Campbells' to savor Dottie's conversational barbs, for fear of being a target if we had to leave the living room, which smelled of scotch whiskey and her poodle Cliché. Cliché slobbered in his mistress's lap when Paul Millard pecked her on the cheek to go elsewhere for dinner. "There he goes," purred Dottie, her cigarette smoke trailing him out the door, "tossing his Shirley Temple curls."

Alan, a soft-spoken Virginian, taught me about toggle bolts and hanging towel racks on Norma Place. He wore work shirts and overalls doing odd jobs and carpentry in everyone else's house, but he never completed his own. Dottie, whom he unaccountably married twice, was an obstacle in his handyman pursuits. Her stacks of unreviewed books for *Esquire* and Cliché's turds cluttered his workspace. The couple's discarded liquor bottles didn't make for good housekeeping either. One morning, I was startled to see Dottie face down in Hagar Wilde's ivy. Alan's terrier Limey was yapping toward home, his leash akimbo behind him. Hagar, a cat person, was glaring from her doorway when I reached Dottie to help her up and carefully walk her along the street. Her breath attested to what would be her limited literary output that day. The front door of 8983 Norma Place that Cliché was scratching on was unlocked. Alan was passed out on the sofa.

Alan died abruptly from too many Bloody Marys combined with Seconals in June 1963. He was fifty-nine. Dottie, anguished and angry, slipped further into sloth. She was more concerned with feeding Cliché strips of raw bacon than with her own nutrition. On one occasion when John and Clem brought her to my place for dinner, she was too feeble to cut her lamb chops, so I did it for her. In March 1964, she decided to move back to the Volney Hotel in New York for what would be her final three years in limbo. Prior to leaving Norma Place, she planted herself in a wing chair, chain-smoking, to oversee a house sale of her belongings. I call my purchase, a lovely crystal piece for long-stemmed roses, the Dorothy Parker Vase. It stands now in an upstairs étagère here in my house, which is adjacent to John Dall's old one on Norma Place.

Dottie had nothing in common with another neighbor, the inordinately healthy Estelle Winwood. Tiny Estelle, delicate but indomitable in her eighties, lived beneath me in Paul's ground-floor apartment. She always wore hats, usually over spit-curled wigs. The purple mascara she smudged on made her enormous trademark eyes more theatrical and surreal. Estelle controlled her tippling, smoked excessively, and left her French doors open so that friends could step through them into her living room for tea, which was replete every afternoon with good English china, sterling silver service, crumpets, cakes, or watercress sandwiches. This ceremony wasn't for me on a regular basis — I preferred sipping my bullshots upstairs — but I came to cherish practical, down-to-earth Estelle.

"You're so handsome, John," she remarked shortly after we met, "have you ever tried ladies?"

She referred to my overhead traffic, which sometimes bewildered her. "Last night sounded as though you were dragging a dead body across the floor." Her tinkling British tones were in resigned amusement. I thought that Maggie and Judy must have been playing and collided with each other. I kissed her on both rouged cheeks, assured her that no body was ever dead, and promised that we would all be quieter.

Estelle was a tireless, veteran coquette. She arched her eyebrows over half-mast lids and added my father to her conquests. Mother and Dad came to visit California during the last loveless year of their marriage, after my sister Ann married Stuart Egerton II in August 1959. I had gone home to Baltimore to be an usher. Dripping inside my formal cutaway at familiar St. David's, I tried not to be overwhelmed by emotion and the humidity, and I succeeded in being moist but engaging at the reception for three hundred at the Elkridge Club. Jimmy's stuffed shirt wilted at the reception too, but we got along for Ann's sake. Her departure for honeymoon and hearth left Dad ever more bored and swinish toward Mother. Their trip to San Francisco and then Los Angeles did not improve his disposition, but Estelle did. On Norma Place, she revived his latent courtliness, and their mock-flirtatious relationship was the highlight of the trip. Mother was red-eyed but resigned, even amused. Estelle took the edge off those searing hours my parents spent alone at the Beverly Hilton Hotel.

I drove the four of us to the Pasadena Playhouse for Estelle's performance in Somerset Maugham's *The Circle*. There was a long lull in the backed-up freeway traffic. Dad found it hilarious that the unperturbed Miss Winwood longed to catch a glimpse of a roadside crash victim. She did not get her wish, but we managed to arrive at the theatre with the disappointed star before curtain time. On my parents' last night in Los Angeles, Estelle was genuinely unhappy to see them leave. She coyly presented my father, whose horselaugh and charm delighted her, with a bottle of champagne. She had no idea that Mother and Dad were miserable, nor did she know that Dad could not drink the champagne. He had, by then, joined Alcoholics Anonymous. When he talked about attending meetings, I thought of other things.

Nina Foch, to conclude this roster of my idiosyncratic neighbors, was the antithesis of Estelle. Estelle took her craft lightly. A painstaking, estimable method actress, Nina was besotted with little else, save for the search for a suitable husband. She bought the small house around the corner from Paul's on Lloyd Place. She did find her youthful mate for a time in the person of Dennis Brite. Dennis, handsome and double-gaited (I know), was a hopeful writer, a household helpmate, and, in the end, unable or unwilling to go the distance with his fierce and concentrated wife. Nina's intellect was blinding. With her comprehensive knowledge of the world's events, she could have been an ambassadress-at-large in designer clothes. She cooked—she could have written cookbooks—and she made sure that she knew, when she became pregnant, more about birthing and raising babies than Dr. Spock.

The Brites and Paul Millard and I drove to Lake Arrowhead for a leisurely weekend. Nina, feeling past the prime of womanhood as it was thought about at the time, was querulous about carsickness and impending birth itself. Her new vulnerability was endearing. Our reassurances were heartfelt and loving. She was a burnished and healthy mother-to-be walking in the snow past the lone Arrowhead Village movie theatre, playing, coincidentally, one of her films, *Cash McCall.* I said the marquee was a lovely perk and good omen for my neighbor, but I thought about my own mother's death during childbirth and felt a chill in the wintry air.

But Nina, luckier than the younger Carlyle, thrived. Her only child was a robust boy. Paul and I, fairy godfathers, were thrilled for Nina. We were saddened when she and a new husband moved Schyler Dirk Brite away from Lloyd Place. The rumor persisted on our block that Nina was fearful that her son's sexual preference would one day be influenced by the preponderance of the neighborhood's homosexuals.

In my continuing regard for *le temps perdu,* I have had a Shermart Market shopping bag framed. It was a gift from Chuck and Tucker, and it hangs in my kitchen. The Shermart was the neighborhood meeting place and playpen, a friendly bastion where romances blossomed in the produce section, hangovers were sustained in the liquor department, and the customer was still considered right. Nina's first au pair girl from France married the Shermart butcher. Norma Varden, Isabel Elsom, Elsa Lanchester, Sara Hayden, and some of the stars they supported shopped there. Peetsie Hayward, Louis's airy ex-wife, rattled her bracelets in the aisles to round up cocktail guests. The first-name clerks who became our friends cashed more of my personal checks than my close-by Bank of America branch. I drove the two blocks to the Shermart nearly every day. Who wanted to smoke, carry bags of groceries across titanic Santa Monica Boulevard, and cruise at the same time? Later, when I did walk to the same Bank of America, I seldom glanced across the street at the brick stronghold of our West Hollywood Sheriff's Station or, further along Santa Monica, at the concrete bunker that houses the RTD. Both forbidding structures blight the block where the Shermart stood.

A good friend in the neighborhood was Paul Jasmin. He slithered into the Shermart after dark. He spent his daylight hours in front of his easel creating bravura oil paintings of faces and figures composed primarily from dots. Their tones were muddy, their backgrounds sparse, one brush prick of color predominated, and I'm sorry that I only own one of them. Paul was edgy, secretive, and another cat lover. One of his cats—called Rose Cat—ran the house he shared with his mother Winnie Ruth a couple of blocks from Norma Place on Larrabee Street. Rose Cat howled in heat for unseemly periods—until Paul calmed her down with the eraser end of a lead pencil. Rose Cat backed up on it and Paul massaged her gently. She made sluttish, gurgling sounds. Paul and Winnie Ruth cackled in unison. I perspired and felt as though I were spying on all three. The other Jasmin felines, Fred and Ethel Mertz, scurried off, offended, to closets unknown.

Paul called me "Star," a diminutive of the nickname that Carleton Carpenter had inexplicably given me: "Black Star." A fairly well known photographer today, Paul was "Jazz" to me—and everybody else.

"Star," Jazz would hiss in whispery tones, "let's go to the bars." We did. Often. Our favorite, hands down, was the Four Star, a real neighborhood saloon that sat on the derelict side of Santa Monica, opposite the Shermart. It was grungy, gay, a sanctum for the haunted, a watering hole for friends, even a haven for the elite. Leonard Bernstein, in evening clothes after a concert, ogled hustlers there. Sometimes Montgomery Clift, and, more often, my pal Johnnie Ray had to be helped off their barstools at closing time. The moment was low if the pawing was good when the bartender hollered "last call" *again,* and meant it. No matter that one had deposited fresh quarters in the jukebox; he yanked out the wall plug to turn it off. Hands left strangers' knees; deflated, lingering customers were herded through the narrow, brick-walled bar and out into the melancholy night. The sensible loners darted home—to avoid being enticed by the lurking vice squad, which meant being vilified on the way to the slammer, being fingerprinted, hiring a lawyer, and drumming up the five-hundred-dollar fine. I write from experience. *Two* experiences. I was lucky to have some small stock holdings to sell. The first time—when the shame was mortifying—Maggie and Judy were glad to have me in hiding at home. The second time, leaving court, from within my lawyer's car, I gave the finger to the prick-teaser who had entrapped me. Most nights, Paul and I skedaddled before the two o'clock crazies. When the jukebox was silenced, the brightened lights inside the Four Star made you blink. One could get a change-of-mind look at a prospective partner. Or vice versa.

Jazz introduced me to one of his friends at a local party. The potluck dinner was pleasant, and the affectionate Gary Campbell was more so. Gary, who loathed the bars, was ahead of his time. It was not monogamy-or-die with him, but almost. I went along with him for two years, with pleasure. He began to come to Norma Place every night, and we took turns cooking dinner for one another. He did not move in because he had a dog and a cat and a diabetic roommate to look after. Gary has had menageries of animals and other unions since, but the lonely roommate, nicknamed Kon Tiki, drank too many beers at the Four Star and went into a diabetic coma. He died in Gary's arms at the old Cedars of Lebanon Hospital in Hollywood, while I watched, as helpless as Gary's grief.

Gary was slender and slightly bowlegged, with green eyes, thick brown hair, and a face like a fawn. He studied and shone in young-boy roles in his innumerable acting classes. Eventually he sensed that his slight stature and too-nasal voice were barriers. He was not hard enough to be buffeted by the acting profession. He chided me for dodging my own dreams. I liked some partying—at Nina's, Paul Millard's, Peetsie Hayward's, or Butler Miles's, where, Hollywood or not, the guests were mixed. Gary termed it carousing. He said that I was afraid of success. He supported Nina Foch's view that I "did not want it badly enough." I thought I did. But for Gary I tried to drink carefully and come home earlier. Except at Butler's, at whom I shall look askance shortly.

Both Gary and I came from families with alcoholics. Our heart-breaking Christmas trip in 1960 to visit his divorced parents in New Mexico strengthened our bond. First we drove, frozen most of the way because of a malfunctioning heater in Gary's MG, to Mrs. Campbell. She lived in a barren outskirt of Albuquerque. She was a skinny, fading-away redhead with a sour mouth and a snarling disposition. A late dinner was flung, and barely eaten, on the kitchen table before we escaped to bed in the face of Mrs. Campbell's mounting, bourbon-fueled invective provoked by the sight of her passive, gamely-smiling gay son. The sounds of crashing ice cubes filled a thunderous silence beyond the cardboard-thin wall—before her scratching voice began to shriek outside our locked door.

"Come out here an' talk to me, you sissy. You little sissy-shit!"

I held Gary harder than at any other time, trying to protect him from her sound.

"You sissy-shit! You ruined my life! I wish to hell you'd never been born! I was pretty before you! Get outta here and live your own god-damned life, you little sissy-shit!"

Gary's body did not relax until she stopped. He seemed resigned. Like me, with Mother and Dad and with Dad and Estelle Bolling. Gary shed no tears, but mine were close. I felt like battering the door down against her rancid mouth.

She was still asleep when we embarked the next morning on a bleak tour of Albuquerque. Did Gary buy his mother a gift? I can't remember. That night, Christmas Eve, the two of us made helpful motions with dinner preparations. It was eaten in a silent, unrepen-tant fog of good behavior. Tinny carols seemed to come from the crack in the plastic case of Mrs. Campbell's portable radio on top of the refrigerator. We were grateful when the house was empty on Christmas morning. I don't care for men's jewelry, but for many years I wore the engraved St. Christopher's medal on a thin gold chain Gary gave me that morning.

We had loaded up the MG by the time Mrs. Campbell reappeared. She walked beside a hardened field toward the house, her stick body hunched over the paper bag containing a bottle of bourbon from the only liquor store that was open. Our toneless goodbyes made small puffs in the chilled sunlight. Our forced "Thank you" was as meaningless as being told, ad nauseam, to "have a nice day."

Our next stop—Clovis, New Mexico—was no better. Mr. Campbell was one of the town's head honchos. He manufactured the glass bricks so prevalent in the Southwestern architecture of his prosaically pretentious house. He was a fire hydrant of a man whose pug-like face exuded welcoming good cheer until nightfall, when his drunken spirits plunged. His attitude toward Gary turned to surly, fist-clenched sarcasm. He controlled his brutality because I was a visitor. His apple-cheeked young second wife served as referee. No doubt she replaced Gary as her husband's verbal punching bag after we adjourned to our significantly separate guest rooms. My own father was suddenly eligible for at least a pedestal, if not sainthood.

We ditched Mr. Campbell and his boiling point by visiting friends and more tolerant relatives in nearby Santa Fe, a town of authentic rustic beauty glimmering in the seasonable snow. We spent a notable New Year's Eve celebrating in one imposing house. Its driveway, entryway, and rooftop were dramatic with welcoming luminaires. These lighted candles, weighted in sand against the wind in paper bags, were everywhere in Santa Fe. They twinkled in their formations of holiday silhouettes as far as the eye could see. The luminaires, which I had never seen before, were the only sight to cherish on our gloomy excursion.

• • •

My grandmother Mum, wary of my movie-star dreams and alert to a budding profligate personality, had instructed that my portion of her estate be dispensed when I was thirty. At twenty-one, I would have escaped to Europe until penniless. In 1961, to the relief and amazement of Mother and Dad, I did a much more grown-up thing: I bought a building. My nest egg, on the point where Norma and Lloyd Place intersected, was a duplex built sturdily the old-fashioned way. It comprised two rental apartments to afford me income. It had a Spanish-style roof, stucco exterior walls, and I salute Paul Millard for hectoring me to become a mini-land baron before it became so financially prohibitive. He negotiated the sale from an elderly West Hollywood couple for thirty-five thousand dollars. I put fifteen down, courtesy of Mum, to open escrow. Whenever I walked out onto my Norma Place balcony, I inspected my acquisition with astonished apprehension. But my monthly payments were never to exceed one hundred seventy-eight dollars a month. So, before it was paid for, I crossed myself daily, in gratitude, for the wisest move I ever made.

Some improvements were in order. Gary planted a Eugenia hedge outside the Norma Place bedroom and den. Squaring off the archways and installing sliding glass doors that led to the patio via new steps of old brick enlarged the living–dining room. All the walls were painted white. Nothing, including new garbage disposals, impressed my upstairs tenant. He moved, outraged, when I upped his rent from $90 to $110 a month. The only headaches during those basically goodwill-toward-tenant days—before rent control—were one or two bounced checks and lovers who went their separate ways when their relationships ended. Oh, and the vexation of too many sanitary napkins down the toilet, or the main line backing up into the tub . . . usually on Christmas morning.

Mum's booty enabled me to give Gary his first trip to New York City. First we spent four days with Mother in Baltimore. The divorce proceedings were ongoing. Mother was alone in a home on Wendover Road that the Poseys had purchased after leaving 617 W. University Parkway. My father was living downtown in his University Club off Mount Vernon Place.

The University Club was the scene of a disastrous lunch witnessed, to my chagrin, by an understandably uncomfortable Gary. Dad would not divulge the name of his new lady friend and future wife—for fear that I would pass it on to Mother, who already knew. Furious and hurt that he would not confide in me, I grew verbally abusive and stalked from the club dining room. Was I going to telephone the *Baltimore Sun* society column, for Christ's sake? I pulled myself together in the men's room in order to retrieve Gary. He, it turned out, was not too taken aback to opine that I had been tyrannical and rude without reason. Like John Paul in the present, Gary thought I enjoyed making a scene. So, who was right, and what else is new? I didn't apologize to either party. My father's new and sober passivity set my teeth on edge. It widened the barrier between Dad and me from that day on. The two of us, when we should have talked it out, never acknowledged a schism.

I chose to commiserate with Mother instead. She and I talked until late that night, after Gary had gone to bed in our guest room upstairs. There were some tears, but Mother was more comfortable, then and afterward, in discussion, and in nipping a bit with me, than she had been for too long a time in the starchy company of my father—after his pivot to lofty abstinence. My heart, not just because of cocktails or absent husband and offspring, went out to her on that visit, which brought us the closest we'd ever been. She missed the happiness she'd had with my father, and she missed Jimmy, who had also married, and Ann. But Mother—I nicknamed her Scarlett—would not take too much time to get over Rowland Posey, remarry, and bury her third husband.

Gary was properly awed by Oak Hill, and by Uncle Herbert and his peacocks, whose iridescent plumage scattered in my uncle's path as he walked across the terrace to greet us, a sepulchral phantom in his long, somber cape. He watched over the gargantuan Aunt Muriel while she presided over tea. She seemed barely in residence after her

years in sanitariums, quivering on the nether edge of sanity in a ceremony done by rote. I had grown up; she was now the child. A nurse
stood by her side, holding a lace hankie to wipe away the spittle that
occasionally dribbled down her chalk-colored jowls. Her confusion
over Gary's surname made us struggle to keep from laughing. "This
is Carlyle's friend, Mr. Gary Cooper," she would repeat. "Would you
like more tea, Mr. Cooper?" asked Aunt Muriel. Gary Campbell
reached for another piece of torte, stared hard at a nearby Miró on
the damask wall, and did not take offense. Uncle Herbert was—until
Muriel died—as buttery toward his heiress wife as the torte. With an
air of genteel distraction, he treated Aunt Muriel like the purebred
Mistress of the Manor in a public show to deflect the damage done
by her minor strokes and shock treatments. He wanted to go on
maintaining those peacocks.

It did not matter a damn to Gary that Judy Garland, in the concert
of her career at Carnegie Hall, was the climax of our trip to New York.
He was country-boy bright-eyed in the rush of experiencing the city
for the first time, more receptive than critical of the Broadway shows
that we attended, and scornfully condescending over the orgasmic
reaction accorded my favorite girl singer. He thought that she was
overrated, especially by me. She was vocally stunning, on her way to
being slim again, and Gary's disdain for her artistry was too bitter a
pill for me to swallow. My contempt for his attitude was lost in the
groundswell of hysteria that would not let her leave the legendary
stage of Carnegie Hall.

The release of the album of her Carnegie Hall triumph fed our
friction after we came home to California. I was as lost in its evoca-
tion of the evening as any record buyer in the nation. Now I have the
compact disc; Judy, in duets with herself in my living room, added to
the scratches on the original LP. Gary could not tolerate my idolatry
of the lady. That was one factor that made him the loser in the diminishing course of my affections. Another was jealousy. He was not
always correct in his perception that my desire had led to consum-
mation. I told him that he was also full of crap when he blamed

Mum's and the Boones' filthy lucre for eroding my acting ambitions, though, of course, the luck of being an heir did make life less stressful. Gary dismissed this fact until, after we had gone our separate ways, his father died. The senior Campbell atoned for his unpleasantness by being as uncharacteristically generous to his only son as he was to his second wife.

The end of togetherness came when I awoke in someone else's bed on Christmas morning, 1961. I returned to Maggie and Judy in the empty Norma Place apartment. My remorse did not quite pack the wallop of my hangover, but I swore on the phone to Gary that I did not even remember being whisked away from a holiday party in Bel-Air. The truth was that I had not meant to pass out. This time Gary was unyielding in his decision to break off our relationship. The anguish of such endings, not always of my own doing, seems unendurable for too long and painful a time. The wrench with Gary, neither the first nor the last, was no different. I pray that age, bad knees, and being with John Paul finally arrested my inclination to repeat the process.

CHAPTER ELEVEN

HIGHS AND LOWS IN HOLLYWOOD

BUTLER MILES WAS the host of that ill-fated Christmas Eve party in Bel-Air. He was a torpid, dead-eyed celebrity collector with a flaccid handshake. Famous faces are herd-like in accepting invitations as long as the address or charity or hostess is right and the free food is edible. Gloria Swanson, a freeloading houseguest, was Butler's bait. His reign as a host was brief. His starry guests started to question his nebulous position in any social strata, even unexacting Palm Beach, where he had snagged Miss Swanson. When he relocated to California, his late entrances and tranquilizer-dulled personality became less than entrancing to those who gathered. They began to wonder what they were doing in the faux French Regency mansion that Butler eventually set afire. When he was accused of insurance fraud, he fled Los Angeles.

I wasted time there because I enjoyed meeting Miss Swanson, Ginger Rogers, Hedy Lamarr, a host of chatterbox Gabors, and others of that bygone breed. They found me mannerly, and there were some moments of exhilaration and middling comedy that made up for being an uncomfortable extra man when the handsome barmen—as they always are in Lotusland—were stingy with their refills.

I basked in La Swanson's favor when she took to my suggestion that she would be grand for the female lead in the movie version of *Sweet Bird of Youth*. The moguls, however, thought that perhaps she had plumbed the depths of the desperate film star to her limits in *Sunset Boulevard*. I pressed no further when she refused to test for the part. Butler, plopped all day in bed like a jellyfish, irritated her more than the youthful executives. So off she went on her energetic way, her outsized head held high, the part-time servants carrying her health foods and exercise bar to the rented limousine that would take her to LAX.

My first sight of Miss Lamarr's matchless profile was a high in itself. Sean Flynn, as dashing in his own right as Errol, leaned over Hedy, who reclined on one of Mr. Miles's rented lawn chairs. Toying with her, he murmured: "What close friends you and my father were." Hedy laughed and looked bemused. The beautiful Hedy and I became friendly. She telephoned, not making Gary's last mornings any easier, to suggest that we go for a drive to search for an apartment building to buy. It never dawned on Hedy that I was merely the owner of a duplex and not a land baron. She was preoccupied with cash, light-fingered, chattered like a child, and, unlike her peers, never said a truly cruel word about anyone. She was a treat to look at and to have on my arm—in small doses.

I drove her into Hollywood one night to see Susan Hayward in *Back Street*. Hedy jabbered in her high-pitched way through most of Miss Hayward's explosive moments. She commented that she had had co-star John Gavin replaced on her own *A Female Animal* because he could not act. When we left the Pantages Theatre, the newsstand vendor at the corner of Hollywood and Vine caught hold of her arm.

"Didn't you used to be Hedy Lamarr?" he asked.

"I still am," she said, shaking him off, exquisite profile staring straight ahead.

She asked me to dine informally at her Beverly Hills home on Angelo Drive. She instructed me to stop at the Shermart for whatever I would like to eat. Well, I hoped, at least I would not have to go to bed for my supper. I bought two filet mignons, broccoli, and something sweet for dessert. The maid relieved me of my groceries when she opened Hedy's front door. I made a drink for my hostess and we sat on her love seat in the den, TV trays at the ready. A swan-necked bust of Hedy looking languid was on top of the television set in front of us. When the maid arrived, I was sipping my second martini to get over being jumpy. She carried our supper: roasted chicken, peas, and a different dessert, nothing of the menu that I had purchased.

"Hedy, where's the food that I bought—brought?" I asked.

"Oh, ve put dat in ze freezer. Ve save it for anozzer night," she sighed. Later she gazed up at me, ready for another MGM close-up. When I kissed her good night I was relieved, I think, that Hedy's large mouth was all that parted for me.

I met willowy Cheryl Crane at one of Butler Miles's parties. The ultra-feminine Cheryl is less a conundrum to me now, seeing her fitfully, than when we became a familiar Hollywood couple in the '60s. Sometimes she canceled our dates at the last inconvenient moment. She was given to tardiness in the extreme. Her non-apologetic demureness when I called her on her rudeness made me debate time and time again whether or not to sever whatever our relationship was. But she was bright, strong-willed, and enjoyable when she was finally dressed and we did go out. She respected me for not prying about her mother or the stabbing of Johnny Stompanato. She also knew that I understood much of the in-hiding hell that she was going through regarding her sexual orientation and being a press curiosity. We enjoyed putting a straight face on things for the fan magazines.

Chic, up-to-the-minute Cheryl, watching her mother swaying solo in the Beverly Hills moonlight, seemed—always—more the sustaining parent than the daughter at a birthday party given for Lana

Turner. Lana had cleared the portable dance floor by her creamy, frozen-in-the-'40s presence. Earlier, the two of us had been drawn to the edge of the dance floor to listen to a familiar voice scat-singing with the birthday band. Ella Fitzgerald went home long before Cheryl and me, and certainly Lana, presumably with her new husband.

Steve Crane, Cheryl's father, owned and operated the exotic Luau Restaurant on Rodeo Drive. Cheryl began to work for him as his hostess. I admired Cheryl for going East to the Cornell University restaurant school to learn the business. I still do, for her successful switch to a lucrative career in real estate. My sister Ann and her husband Stuart visited California while Cheryl was at the Luau. Cheryl picked up their dinner check and the bar tab—for the most lethal mai tais in Beverly Hills. My sister was reeling, but impressed.

Steve Crane gave mammoth, extravagantly catered New Year's Day "hangover" parties at his neo-baronial Tower Grove estate. One year, I took Cheryl. Some of Hollywood's not-so-beau monde climaxed these events by frolicking nude in Mr. Crane's tented pool. Cheryl and I, lightheaded, provided our own gleeful clincher at one soirée. We made a spur-of-the-moment announcement to a voracious member of the fourth estate, Harrison Carroll. "Cheryl Crane to Wed Actor John Carlyle" was the headline of his column in the next day's *Herald-Examiner*. There were some anxious calls from Baltimore, the only quarter to take us seriously. Lana Turner was quoted as saying that our plans were news to her. Columns and movie magazines kept abreast of our betrothed front for months. Even our own interest waned when no date was set for the big event.

Miss Turner was barely on time for the 1966 premiere of her remake of *Madame X*. Cheryl and her grandmother Mildred did not set any records either, but our group finally managed to convene in our back-row seats. Constance Bennett's last performance in the lachrymose woman's picture could not distract me from my aching bladder, un-emptied during yeoman escort duties. Because our nervous star had been on the aisle, my tear ducts are not what burst after the film. I have begged, manipulated, and paid to sit on the aisle ever since, in planes, trains, and at the theatre.

The event most publicized during my saga with Cheryl was her twenty-first birthday party in July 1964. Her mother took over the Galaxy nightclub on Sunset Strip. Cheryl cut a four-foot tiered cake to the applause of two hundred well-wishers. There were mostly reporters, friends like Agnes Moorehead and Sybil Brand, Steve Crane, one former stepfather, and grandmother Mildred—a nice woman who told me how hard Lana had worked over the years. Cheryl and I stood side by side to receive her guests. Our aplomb went out the window when Frank Sinatra appeared in front of us with some other gangster types. "How does it feel to be a twenty-one-year-old broad?" he asked Cheryl. He presented her with a tiny gift box and left as suddenly as he had arrived. We took a brief break from the receiving line in the nightclub's kitchen. Cheryl excitedly ripped open the box containing a gold and diamond St. Christopher's medal, one of the evening's highlights for the statuesque birthday girl.

The suntanned Lana, wearing trademark white and sipping vodka, undulated away the night. She tried, unsuccessfully, to teach me the provocative watusi. "Just go, John!" she urged, in her rose-petal voice. The bar area was stacked with admiring men ogling her mother when Cheryl and I said thank you and good night long after two o'clock. Outside on the Strip, the photographers still awaited Lana—like they did until the end. I feel sad for Cheryl and bereft at the loss of glamour whenever I drive by the high rise where Lana lived.

My television roles were becoming scarce. I complained to my agent that they were also smaller. I did not comprehend that my name in the drivel of a gossip column could be harmful. The old-fashioned trade paper announcement that I had been hired for a job was another matter—maybe. Did anyone remember the specifics of either mention? The truth is that I was only irritated if my name was misspelled.

I did two plays for nothing at the Players Ring Gallery. The Gallery, ten minutes away from home on Santa Monica in West Hollywood, was the most eminent among many small theatres in Los Angeles. Actors have always stampeded for showcases, and in the '60s we kicked back our meager salaries to management like the proverbial herd of cattle. With "waiver" houses, Actors' Equity sees to it that we can keep our pittances. The Gallery became the Coast Playhouse, where, presently, I shall tell about returning to perform in Martin Sherman's *Bent*.

The Heroine was a not-so-funny comedy. I supported character actress Virginia Vincent, who conducted herself like a nettlesome leading lady. Perhaps her bitchiness was because she was far more adept at farce than I. We were well along in the run before I stopped working for my laughs and sitting on hers. When John Dall came to see the show, he zeroed in helpfully on my loosening-up process. "Keep your legs farther apart and you won't look like you're standing at attention," said he.

I never left the stage during *Catch Me If You Can*. On the night that I replaced the leading man—with the second show on a sold-out Saturday night—I did not want to go on at all. The rehearsals had been hellish. Paul Levitt, the dour owner of the Gallery, often looked on as though he were wondering if he had chosen the wrong replacement. Alan de Witt, a lovely director, patiently put me through my paces. They were largely little more than line recitations of my endless words. Corban, the missing wife murderer, had to be essayed, until the final dramatic scene, as lightly as a soft-shoe routine. My approach in the workhorse role would have stunned an elephant until the technical rehearsal, when there were actual titters from the heretofore sullen crew. Then, during dress rehearsal, I could sense "Boomie" de Witt smiling, finally. I hung on to his last-minute notes with my first modicum of confidence.

The actor awaits his first reaction from the audience. Be it good or ill, silence or laughter, it puts him in touch, makes him begin to relax, and enables him to feel. My late-show crowd, some tipsy, had duly noted the cast change in their program, but they were there to be supportive and to have a good time. They always are. This fact does not sink in with some performers, and it never obliterates the good actor's initial terror. Nerves are a given in the acting profession. The players who profess to be without them are cold fish, or liars. The art is to keep the quivers under control. I was astonished years ago by Frederic March's trembling hands at the start of his Broadway opening night in *Long Day's Journey into Night*. I admired him all the more, and his performance took hold and soared. My *Catch Me If You Can* took flight in a tinier arena, but you get my presumptuous idea. That rowdy and receptive first audience got me off the ground at last. Paul Levitt burst my buttons by pronouncing my performance "as funny, in a more realistic way, as that of my predecessor." I had stopped trying to emulate the latter's loopy antics, and the house stayed packed throughout the eight weeks remaining in the run.

I couldn't help spotting friends in the theatre in the round setup at the Gallery; they were practically in my lap. One night, actress Susan Cabot sat dead center on the front row. I had not seen Susan since classes at Estelle Harmon's and taking her to parties at Carroll Righter's. After a terminated contract at Universal and a turn as the Wasp Woman for Roger Corman, her career had waned. Backstage at *Catch Me If You Can*, the hardness was just beginning in her weary monkey face. We hugged each other good night, and I never saw black-eyed Susan again. She died at the hands of her dwarf son when I was researching this book. I shuddered and shoved the happy photographs taken of Susan and me at Pappy's back into a drawer.

My *Catch Me If You Can* cockiness, and concentration, suffered a setback the night that Ann and Stuart sat as close as Susan during their first visit to California. California's choking month of September brought its usual tormenting heat. I prefer to act for strangers, and, like Joan Crawford, in a cold climate. She could demand it. The Gallery's air conditioning collapsed the night Ann and Stuart were on the premises. My sodden performance took on plowshare symptoms. My sister told me afterward that I sweated

right through the snappy plaid cloth of my summer sport coat from
Carroll and Company.

I roasted again through the first night of *A House of Pomegranates*, a
concert reading inspired by four of Oscar Wilde's fairy stories. I
stood before a posh audience jammed into the McKenzie Gallery on
La Cienega Boulevard. Rivulets of perspiration ran down the inside
of my evening clothes. Four of us, organized and led by actress Molly
Dodd, looked wilted but elegant upon a raised platform, timing our
Wilde witticisms carefully as orchestrated by our erudite, frog-
voiced director, Robert Laning. Communicating the poignant
heartache of "The Happy Prince" and "The Nightingale and the
Rose" was very much my responsibility. Despite the heat, my work
was seldom more highly praised. I took to the stylized recreation
and the platform presentation of the fables we brought to life that
evening, the first of many. Molly named our group the State Repertory Theatre. We toured California with the magical works of Mr.
Wilde until late in 1969.

I invited Judy Garland and Mark Herron to the McKenzie Gallery
in 1965, but the newlyweds were a no-show. Judy swore later that
their absence had not been her fault. Fault? She would seldom admit
to it. "Don't put *me* on the mat!" came the cry. And who could?

I had known Mark Herron slightly since the early '50s. We met
again through Robert Osborne. I had lost the lead in *The Sleeping
Prince* at the Pasadena Playhouse to the jittery, charming Mark. He
had the good grace not to crow about it after Robert brought him to
Norma Place in 1962. Robert, through his love and encyclopedic
knowledge of the motion picture business, was just starting to forge
his path above and beyond a nebulous acting career. Today his good
will is evident in his coverage of the industry; he is the only successful *and* contented ex-actor that I have ever known. Mark and I
discovered that we shared a sly sense of humor, a great fondness for
stalwart Robert, and a genuine passion for Miss Garland. His passion
was paying off, which he did crow about.

Besides Carnegie Hall, I had followed my star to Las Vegas, Long Beach, Pasadena—wherever I could drive to buy a ticket. I had been appalled by her blowfish appearance at the Cocoanut Grove in 1958. Carleton Carpenter, who had worked with Judy in *Summer Stock*, took me to her opening at the Shrine Auditorium in 1959. That had turned out to be quite a night. She waddled on stage to sing wondrously in a pouch-lidded trance. Her torpor only served to further galvanize her brute-force audience, primed as always to strengthen her. Between her gilt-edged songs, we were her lifeline. When she changed into her trademark tuxedo jacket, her lovely legs began to prance as of old. The illusion of Little Nellie Kelly replaced the top-heavy diva before us.

Vern Alves was backstage after the show. Sid Luft authorized him to invite Carp and me to the first-night party at the Luft home in Holmby Hills. Carp did not have to twist my arm. 144 South Mapleton Drive was a pseudo-English manor house. The sparse furnishings inside were from the beach-house set of *A Star Is Born*. The guests—including all three of Judy's husbands—were gathering in the living room. Mr. Luft welcomed David Rose and Vincente Minnelli, who stood shyly at the periphery of the party throughout the evening. Eventually, Sid guided his smiling wife through the applauding crowd. Judy's laughter turned her eyes into slits as she bade us to have a good time and make ourselves at home.

I did both with rapidity. The buffet and bar were sumptuous. Little Liza Minnelli took me by the hand almost immediately. She showed me her silver-framed photograph of the boy she had a crush on, the actor George Hamilton. Then she led me on a tour of the expansive, empty backyard area where, she said, "Papa Sid" was planning to build a pool. She was all enormous eyes, dressed in white, with her dark hair drawn back by a white satin ribbon.

Liza danced that night, beautifully, all around the living room. She was like a startling white butterfly. She attempted, not so beautifully, to follow her mother in song. Mama, warm with the Palace and *A Star Is Born* remembrances, looked on from my lap, a large but loving load to heighten my sozzled delight. "My god," Judy laughed in my ear, "Liza's got a voice like chalk on a blackboard." At a later point, I was presumptuous enough to ask David Rose how he could have divorced our hostess. His patient reply remains a muffled politeness. My final image of Judy Garland from that night, while Vern Alves and Sid Luft helped her up the movie-star grand stairway to bed, was her whispered, collapsing goodbye to the house at large.

On his visit to Norma Place in 1962, Mark Herron talked—and talked—about his escalating relationship with Judy. Robert Osborne was astonished. I was jealous. Mark had met her through the costume designer on her television show at CBS. I attended as many tapings as friends in high places could get me into. Mark regaled Robert and me with backstage stories and darted off to resume new fiancé duties at 129 South Rockingham in Brentwood. Judy had moved there with her children Joey and Lorna after divorcing Sid Luft. Liza was off reaching for the brass ring in New York. The thought that fey Mark could be anybody's stepfather left me incredulous.

That did not keep me from accepting Mark's offer to follow the yellow brick road to Judy backstage at CBS. It was painted on the floor outside her dressing room. We selected fans gathered to be received in the outer room of her own private bastion that was anchored onto the outside of Television City. Lathered in TV makeup, her hair lacquered, she was charming and skinny now. Her cascading cackle of thanks for our compliments and her trembling hand dismissed us, backward, out to the yellow brick road again.

When her series was canceled, there was no merriment backstage or anywhere else following her torturing final show. Emotional exhaustion set in with her delays. The bored orchestra members stretched and nipped, and the sun came up. Judy, her eyeballs black marbles, looked like a trapped bird ready to flutter wildly into the rafters. She could not try *again* to finish the taping. She knew it, and she said to hell with it. Mark accompanied her home to Brentwood. Her infinitely patient audience straggled into the dawn, miserable at having witnessed the sad conclusion of her first professional failure.

I cursed *Bonanza* and the fools who would rather watch Westerns as I crashed for a few hours back in my apartment. My own uppers had sustained me through Judy's long night. When I awoke, too soon, still troubled, I took another Dexamyl spansule. I slugged it down with a Nutriment drink laced with vodka to jump-start myself going again. Judy had nothing on me. Well, yes, she did. But my own more intermittent, new practice that I had not yet mastered would also take too long to get the better of me.

Another bad habit was useful in a couple of good jobs. I lucked out being cast in two cigarette commercials when they were still common on television. In the first I looked sartorial puffing away at a polo match being played and photographed in Fox Hills. The second, several months later, was for Bel-Air, the brand name that I remember because it was an assignment best forgotten. A pretty girl and I were filmed dancing dreamily together on the terrace of a Malibu beach house. Next we were to waft down to frolic beside the moonlit ocean, Bel-Air cigarettes in hand. The trouble began when my bellows-like cheeks made my inhaling over her shoulder look like too much work. One should smoke oh-so-effortlessly on camera. I could not smoke and glide gracefully to the music playback at the same time either. Wondering how I had gotten the job smoking on the audition, I popped a little green and white something during a coffee break—to warm myself up and forget my awkwardness. The result was that my agitation, not my confidence, increased. The director shot more close-ups on the exasperated girl than planned. When we abandoned the porch for our barefoot-in-the-sand bit, we were over schedule and close to freezing. On the beach, tossing bits of driftwood seaward in not so playful a fashion, I became a sullen stick, ready to flatten the fed-up director. He finally called a wrap after some ungainly long shots. I could not stop talking on the endless ride back into the city in our transportation van. The cold, I repeated to the silent actress, had destroyed my timing. At home on Norma Place, the affair of the moment was fast asleep in my bed and wanted to stay that way. I wanted TLC and a sympathetic listener. His silence irritated me enough to blast Judy's Carnegie Hall album for what was left of the night. It was not one to remember, except for the excellent money that I made off the commercial, some of which was for overtime.

The round-the-world peregrinations of Miss Garland and her unlikely companion Mark, following on the heels of her television series cancellation, made for unsettling newspaper reading. The again-skinny legend and the edgy aesthete were a road show variation on Elizabeth Taylor and Richard Burton. Judy's public image was trashed; Mark had none. He wrote me drunken, rambling letters from their various ports of call, culminating on May 31, 1964, in his wooly, wildly thankful reply to the most expensive and urgent telephone call that I had ever made—to Hong Kong. My car radio had announced that Judy Garland was near death there, so I frantically placed the call. Mark's convulsive voice, from some faraway hospital where he thought the nurses were eavesdropping, cried that she was recovering from pneumonia. He prayed that she would pull through. So did I. When she did, he scrawled hysterically that he had saved her life. The press could beat him to death before he would tell what had happened. Mark, to his credit, never confirmed the accidental overdose that I imagined. He wrote that she was "sitting up in bed, ordering trays of jade and pearls to choose from, and once again playing the very big star."

Further assurances of happiness came from England and even Greece. Mark was the referee and producer when Liza Minnelli joined forces with her mother at the London Palladium. He mailed me a 45-RPM Capitol Record of "Judy Sings 'Maggie May.'" I wore out the lost vibrato on the four charged singles. The Garland–Herron idyll culminated in a London "marriage" that was pronounced humbug by the media. Sid Luft proclaimed it illegal. They were both correct. I was relieved—temporarily.

When I read his recent obituary in *Daily Variety*, I thought "there but for the grace of God go I." It dismissed him as one of Judy Garland's husbands.

I was beginning to exhibit some physical signs of my bad habits, so I made my way to Brad's Gym, with its weights and pulleys and all-male clientele. That small, clubby sweatshop became a Monday-Wednesday-Friday constant in my West Hollywood life. I sweated in vain for total fitness, but I felt light-headed from the discipline of exercise. It more or less offset my hamster-like sexual activities and hedonistic weekend pursuits that were buttressed by booze and more frequent pill-popping. The knowledgeable and kindly instructions of owner Brad Moore, and the company of fellow members Robert Osborne and Tucker Fleming, made working out bearable.

My old friends Chuck and Tucker had settled permanently in California. Their house, the scene of upcoming crimes, was in the fashionable "bird" streets, in the hills above Sunset Boulevard on Warbler Way. Tucker kept fit gardening and doing heavy-duty landscaping, as well as by pumping iron at Brad's. The only weight Chuck lifted was the current book, a cocktail glass, or cooking utensils. My European traveling companion and his friend took pride in serving—weather permitting, outside by the oval pool—intimate gourmet dinners and Sunday brunches. Their hospitality has been impossible to reciprocate fully. I serve one of four or five simple menus, to no more than six, a few nervous-making times a year. I look forward to the hopefully *Good Housekeeping* evening drawing to a close more than I enjoy displaying my mother's sterling service.

My Boone trust checks were moderate, the property taxes on Lloyd Place were soaring, and the paucity of acting jobs made part-time work mandatory. After all, I had to clear enough to pay Paul Millard his rent for Norma Place, now one hundred seventy-five a month. He swore not to raise it again.

An acting interview during this penurious period is worth noting. I had a preliminary audition and interview with a couple of go-betweens at the William Morris Agency. Afterward, my agent telephoned. He instructed me to drive Pacific Coast Highway the following day to a Malibu address. He did not know whom I was to

meet. He told me to dress up. A jacket, tie, the works, and tight-fit-
ting pants—padded, perhaps, with a pair of socks? He laughed the
way agents do, sweating on his end of the line.

When a shriveled butler ushered me into a Belle Watling vestibule
the next afternoon, I knew at once what was about transpire. Trompe-
l'oeiled musclemen in loincloths, bearing jewels and gifts along the
wall beside us, led our way up the fluted, curving stairway. He
showed me into an every-shade-of-pink bedroom with a satin circular bed. I gawked nervously at an acre of rosy coverlet and shiny,
fluffy pillows. I turned around to see that an equally decrepit appari-
tion had replaced the butler. Silently, and as if by magic, Mae West,
in something peachy white and gossamer, had arranged herself
provocatively in all of her bewigged blondness on a chaise longue
behind me. Her little white hands indicated the script of her own
play, *Sextet*, on a gold-leafed table nearby. Competitors who had gone
before me had earmarked the two scenes that I had taken a stab at
in the Morris office. I read them aloud again with, or rather, *to* Mae,
turning the purple pages that I held aloft with nervous hands. Mine
was, of course, the straight role, a young movie star befuddled and
mad for Mae. He praised her lips, her eyes, her entire pulchritudi-
nous persona, in the kind of florid sentences that went out of fashion
with the demise of Oscar Wilde. Mae's breathy replies were trade-
mark-terse in her patented speech pattern and were delivered with
her rolling, cloudy baby-blue eyes looking directly at my—
unpadded—crotch. She sweetly, and discreetly, without undergoing
the difficulty of uncurling, waved me away when I finished. Driving
home, I succumbed to cannot-wait-to-tell-someone laughter, but the
pity is that I was neither a stud nor a body builder.

Instead of Miss West, the notably less glamorous *Life* magazine
assisted in my financial bailout. A swaying earthquake scare was the
most stimulating event in my short history of trying to sell the weekly
magazine on the telephone. We were too briefly evacuated from the
grubby office suite in a Wilshire Boulevard high-rise where, from
five until nine on weekday evenings, I hustled for new and mostly

irate subscribers. The dinner-hour hang-ups of the more volatile prospects remain vivid. My hours left me free for decreasing acting interviews and performing the Oscar Wilde fairy stories on infrequent weekends. My sixty-dollar pittance for selling the once-prominent and now-turning-tatty *Life* took up where my exhausted unemployment benefits had left off. I rattled off the printed spiel. I became expert enough at closing the deal, thus earning a meager bonus, to be asked to join the bored ranks of the Willy Loman types who managed my cohorts—mostly actors like myself, and prone to frivolity. So for a while, I coached and cajoled and hammed it up—on a more controlled treadmill.

At home I turned in early in order to look pretty posing for a modeling gig for the May Company. Robert Osborne had arranged that I replace him as one of the May Company men's wear models. Sometimes full page, often stiff, and always flattering photographs of me ran regularly in the *Los Angeles Times*. They fed my scrapbook and my ego until a new advertising department boss-lady hired my replacement, one she had a yen for.

I had occasional blips of creativity, using my mind instead of my looks, for once, also with the assistance of Robert, who got me an assignment to write a biography of Humphrey Bogart for a now-defunct film quarterly. *Films In Review* took notice, and I wrote two other career articles, on Joan Fontaine and Lon McCallister, for their editor, the avuncular celluloid expert, Henry Hart. Joan cooperated with corrections relayed from New York through her business manager. My friend McCallister volunteered every other factual word about himself over my shoulder. The pacifying hours learning more than I ever wanted to know about Bogey, Joan, and Bud at the original Motion Picture Academy Library on Melrose Avenue passed much faster than the ones at *Life* magazine.

I was still toiling for the magazine when Judy Garland and Mark Herron returned from their European hegira to nestle stateside in Brentwood. Mark wanted to familiarize his—still—intended with his own circle of friends. I leapt at the idea and headed out to 129 South Rockingham in Brentwood. Judy was petite in mink-trimmed black at our first gathering, healthily svelte at this juncture, her piquant prettiness at its most beautiful in minimal makeup. Almost forgetting that Mark was in the house, I hastened to reminisce with my hostess about our time together at the Palace and on *A Star Is Born*. Her receptiveness was open-armed and her hospitality boundless. The Garland guffaw burbled up from her toes over the monologues of two other friends and wonderful performers: Patti Regan reciting something priceless from the Billy Barnes Revue, and actor Bob Ridgeway camping outrageously through his tale of "The Gay Caballero." The two never had a more demonstrative audience than Judy, and none of us ever had a better time—until long into the night, when Mark wanted to go to bed. Judy craved the laughter and company indefinitely. Wanting to steal Mark's thunder, I was on her side. Always.

That was the scenario on subsequent occasions that I tried to pro-long. I staked my claim, until the day she died, on Judy's conscious-ness through as many dawns as she demanded. Mark, the arbiter in 1964, accused me—correctly—of trying to unsettle their relationship when I telephoned at four in the morning for a Rockingham invita-tion. Judy answered and the shock was not that she said no, but that she was sleepy. She was right when she told Mark afterward that "the drunken Carlyle" had called. I don't know whether he was out or asleep, but he never let me forget the intrusion. From then on, I waited to be asked, preferably on weekends. Going chez Garland after locking up at *Life* could be a killer. Everything would be okay, I told myself, if I did not take Dexamyls on weeknights.

Even after Mr. and Mrs. Herron actually did make it legal in a Las Vegas wedding chapel, thus guaranteeing the erosion of Mark's stamina, and their relationship, their calls for nocturnal frolics on Rockingham continued. They included poolside nights with Judy stepping off into the deep end, wearing tummy-covering, diaphanous-topped bathing attire from Jax in Beverly Hills, and rejoicing in as many revelers as possible. Exercise, much less swimming, was as alien to her as to Mark Twain. So she clung, clowning, coquettish, frequently to me, along the kidney-shaped poolside. She distributed bath towels; liquor and pills gave me the courage to preen in front of the fire that Mark had been requested to light in the sunken living room. Judy murmured that I looked "very pretty." I didn't hurry getting dressed.

One particular night was a debacle. Robert Osborne and I joined Mark and Judy on the carpeted floor to form a Monopoly foursome. Our talk turned to Liza as we made our moves. I was focused on the game, and the burgeoning hint of mother–daughter competition in the air. I suggested that Miss Minnelli, albeit talented, did not deserve anything so exalted as a Tony Award for her work in the New York revival of *Best Foot Forward*. I learned the hard way that Mama could make such a critical observation, not an outsider. Judy, in a flash and in fury, emptied her goblet of vodka and orange juice over my head and down my front, howling at me at the same time to leave her house. She raced down the hallway in her peignoir to her bedroom and slammed the door, hard enough to disturb Joey and Lorna trying to sleep in their wing beyond the kitchen. I would later learn that the children were accustomed to Mama's mood swings, but I was not. Yet. Robert escorted me, stricken and sopping, into the Brentwood night. Mark promised to deliver my abject apologies to his bride, but many days passed when the only news of Judy Garland was through the placating Osborne as we worked out together at Brad's Gym.

Of course I was reinstated. I was, after all, like a dog with a bone in my efforts to become a part of Judy's life. She knew that I loved her, and, after the Liza upset, every subsequent tumult only afforded me a rest period from an exhausting, kindling relationship. The one that she was currently in, her marriage, together with the laughter that Mark had brought to it, began to wind down.

There was an opening night get-together in Judy's bungalow after her show at the Thunderbird Hotel. Mark had formed a mini-junket to fly to Las Vegas, and we were vociferous in our praise for her performance. I had wanted to hold her when her fingers trembled so badly in her dressing room before she went on stage, but, with the reflection in the mirror of Mark sipping a vodka, I could only button her blouse for her. There was scant relief from nerves in the rain of flattery after she had sung, and too much laying on of hands, orchestrated by her fluttering, frantic husband. Judy rose like a cry. There was a wrenching wail of "I can't say thank you any more!" She fled from the room. Mark, temporarily latched out of their sleeping quarters, was left to serve the stale catered food.

When his turn came to flee in order to appear in a play, and to take the necessary hours away from Rockingham to rehearse it properly, Judy complained that she could not find her husband. She soon stopped looking, and Mark moved out of the house. She claimed that the marriage had never been consummated. After the breakup, she told me, "Mark never did any real harm."

Mark disappeared from my life too. Like a mesmerized moth drawn to a dimming flame, I gladly, willingly took his place in Judy's life.

CHAPTER TWELVE

IS THIS MR. GARLAND?

MY GARLAND TIMES, the most heightened hours and, God knows, the heterosexual heights of my life, began in earnest when I took Judy to bed. Or was it the other way around, for a lady who was accustomed to conquest?

"You're not going to get rid of me."

I knew she meant it, curled beside me in the Hillman Minx that had replaced my Oldsmobile, as we twisted out Sunset toward Rockingham.

"Don't drive too fast, darling." That would become her whispering, unnecessary entreaty whenever I was behind the wheel. The chance of Judy getting injured while a passenger in my car terrified me—as did the thought of discovering her dead beside me in bed, which was, unfortunately, never an unlikely possibility.

We were finished with a midnight meeting with some deal-maker–lawyer at the Polo Lounge in the Beverly Hills Hotel. Such persons abounded. They were seldom able to pin Judy down and usually vanished, befuddled by her night owl's time clock and con-founded in the face of her greatest weapon: vagueness. Sid Luft, the most effective chargé d'affaires she ever had (not counting Louis B. Mayer), once told me, in a moment of pique, that "Judy couldn't do any-thing right, except sing a song." But, unless supine on Seconal or crashing from Ritalin, she could do absolutely anything she set her mind to, from concocting her own hats and cooking Thanksgiving dinner, to being the most careful and caring mother in show business—or, on the night in question, wooing me.

Lionel, her houseman, went drowsily back to bed after closing the electronic gates behind us in the driveway. "Obey Mama!" was chalked on the pantry blackboard. Joey and Lorna were asleep in their room beside Lionel's. I nervously filled an ice bucket to take to the bar in the living room while Judy went to change. I vacillated between fear and determination in my certainty that I was at that moment, at last, the more-than-willing—and hopefully able—object of her affections.

She returned, an alluring child in her chiffon peignoir, her aroma the seductive scent of her favorite fragrance, White Shoulders, her eyes waiting, like a calf's. We sipped, we talked, we embraced, and I told her that, yes, I would stay with her until she went to sleep. Her fingers were like the wings of a small bird against my cheek and around my waist as we walked down the hall to her bedroom. The only light came from outside and we went to her bed, where I need not have been afraid.

The sound of that voice sighing endearments while I gave her pleasure was the stimulation that enabled me to have one of my only successful times with a woman. My lifelong fixation manifested itself physically, to my relief and to my delight. My tongue and my mouth and loins belonged to someone new. Her noises and her body that had no limits for me were astonishing. She wanted me to stay by her when we were finished. When she drifted off to sleep, I slipped out through the bedroom's sliding glass doors. I felt bashful about being seen by Joey and Lorna, and I was concerned about Maggie and

Judy being hungry at home. I was also wide awake, restless with incredulousness.

The electric gates stood open. Judy's maid Alma had reported to work. Lionel was preparing to drive the kids to school. I glimpsed the two of them — who would have committed hara-kiri for their mistress — looking discreetly through the kitchen window as I drove off the property. All three of us were well aware of the Pandora's box that had been opened.

Judy, euphoric, telephoned that afternoon and nearly every day after. At any hour she pleased, sometimes after she had just hung up. Maggie and the other Judy had to adapt to more nights alone than usual, meowing side by side at the top of the stairs when I finally did return to Norma Place, often with the latter's namesake. Judy was adorable and devouring, and for a long, helter-skelter time, I was puffed with pride at her infinite, tactile capacity to make me feel like the number one, indispensable male in Judy Garland's universe.

I was thirty-six in 1967; Judy had turned forty-five in June, a birthday to remember because I had gone to the party that Peter Lawford gave for her at his beach house on Pacific Coast Highway. The place had been JFK's so-called Western White House and, before the Lawford–Kennedy connection, the former home of Judy's boss at MGM, Louis B. Mayer. Judy, sharing my gallows humor, chased me around the sprawling, ghost-ridden premises. She brandished my gift, the unexpurgated *Hollywood Babylon*, which sleazily recounted each of her supposed suicide attempts. The grisly book was replete with decapitations, photographs of dead celebrities, and nudes of Joan Crawford.

Judy was not political, but she was a champion of the Kennedys, and the feeling seemed to be mutual. Robert Kennedy swam in his skivvies one sultry night at Rockingham after the kids had gone to bed. He was toothsome, tough, and attractive. I took care to concentrate on my hostess. Flower power, hippies, and their music were beyond her. She was too self-centered to be more than mystified by student activism and Vietnam. The same could be said of me.

One morning, I marveled at her weight loss, silently wondering where the flesh had gone. We were standing over adjacent wash-bowls in the master bathroom, mid-morning disheveled, and scarcely covered. She saw me staring.

"I consider myself a fairly attractive woman now. I'll never be fat again!" She had read my mind and she was right. I hugged her, fondling her bare belly. She burst into an a cappella version of "Three little scars. . . ." I reached, cocky, for a toothbrush, contemplating matrimony.

There were times when, exhausted, or needing to regroup for my *Life* work, I went home and turned off my telephone. It was the only way, and Lionel understood. Sometimes he conspired with me to inform his searching mistress that I was away, or at least that there had been no answer when he knocked at my door as I sought refuge in two or three much needed recuperative days. Judy would have been a frothing pit bull in the latter age of answering machines and cellular phones.

I did go to Las Vegas again—that citadel of bad taste and stadium-sized casinos, where clocks are nonexistent. I won the trip on the television show *The Dating Game*. Judy thought the whole thing was a scream until I told her that there was no way that I could take her with me. Being a contestant as "myself" was unnerving. The turntable I sat on swung into the lights before a screaming mob of teenagers. The double-entendre banter that made me their favorite remains a blank in my memory. The off-camera floor manager had to prod my foot when my name was announced. I had been instructed as a winner to wave joyfully from the stage apron. Friends in the Sher-mart the next day told me that the live microphone, and thus the country, had heard me stage whisper "I hope you like to drink a bit" to my date and startled partner. She was a horny, dark-haired Latin lovely, and within a few days my gleeful Norma Place neighbors saw the two of us transported off to LAX in a white limousine, THE DATING GAME decaled on its side in foot-high letters.

We were chaperoned in Las Vegas by a rotund photographer, where, at Caesar's Palace, Juliet Prowse and Chita Rivera in *Sweet Charity* were part of the bargain, dinner included. It was a busy evening, watching the photographer's food dribble from his mouth, avoiding the nudging rub of my date's ample thigh, and getting up and down to answer Judy Garland's pages. Judy, restless and scheming on Rockingham, implored me to stay on at Caesar's Palace. She declared that she could join me after the *Dating Game* sojourn for a longer stay. The photographer and my date were thunderstruck. The latter accused me of being a tease when I escaped upstairs to bed.

The next day on a wordless drive from LAX back into Los Angeles, I planned a placating rendezvous with Judy. Madame Gumm—that's what I called Judy when spirits were high enough to get away with it—was a chatterbox. So was I, especially on uppers. We talked of everything from mothers to Joseph L. Mankiewicz. She admitted that the director–screenwriter had been the long-ago love of her life. I refrained from asking why. A guru, perhaps, in her rush to sophistication? Judy's loves came in all shapes, sizes, and sometimes, it was rumored, sexes; I was enjoying my turn. She commiserated about stepmothers, loss; in her case, her father who was dear to her, and she was less than charitable toward her punishing stage mother. Her organic wit was sharp and contagious.

We grew limp from laughter; humor was the predominant, sustaining emotion in Judy's life. It was her weapon against the doldrums, which could catapult her into cataclysmic rages that were overwhelming in a tiny woman who could blast you against the wall with a guttural growl and a Joe Louis fist. We lay complacently in her king-sized bed one night, her head tucked like a sparrow's in the crook of my arm.

"Do you really love me, John?"

"You know I do."

"Are you really in love with me?"

"I've loved you all my life, Judy. I don't know if I'm in love with you."

"I understand, darling." She turned out the bedside light and I was fast asleep.

I awoke with a book slamming beside my head, against the tiny roses embroidered on the quilted headboard Judy had designed. More volumes followed from the hallway bookshelf. A small picture frame flew though the air. An ashtray was hurled against the wall.

"You don't love me!" screamed the bobcat in the hall. "You . . . said. You said you . . . you didn't love me!" Her stammer made her angrier.

She raced toward the living room with me in nude pursuit. I tackled her there, before the fireplace, fearing for my life. Judy as Esther Smith, demure in delicate oils, holding her parasol and wearing her white *Meet Me in St. Louis* picture hat, looked down at us from above the mantel. We collapsed in a thrashing heap on to the carpet. I was a flailing spider caught in the folds of Judy's nightgown, yelling that I did love her, and it began to make her laugh. Humor, as I said, is catching. In an instant we were a tangled lump of clutching, fondling hysteria until I disentangled myself, self-conscious at being naked, to go find a bath towel.

I regularly joined Judy in her nocturnal prowling. We could both be tireless in the grip of amphetamines. Uppers can be confidence-enhancing, but theirs is a sleepless hold whose clutches she had tried mightily to escape from. She was delighted to appear on my Norma Place doorstep when I telephoned, too sun-up shaky to drive to Brentwood. A gawking taxi driver, or patient Lionel, stood behind her, holding a covered dish of something light, like hearts of palm.

She was only hungry when she first woke, before what she called her "medication" could take effect. Otherwise she was a distracted bird, pecking at meals. The food wasted on her in restaurants, especially when I had to pay for it, and at home, was sinful. I did not know that she would never be plump, and therefore healthy, again.

Her visits to me almost always lasted twenty-four hours or more. Our quest for amusement could be non-stop. We assaulted the neighbors through the night playing records, usually Judy's own.

Friends, impressed and entranced at first, and then exhausted, came and went.

Our Hollywood name games provided much merriment. Paul Millard's given name of Fink had provoked hilarity; Judy thought a "Fink, Posey, and Gumm" vaudeville routine would bring down the house. On one jubilant occasion, while Paul's stamina held out, my landlord and I sat slap-happily on my living room floor listening to Judy's voice soar in accompaniment to her Carnegie Hall album. She often felt like singing when it was not for her supper, and no thought had to be given to being on time. In the midst of this double dose of gratis Garland, there was a sudden, intrusive knock on my front door. I thought, in the instant hush, it was surely the police. Judy, bright in my red Brooks Brothers bathrobe, crumpled modestly into the sofa. I crept down the stairs to open the door. There stood a middle-aged lady. She too was wearing a bathrobe, with pajamas and slippers. She told me that she had followed the sound of Judy's voice from around the block, on Keith Avenue. The signpost to what she could not believe she was hearing was the telephone pole in the trees outside my kitchen window. She was certain that the voice was the real thing rather than a recording. Could she please, please come in for just a few minutes? It would mean everything to her. When I went to ask her, Madame Gumm said yes, but only for a moment. Timorous Kate sat down upstairs. She told us she was a schoolteacher. We insisted on calming her with a stiff vodka tonic. The concert resumed. The stunned and rapidly discombobulated Kate listened until Judy took me into the bathroom to whisper that Kate was making her nervous and that I should take her home. I walked our visitor as far as the corner. Both of us, blinded by the morning sun, strained to look like upstanding citizens. I watched Kate drift down Hilldale in her bathrobe and returned to see Paul off to his own apartment downstairs. Judy and I, laughing, drew the window curtains closed beside my bed.

At such times, with the witching hour finally winding down, we chattered our way toward sleep. Judy's drifting-off time was mine to try to rest alert. I monitored her breathing for a while. I slept lightly, making sure that she did not float to the bathroom to rummage in her purse for *more* Seconal. If the fluttering rattle in her throat meant only that she was sleeping on her back, I turned her gently onto her side. Nightmare imaginings of something more serious were never far away. But during our nights together she lay peacefully, like a snoring chipmunk.

Two days after our visit from the schoolteacher, when Judy had returned to Brentwood, I found a note slid under my door: *Dear Judy and John, I told you no one would believe me. Thank you! Kate.*

Paul, from his tiny summer rental at the beach, called his actress friend from adolescent days in Ohio, Jean Peters, for Judy. She was delighted to talk to Miss Garland, who took the receiver to ask Mrs. Howard Hughes if she could persuade her husband to finance a motion picture of the life of Aimee Semple McPherson. Judy longed to play the flamboyant, non-singing evangelist. The vehicle would have been ideal had Mr. Hughes or anyone else cared to produce it at that faltering stage of her career. Judy's charm and enthusiasm were persuasive in the moment; she crowed after the conversation that Jean Hughes had promised to do everything she could, which, alas and understandably, was nothing.

The two of us were elated and mischievous when we left Paul's and drove along Pacific Coast Highway. We had no intention of going home so early. I was certain that my friends Don Bachardy and Christopher Isherwood would not be averse to a one-in-the-morning drop-in with Judy Garland in tow. Judy was delighted with the idea. We turned into Santa Monica Canyon and headed for Adelaide Drive above the beach cliffs. When we knocked on the front door, Christopher answered, already dressed for bed.

"Oh, no!" he said, in his high British twang, "certainly not!" He slammed the door shut in our faces.

We walked, outraged, back up to the crest of his driveway. We fetched our vodka glasses from the front seat of my Hillman and hurled them down the incline to smash in Christopher's entryway.

Like two hyped-up adolescents, we drove away fast. Mr. Isherwood took much more time to accept my apologies than he had coming to the door; we were never genuinely friendly again. Don Bachardy later told me that matters would have been different if he had answered our knock.

I performed live on *Divorce Court*, a local, largely improvisational television show. Judy watched with Joey and Lorna, and she invited me to dinner afterward. My usual post-show qualms, quadrupled, accompanied me to Brentwood; Miss Garland had watched and judged my work under low-budget circumstances. I may as well have been an Oscar nominee. When she threw open the front door, she compared me to Robert Walker and Dirk Bogarde, her favorite actors. The kids were touching and hugging too, and Judy prepared her specialty, shepherd's pie. Alma looked on balefully from a pantry chair, resigned to chaos and cleaning up. Her employer managed to dirty every pot and pan, grabbed off no matter how high the shelf. Judy did the same thing in my kitchen on Norma Place.

Judy often felt forsaken in Brentwood, a state she usually brought upon herself. "Where the hell is everybody?" she would ask in her echoing living room. Joey and Lorna were asleep or at school and her phone had stopped ringing. "This house used to be filled with people," she cried, "even if we hated each other." The pleasure was mine, when *Life* or my sanity did not take precedence, to fill the void. Off we would go, like eager prom dates, to a movie and dinner.

"And is this Mr. Garland?" asked a lady maître d' in a high-rise restaurant at Sunset and Vine. We had just shared popcorn in the balcony of the Pantages to see *Hotel*, a movie as slick as our thoughtless hostess. "He is not. This is Mr. Carlyle!" pealed Judy emphatically, undermining the lady and riveting the attention of every other diner. There was the occasional, welcomed freebie because of Judy's presence, sometimes courtesy of Cheryl's father Steve Crane in his new restaurant atop the 9000 Sunset building. But mostly I showed Judy off at the Por Favor, which was within walking distance of

Norma Place, and where the management knew me. The bar was gay and crowded. The cuisine was good affordable Mexican, and the dining room clientele was mixed. The Por Favor's affection and red-carpet treatment for my lady friend was embodied by John, a waiter whose eyes grew almost as luminous as Judy's whenever she appeared. He maneuvered us past the bar and diplomatically fended off intruders. He was gently deferential and never the sycophant. He was also a victim of the drug culture, a fact that I did not know until twenty years later when I saw him last walking down Doheny Drive in West Hollywood, burned out and mindless. Having recognized him, I drove around the block, but he had already disappeared. I wanted to help him, to remind him of those Por Favor evenings that he had added to, to thank him again for a heartfelt letter he had written to me when Judy died, a letter I'd saved.

My sortie with Judy to see Vanessa Redgrave and David Warner in *Morgan* was more indelible than the avant-garde film. It was playing in a so-called art house theatre in Westwood. The village was still safe and small, rife with low-rises and wholesome UCLA students, and a friendly, campus atmosphere. *Morgan* was more or less incomprehensible. Judy's first observation was, "I don't know anything about the movies any more."

Her next titillated at least two rows of the audience: "Vanessa's father likes to be flagellated."

Beside me there was a sudden, ominous snapping sound. "Darling," Judy whispered, thrashing about, "I've broken my glasses." I shushed her and told her to be patient. She went to any lengths.

"I'm not sitting through this," she pronounced.

"Go on, then," I hissed. We had, after all, paid four bucks to see the lousy thing.

With that, she made her exit, imperious in a flared white blouse, black slacks, and clutching a pair of deliberately broken granny glasses. To hell with her, I thought. I had the car keys, so I stubbornly sat through the rest of the movie. I rose to leave, hoping that Judy had not called Lionel or hailed a cab to Brentwood. I swung through the doors into to the lobby, where Judy sat, holding court on a love seat in a flattering pool of light, a semicircle of enraptured young people crouched at her feet. Her laughing eyes glanced off mine as she serenely answered their questions, leaving me to cool my heels in the men's room and then on the street until the star was ready to make her exit. She waved and blew kisses when she swept outside saying goodbye. She deigned to hold my arm and pranced beside me down the sidewalk, triumphant.

Chuck and Tucker's endurance of Miss Garland was exemplary. They were among the "proper" people and new places I searched out to distract and entertain Judy—sometimes to delay our going to bed. I was not always up to our sex life. At the same time, I was hell-bent to prolong Judy's desire for my company. Judy was voracious and unselfish in laying bare her need for devotion; that's what had to be limitless, not my capacity. We seldom discussed homosexuality, mine or anyone else's. She brushed it aside and never, ever judged me for being gay.

"I'm with an Irish lady that I'd like you to meet," I told Chuck, seeking an invitation. Judy believed in good manners. She would have been in shock if we'd arrived unannounced. Chuck, suspecting, because he knew whose company I was keeping, told us to come on up.

First we stopped to buy two azalea plants to take to Warbler Way. The traditional Cape Cod house was tucked into a cul-de-sac a few short streets above Cordell Drive, where George Cukor lived. Judy, on the shelf professionally, fled from the critical and *veddy* correct presence of her last major director, but she took to the informally decorous residence of my friends. Judy was charming to Chuck. Our air-conditioned spirits, without going for a swim, were manic when unsuspecting Tucker parked in the carport and walked in from the kitchen. More sober-sided than Chuck, Tucker's pumpkin smile flummoxed—he never did get over the impact of Judy. He came to

care for her deeply in his own courtly way, more cautiously than
Chuck, and with better sense than I. Beginning with that cloud-nine
first gathering in the living room on Warbler Way, Tucker kept Judy,
Chuck, and me grounded. Or he tried his best to.

Warbler Way became a safety zone second only to Norma Place for
Madame Gumm. At Chuck and Tucker's, she swam, sang, and even
cooked. One Sunday morning, she made do with four eggs for our
brunch. She added butter and milk and decorated the eggs as well,
with fresh parsley and slivers of pimento, and a ring of encircling
bacon strips. The platter, emblematic of Judy's approach to life in
these, her last, lackluster years, was pretty and colorful, fit to be photographed, but barely adequate nutritionally. She would grow more
impoverished, lowering more strata, when she sought shelter after
leaving me and California behind.

"Don't stay in the sun too long," I counseled her beside the oval
pool. Bright sunlight, like running out of Ritalin, made her blown up
and lobster-skinned.

"It's okay, darling. My freckles were famous at MGM."

"Yes," I replied, "so were my blackheads at Republic." She fell
about, her laughter echoing up through the hillside foliage. The
beach towel that Tucker had wrapped around her kept slipping open.
A curious housepainter almost toppled off his extension ladder.

We impulsively telephoned my sister Ann one Saturday morning
from Norma Place. We told her, with Maggie and Judy glaring on, that
we were going to be married. In Las Vegas. Almost immediately. No,
there was no definite date set at that moment. "We just wanted you
to be the first to know."

Judy, taking up cat space on the side of the bed, wearing my red
robe, took the receiver to introduce herself. There were assurances of
how much we loved each other, a discussion of the spelling of my
sister's name (with or without an e); then, prompted by Ann's disclo-
sure of her pregnancy and the question of what to name her second
child, a knowledgeable discussion of English Royals. Stuart III if a

boy? (He was.) Then Judy said that she had three kids of her own, Liza, Lorna, and Joe.

"Yes, I know," laughed Ann.

"Where is your husband?" Judy asked.

"He's out fixing the mailbox."

"Is he really? Oh, how wonderful! I wish I had a husband like that." She smoothed back my tousled hair with her free hand.

Ann, not easily floored, was sufficiently tantalized to break the news of this whimsical conversation to her parents. By now Dad was living with Jean, his fourth and final wife, in an apartment on Mount Vernon Place. Mother had moved into a smaller house of her own on Bellona Avenue.

My undaunted father, trying, not for the first time, to gauge the depth of my feeling for Judy, called on Sunday evening. He said that he had always accepted and tried to understand my devotion to Miss Garland, but he attempted to make certain that under no circumstances would I go so far as to marry her. He assumed that I had better sense. When I waffled, he was alarmed. There was a feeble part of me that felt that I could succeed in making and keeping her happy. No one could, of course, which is what my father, based on his reading about Judy's troubles, tried to make clear from three thousand miles away. He did not need to tell me that Judy's bottomless need for love surpassed the capability of any man, of whatever sexual persuasion. He did not speak of my homosexuality; he spoke of my ruining my life, and the apparent erosion, because of her publicized erratic behavior, of Miss Garland's own self-worth. That I loved her despite her foibles cut no ice; he said he had been through enough analysis to know that our marriage would be doomed. Mother, aged sixty, wrote eloquently that I "should proceed with great caution. People at Miss Garland's age rarely change."

I knew they both were right. Judy had tried to change, but her resolve had lessened. The support system of her dependence on daily Ritalin—and Seconal to counteract it—had begun, like her voice, to fail her. If only such a tragic habit and its consequences could have been addressed publicly back then, my enchanting lady friend, from whose shortcomings I turned a blind eye, might still be with us. While it amused both of us to talk of marriage, I never proposed again.

Mark Herron once accused me of taking his ex-wife to the Four Star. It never happened; I told Mark that I had more class. Peetsie Hayward triggered the rumor when she saw Judy and me on a daytime walk to the Orange Julius stand further along the block where the Four Star was located. We stopped at Propinquity, a gift shop whose flighty proprietor presented Judy with a little colored windmill to carry on our way. Pedestrians observed us and retraced their steps. Drivers circled the block. We passed the local record store. Its owner, hoping to lure her inside, bobbed feverishly in the window that displayed the album of Judy and Liza at London's Palladium; my companion paid no attention to either.

She took it graciously for granted when an admirer picked up the tab for our dinner and drinks at the Raincheck on Santa Monica Boulevard. He materialized beside our booth to tell Judy that she was "the most beautiful lady in the world" before he vanished out the front door.

Reactions were not always so benevolent. Judy liked to play pool. We went to the local billiard hall. "Look," muttered a plaid-shirted pool shark as we passed by him inside, "Judy Garland!" "Who gives a fuck?" snarled a layabout beside him. She was like cats, I think, at the end, and still: either loved or hated.

We attended Jack Jones's opening night at Cocoanut Grove. Judy wore a long, hobbling gown encrusted with white sequins. No last-minute hairdresser would accept a check on Rockingham, so concerned Alma had insisted on covering the back of Judy's short brown hair with a softening ostrich feather ornament that matched her dress. Alma told me, "I hate to see her going out like that, without her hair done. It's just not right. She's still a big star."

Arriving in front of the Ambassador, we lost our vodka glasses in the limousine's armrest containers. We made an entrance through

the lobby and descended the stairway to the Grove. Fans and photographers, telling Miss Garland how well she looked, parted in our
wake. The trick, said Judy, smiling delightedly, was to always keep
moving. Mr. Jones, the new rage, was first-rate, and the night proceeded without mishap until, on her way to the ladies' room after the
show, Judy stumbled slightly in the carpeted foyer.

"Well, I see your date is drunk again," said a producer nearby,
casting a smarmy look.

"She is not!" said I, incensed. She had nursed one drink all
evening. She tended to be awkward, and the dress didn't help.

He laughed derisively, and, by way of furthering my career, I
shoved him backward three or four feet, glaring at him as he went
totally off balance to the floor. He arose, unhurt, to stalk off and
spread more rumors. Judy, glowing, treated me like Sir Walter
Raleigh when I told her what had happened.

There are photographs taken of us that night, and I have never
looked so happy. I always do in pictures with Judy. Is it true, as her
biographer Gerald Clarke suggested, that she was the biggest thing
to ever happen to me? Without meaning to be ungallant, I hope not.
I mean this to be my story, not Judy Garland's. But she sure as hell
made a dent.

We kept the same limousine to go and visit my friend William, who
was also Judy's neighbor, in Brentwood. It was a hot night. Judy
crossed through the Neutra-designed living room and one-stepped
outside — straight into the shallow end of the pool. Most of her white
sequins sparkled to the surface. Jack Owen, jealous of our conviviality
and disgusted by Judy's behavior, watched in the darkness by the
guesthouse, glowering from tree to bush. The next day, he destroyed
every recording that William had collected of his guest. William
donated one of his white shirts and a pair of slacks to Judy to replace
the wet evening gown. He was too polite to ask for them back.

Now and then, I gave a party on Norma Place. Paul Millard talked me
into hiring a couple to tend bar and serve — twice. There was a less

expansive affair for my sister and her husband Stuart. A good thing, too. They sat owl-eyed and shattered through a drunken actress's disillusioning diatribe concerning the self-destructive homosexuality of Montgomery Clift, whom Ann'd had a crush on. Barbara Rush, who knew when to go home, redeemed another group. Seventy-four others stayed until three in the morning while I, sitting on the back porch beside the freaked-out, caged Maggie and Judy, prayed for my guests to leave.

The smallish party that is still talked about was for Judy. She stayed for three days. It started remarkably enough, as I accidentally slid down the stairs to greet my guest of honor. She had finally appeared on Paul's arm in my front door, thus appeasing my fortified anxiety. Paul had driven to pick her up in Brentwood. Festivities were off on a merry course when I greeted them on my bottom. Judy flattered me by looking glamorous in pearls and floor-length black velvet. Cheryl Crane attended with a lady friend, in lieu of Lana Turner. A casting-director acquaintance came to the top of the stairs with Hedy Lamarr, thus quasi-completing the distaff trio of the MGM *Ziegfeld Girl* stars that I had invited. Hedy's hair was dyed orange and she wore a fur jacket with slacks. She took in Judy's formality and sweetly told her how "*zilly* you look."

Ramona Rush Hennesy, Barbara's sister, was amenable as always when her husband, art director Dale Hennesy, telephoned their baby-sitter so that the two could stay later than they already had. Dale wanted to further observe my pair of ladies who had contributed, in his words, to "motion picture history." John Dall, feeling no pain either, agreed. Judy and Hedy, oblivious, spent a long time huddled on my bed, chattering about what better mothers than Lana they could have been for Cheryl. Judy, as the evening wore on, wanted to be less constrained. She went into my bathroom where Hedy helped her to change into my familiar red bathrobe. That is when a favorite ashtray, labeled with my Capricorn birth sign, disappeared from my toilet top, never to be seen again.

Judy tapped the overly talkative John Dall's skull with her high-heeled shoe that night. His lionizing position slumped at her feet beside my cocktail table barely changed. Things wound down, but not before Hedy requested Judy to sing "Somewhere Over the Rainbow." "You sing it," Judy replied. She led the "oh my god!" howl, and the laughter, when Hedy did, in a Viennese accent. It was time for everyone but Judy to say good night.

With Judy, there was pandemonium; there were scenes and schisms. "You deserted me! Like everybody else! That's the ball game! You can go to hell!" Judy's phone slammed down in my ear. I had left Rockingham at three in the morning, pleading exhaustion. We had hugged each other good night; now I was too tired to give a damn. The phone rang again.

"Oh, darling, I'm sorry. I . . . I do that . . . with . . . everybody I care about. Please forgive me. I love you." I forgave her and fell into bed.

Judy's California coda was prolonged. Her cars were being repossessed. The gardeners at Rockingham were not being paid. One intrepid process-server climbed the wall and popped up in the kitchen window. After she let him in to do his dirty work, he asked for an autograph! Even faithful Lionel and Alma were eventually unable to stay on. They could not survive on their unpaid salaries. There were imploring phone calls to Liza in New York for financial aid, if only to pay the utility bills. Liza did finally pay Mama's debts—after she died.

Judy was incapable of performing in *Valley of the Dolls*. Out of financial desperation, she had signed to do what was to be an ultimately dreadful film. I watched her delaying tactics at Twentieth Century Fox. She claimed to have lost a boxed set of four front caps, requiring an emergency trip to the office of a Beverly Hills dentist for temporary replacements. She spent long, expensive hours holed up in her lavish dressing room, complete with pool table. She was flat-out terrified and bereft of confidence. She felt "trapped" in her becoming chestnut-colored wig. The respectful crew and the grips in the catwalks applauded her when she appeared on the set—hours late.

Mark Robson's no-balls, hands-off direction was the coup de grâce.
Judy retreated to her dressing room. I went home with a sinking
heart. After four stalled days, she was fired. At my instigation, she
placed a few desperate calls to ask the head of the studio, Richard
Zanuck, to be reinstated, but he refused her pitiful pleading.

One night while visiting me at Norma Place, Judy sat watching
herself in *A Child Is Waiting*. I had seen the film. I went to make my
bed—which, two seconds later, Maggie and Judy went flying under
when my bathroom door slammed. There was silence, the TV had
been turned off, and the lady had locked herself in my bathroom. I
knocked and asked what was wrong. "You walked out during my best
scene! You're not interested in my work!" she screamed. "Judy, I've
already seen it," I protested. Loud Lily Mars sobs followed, finally
subsiding after a lengthy, coaxing time to make her come out again,
so that I could throw my arms around her and repeat that she was a
great, astounding actress. Almost as good as Lucille Bremer, I said.
That brought her around.

One polemic at the Por Favor was hell. "There is no Judy Garland
any more!" I said, bolstered by amphetamines and vodka Gibsons,
worn down by Judy's complaints concerning professional calamities
of her own making. We were dining with a nervous nightclub comic
whose tic accelerated. I told her that the *Valley of the Dolls* debacle
had been her own fault and that she did not take care of her voice,
much less herself. I brutally called her on her excesses and excuses.
In a flash, left-handed Judy, her eyes vengeful with black rage, socked
my jaw with one connecting blow that pitched me out of my cane
chair onto the floor. The twitching comic and the astonished patrons
of the Por Favor were not half as embarrassed and aghast as I was. I
stood up, threw some money on the table, and made a tail-between-
my-legs exit. I practically ran around the corner to Norma Place. The
lady got a ride home—to Brentwood, of course—with the comic.
Later, in New York after our estrangement, she let the comment hang
in the air that the comic had *longed* to drive her home in the first
place. I ignored what she implied, but we both laughed when she

told me that she had only struck me with the certain knowledge that she had substitute transportation.

Around this time, Judy's new publicist, Tom Greene, had come on the scene to help with Judy's tangled affairs and disordered life. I thought about myself and did not care that he would become a fresh contender in the marriage department.

Some mornings after the Por Favor falling out, I joined John Dall in the Hilldale Coffee Shop. He asked me how Judy was. I told him that she was an unreasonable, hopped-up madwoman and that I never wanted to see her again. He told me time would anesthetize my choleric feelings. It did. I missed the sleepless nights that she had once sung about. I wrote her a letter of apology. In answer, Tom Greene telephoned. I was certain that Judy was within earshot, maybe even eavesdropping on the extension phone as was her wont. Tom said that she had lost the Rockingham house to creditors. They were packing. Judy was on her way by train to appear at the Westbury Music Fair in New York. I asked that she come on the line. She did not.

I was not contrite enough to drive to Brentwood. The loss of the house had seemed inevitable, but I was certain that she would return to another domicile in California—perhaps my own. Tom called back again. He told me that he had arranged for her to travel East in a railroad car painted pink. How or why that was managed, I never learned. They were stopping en route in Chicago to celebrate her June 10, 1967 birthday at the Pump Room. Tom suggested that I call her there. I did, of course. I told her how much I missed her. She had already melted. She was childlike with gaiety over my call. She exulted in the joys of a cross-country railway trip, and she startled me by expressing zealous optimism over new plans for a fresh start in Manhattan. It turned out that that was where most of the too brief, mosquito-like existence remaining for her would indeed be based. I wished her love and luck and hung up, awash with turbulent feelings: surprise, guilt, relief, and a pestering melancholy.

My tristesse was short-lived. Trade and newspaper blurbs announced that Judy Garland was returning to the Palace for her

third engagement on July 31. Sid Luft was back on the scene as her
producer. There was no question that I had to be there. The trip had
to be planned between dates of collecting unemployment claims. I
had obtained new benefits, not through acting, but courtesy of an
obliging *Life* magazine manager who had agreed to fire me—to
enable me to be eligible to collect benefits. An employer had to be
finished with you, not vice-versa. Within earshot of the phone banks,
I threw a premeditated fit, overturning a file cabinet in an outer
office. My cohort deemed me overwrought. He might have added
underpaid.

I made airline reservations between my shock-to-the-system 8:20
A.M. Tuesday unemployment reporting appointments. My old New
York friend Paul Phillips said that I could stay in his walk-up on
Eighth Avenue. He was, coincidentally, going to be Judy's stage man-
ager at the Palace. Since *Mr. Roberts*, Paul had come up in the Great
White Way world. He promised not to tell Judy that I was coming.

I was hauling out a suitcase on a sweltering Los Angeles evening
when Judy, plaintive, telephoned me from New York. She was forlorn and friendless—Tom Greene was on his way to being permanently persona non grata—and she wanted to know what I was up
to. I told her she'd spoiled my surprise: I was packing to come to her
Palace opening. She bubbled over, wrote down my arrival time, and
insisted on meeting my plane. I would be her escort on opening
night! Now I jumped for joy—and gathered extra Dexamyls to store
in my toilet kit.

I left Maggie and Judy in the care of my neighbor Dick Dobyns
and boarded my supposedly non-stop flight, which began with all of
us passengers growing hot and apoplectic while waiting on the
tarmac for more than an hour's delay prior to takeoff. When we were
airborne, the pilot notified us that a stop had to be made in Kansas
City to deliver a coffin. He promised that he would do his utmost to
make up time once we were aloft—again—depending, of course, on
the wind factor. Midway through this fiasco, a wide-eyed stewardess

lurched her way from the front cabin toward my seat. She hunched down in the aisle to ask if I were Mr. John Carlyle. I said I was. She informed me that Miss Judy Garland, having contacted the pilot, wanted me to be assured that she would be waiting at the airport, regardless of the delay. Which, when we finally landed, was four hours later than our scheduled arrival time.

The crew and attendants jostled to get a look at Judy as she welcomed me. She did not look too rumpled in a Mondrian-trimmed shantung suit. Her hair was cut gamin short, and she waited, somehow, on the ramp, at the very door of the plane! I felt proud as a peacock. It was lovely to see her again.

"I like your new hairdo, darling." My hair was shorter too, middle-aged preppie-fashioned, with barely enough falling over my brow for Judy to smooth back.

She was affectionate and so grateful for my coming that she felt compelled to return to the VIP lounge to introduce me to the bartender who had accommodated her with two drinks and four hours of midday conversation. He was a beaming Frank Morgan type who told me he was delighted to meet the gentleman for whom she had waited so long. Judy's restless, waiting limousine driver did not appear quite so convivial, but we floated back into Manhattan nonetheless, snug in the back seat, with the partition closed. At a couple of stop lights, some Big Apple pedestrians waved their good wishes for her Palace opening before we pulled up to the theatre's backstage alley entrance. We went through the stage door and walked out upon the fabled stage. Judy shouted "Look who's here!" to the onrushing Joey and Lorna. They were to make their Palace debut on the bill with Mama. Paul Phillips lugged my suitcase into the wings while discordant instrumental noises rose angrily from the pit. He reminded me that the orchestra was on golden time. I told Judy that no, she had no time to play, that I would go home with Paul and would see her from the front row the following night. Tardy rehearsal music sounded as my impatient host and I trudged off toward Eighth Avenue. Paul stopped to have a duplicate key to his apartment made, showed me in and around his flat, and rushed back to the Palace, leaving me alone to regroup.

After a much-needed nap, I rediscovered Manhattan, barhopping until dawn. I passed out through the entire next day, ignoring Paul's comings and goings. I likewise ignored Robert Osborne when he pounded on the door after trying in vain to telephone me. Judy's calls went unanswered as well. I awoke so late that there was barely enough frantic time to revive myself with an upper and dash to the East Side—where Robert, in town for the opening too, had instructed me to go to rent evening clothes. The fact that there were a few minutes left for the establishment to stay open to fit this per-spiring wreck is one of God's mercies.

Paul, aghast with disapproval, passed me on the stairway on his way back to work after his supper. He promised to reassure the alarmed, nervous lady I had traveled thousands of miles to see per-form that I would be on hand at the Palace.

During Judy's overture I sat like a shored-up robot. I began to gain strength in the front row, as Judy was no doubt doing offstage. My medicated fog lifted the moment she made her entrance down the center aisle. I wanted to touch her, but she was too far away. My sweaty hands slapped in the air over my head like the Scarecrow in *The Wizard of Oz*. By the time she'd finished her opening number, "I Feel a Song Comin' On," I was as supercharged as every other fanatic in the rabid, ferocious audience. "Louder!" they demanded. Judy's voice—like smoke in the beginning, and unbeknownst to me sitting on the front row—was almost lost in the roar of the orchestra's over-amplified sound system. The demand was a first for her, a jolt that, despite jagged notes and a crazed vibrato, galvanized her soaring momentum for the rest of the night.

When the dancer John Bubbles came on to soft-shoe "Me and My Shadow" with Judy and her children, I was enchanted. Having Joey and Lorna smile in my direction made me swell-headed. When Judy sang directly to me, I was cock-of-the-walk. I was also too high that opening night to perceive that this driving seductress was a wasted cry from the apogee of the Judy Garland that I had held a flashlight and ushered for sixteen years earlier. But that did not matter. Explosions of bravos engulfed her like before, and this time I headed for the backstage area instead of the locker room of the Palace—to take Judy to her opening night party at El Morocco.

It would be easier to dislodge a pearl from an oyster than it was to get Judy to leave her dressing room, a sanctum—it included bathrooms—that she was always loath to depart, especially the one at the Palace. I was summoned into this safe-hold from among a crush of well-wishers and allowed to wait with Joey and Lorna until Mama, resplendent in tailored white with matching boa, was prepared to make her leisurely exit. When she was ready, she sent the kids off with their father through the stage door. I took their mother's arm to lead her outside through the glass front doors of the Palace lobby. I wished the theatre's old janitor Turner had been alive to hold them open for us. The sight that greeted us, a taken-for-granted given throughout most of Judy's life, has always exemplified for me the awesome impact of fame.

New York's finest, mounted on horseback, could not control the Times Square mob that massed forward to catch sight of the star they had waited too long to see. They surged and swelled, screaming around us, touching and grabbing at their prey. Judy was the only person present who was not on the brink of panic. The star was in her element, moving steadily forward toward our car, smiling, waving, God-blessing, making her way through her bludgeoning public as though parting a tumultuous Red Sea. I was glad when we were safely inside our limousine, though I was not convinced that the crowd would not succeed in their apparent effort to rock it over. Judy, however, commanded the driver before driving off to "turn the inside lights on—so they can see me!" He did, which generated more frenzied window tapping and spectator applause. Then he began to carefully drive our way out of the bedlam and maneuver us toward El Morocco.

The party had been in full swing for upward of two hours by the time Judy made her entrance. Festivities were halted for hugs and hosannas, and we were led to our place-of-honor banquette. Snuggled against the zebra-striped motif, we smiled and embraced in the glare of the flashbulbs. We kissed for the cameras. Judy told the press that we were dear friends, and that her rumored engagement to Tom Greene was off. Then we got up to dance.

Bert Lahr cut in on me. The minuscule dance floor was cleared to watch Dorothy move into the adoring arms of the Cowardly Lion. They were two imp creatures, lost in one another's laughter, and oblivious to the moist eyes of some, looking on from among the fake white palms. When Judy and I had sat down, Angela Lansbury made an even later entrance after her star turn in *Mame*. The two talked across me about *Harvey Girls* and things unknown. I blew smoke and made faces at sleepy Joey and Lorna, biding their time in an adjacent booth.

I have always treasured the photographs from that El Morocco night, some of which are framed on my bathroom wall. I did not welcome the item in Earl Wilson's column the next day, carried in nearly every American newspaper, noting that John Carlyle had been Judy Garland's escort the night before. My paranoiac imagination ran away with me, as I feared that everyone at the Department of Unemployment in California was bent over the gossip column, taking note of the publicity that I would ordinarily crave. I was also fearful of hurting my family's feelings if they read that I was on the East Coast but didn't come to Baltimore. I telephoned Ann to ease my guilt. Judy had paid my way, I lied; there was simply no time to visit Baltimore. She understood. Ann doubted that either Mother or Dad read Earl Wilson. They never told me they did. Apparently, the good folks at unemployment didn't either.

Judy insisted, throughout our brief romp from P. J.'s Saloon to various penthouse parties, that I would be wondrously better off living in Manhattan. I gently changed the subject. I cradled her against my chest as of old until she went to sleep at dawn in her suite at the St. Moritz.

One manic morning, in our idea of mischief-making, we played a joke on Sid Luft. I told him his former wife had grown bored with it all, that Judy and I were calling him from Los Angeles. For a moment Sid believed me. We pictured him turning white and grew hysterical laughing. He was backstage, his composure regained, when I went to the Palace on my final night in New York to bid goodbye to Judy.

She came offstage a wet wreck, grabbing for air and a towel and a slug of water, tiny and slippery when I held her in my arms. She fully counted on my coming back to her after making the necessary arrangements in California. I had been too chicken to turn down in person Sid's offer to be a "companion" to Judy for five hundred dollars a week. I hedged that I would think about it in California for another week. As I watched her lonely figure walk back into a buffeting thunderclap of applause, I was torn. She was a weary warrior, dwarfed by the cavernous Palace stage. I whispered my thanks to Paul Phillips and repeated the familiar route, carrying my suitcase through the theatre alleyway, this time to take a taxi to the East Side airline terminal where I boarded a bus to take me to JFK.

On August 26, 1967, I wrote to Sid:

> *After carefully thinking over your offer, I've decided to reluctantly say no.*
>
> *This decision is in spite of the need for extra money, together with the desire to be of any help to you and Judy that I could. Not to mention the prospect of traveling around the country with my favorite performer.*
>
> *But, I'm an actor, Sid, and I must pursue it. If job offers don't materialize, I will consider a six months' stay in New York at the end of October—which is also when my current unemployment claim expires! There is also my apartment to be sublet, animals to consider, and my duplex to be dealt with. These details cannot be settled in a week's time.*
>
> *Finally, I guess I love Judy too much to become an employee. Relationships can change under those circumstances and I want ours to remain intact—always.*

Show her this letter if you would, Sid, and ask her to understand.
I hope you both do.
   My best to you both, hope Boston is another smash—and perhaps
I'll be seeing all of you in a couple of months.

This marginally soppy epistle that I may as well have never sent was meant to be understated and diplomatic. It ended by my calling attention to a letter to the editor that I had also written, in response to a semi-derisive piece on Judy's Palace stand, to *Time* magazine. You can gather the inference that I took umbrage to from the extract that was published in the issue of September 1, 1967: "The lady is about as masculine as a buttercup—psychiatrist's pronouncements notwithstanding."

I waited to call Judy—until she had had what I nervously hoped would be sufficient time to absorb my flying the coop. When I did, she flew at me through the phone, her voice like a blowtorch: "You promised me! You deserted me! Just like everybody else!" On and on she went, her victim's fury mounting with each familiar, sledgehammer accusation: "You said you'd be here for me! You bastard!" She hung up on me. I stared at the phone, embarrassed for both of us.

I felt some relief as well. I was the one who was not ready to self-destruct.

I came close. I dove into debauchery in the darkness of bath-houses, without remembering the many with whom I slept. I drank too much in order to fuel my pills. It took me until mid-week to recover to half myself for my more and more inconsequential acting interviews. I hid away to pull it together for Maggie and Judy and the company of one or two close friends. I lost myself for hours reading—my film reference books and fiction. Later, it was biographies, and I have always been reclusive. But then I did not care enough for any one thing, including myself, to maintain direction. It was my prolonged male menopause. I was without love. I missed being the object of it and the turmoil of it—with Judy.

In this period, Charlie Cochran, the friend who was with me when

Judy died, abetted my escaping. He sang, in a nasal and distinctive style, accompanying himself on the piano, what were once revered as cafe-society songs. He performed at two ocean-lapped hideaways off Pacific Coast Highway, La Mer and the Holiday House. I frequently enjoyed his wit and bonhomie. Drinking together after his sets sent me into boozy rapture over his perfect diction and comfortable presence. Once, he disappeared off his fourth floor Holiday House balcony, landed in the sand below, and walked back in, unscathed, his half-mast blue eyes still twinkling. He has since reformed to become a pillar for the salvaged, but not by musicologists. Sometimes he telephones me from his home in West Palm Beach—on the anniversary of our telephoning Judy in London on June 21, 1969.

CHAPTER THIRTEEN

THE LAST OF JUDY

IN NOVEMBER 1967, Judy raised her delicate head once more. I saw to it when I telephoned her in Las Vegas. I told her that Chuck and Tucker and I would be flying up for the night of her opening at Caesar's Palace. She could not remain angry for my New York no-show. I knew my way was softened from a letter that casting director Michael Shurtleff had written me earlier in the month. There was poignancy in his account of an evening in Manhattan that made me want to be with Judy. He was in the Salvation, his favorite discotheque.

"Miss Garland was there," he wrote. "With me were two of her worshippers. I'd never have imposed on her, except that at one point everyone in her party left her all alone. She did her face three times and then was left having to sit looking very much alone, so I went up to her and said I was a friend of yours and Chuck and Tucker, and she was lovely and sweet and we had a fine talk. She came out on the floor and we danced together, and now my friend is never going to wash his left arm again since she held on to it. I am to deliver urgent messages to you to come East 'where the life is and stop decaying out there.'"

Instead of going East, I went with my two friends to Vegas. Chuck and Tucker waited in a bar area of Caesar's Palace while I telephoned upstairs. Judy told me to come up, saying she longed for my company before her opening in the midnight show, which turned out to be the only one she would perform throughout her engagement. I was jubilant that she wanted to see me before she went on. Wearing a white terrycloth robe, she threw open the door to her suite, her hair—dyed the old MGM auburn—in curlers. She buried her pale face and metallic head against my chest. She took my hand and led me through the gaudy living room bedecked with the requisite flamboyant star's flower arrangements to the dressing table/makeup alcove. En route, she informed Sid Luft, in attendance as of old, that there would be no show unless she had more Ritalin. I rose above the banter that ensued. I checked my own Dexamyl supply in my jacket pocket, talked of some pipe-dream acting possibilities, and reiterated how good it was to see her again. I told her that I had to be back in Los Angeles the next day for a probable interview and made no mention of our contretemps regarding New York. While we spoke, she applied with adroitness, despite trembling fingers, the Judy Garland visage. I reminded her that Chuck and Tucker were waiting, hugged her good luck, and left her to dress for the show.

Downstairs, our showroom table was okay, but not ringside. There was a sudden commotion from that area. A flighty maître d' scampered, ashen-faced, up the tiered steps to where we were seated. He told us that Miss Garland had threatened not to go on until we changed places with the disgruntled group down front—which was headed by the owner of Caesar's Palace. The re-routed group had no choice but to pretend to be cavalier as the three of us carried our drinks down to the best table in the house.

The Garland pizzazz still held. It was fortified now and then with a sip from my drink when I handed it up to her. By now her program of songs was truncated and her arrangements simplified to allow her to sing in a lower key. Judy sang without strain when rested, and, whether she was or not that night, she seemed refreshed by our presence as much as by the Ritalin, and high and happy too on the adrenaline that surges on opening night. We were on our feet when she tilted her hand microphone skyward, snapping its long cord like a lion tamer, the instrument almost swallowed with the towering sound of her last lament.

We did not have to twist Judy's arm to go on celebrating after a lackluster party in her suite dominated by Nevada businessmen and their flashy wives. The only redeeming company was jocund Mama Cass, who had to leave early. I tried not to think of the old days, when every other lionizing star on the Strip would have been drinking Judy's liquor. Sid, yawning, told us to take good care of his meal ticket. Off the four of us went, unmindful of a return flight to Los Angeles.

A while later, the Garland–Williamson dance team refused to leave the floor of a downtown Las Vegas dive. They had become a tiresome spectacle in the one dump in town that wanted to close. All of us were asked to leave. Judy and Chuck and I, beginning our slide off stimulants, were outraged. Tucker forbade a public explosion of anger and called a cab. Back at Caesar's Palace, becalmed in Judy's suite, I went into her bedroom to lie down — and promptly passed out in her oceanic bed. Chuck and Tucker chatted up Judy in her living room before feebly suggesting that perhaps it was time to wake me up. Judy opened the door to the bedroom and immediately barred entry to it.

"Look at John, we couldn't possibly wake him up."

My friends protested.

But Judy said, "No. He's got to sleep. He can stay with me. I'll take care of him. We can get married here in Las Vegas."

Chuck and Tucker were past fading, and even Tucker was buffaloed. They headed for the airport.

My awakening the next afternoon with Judy pressed dead-to-the-world against me was not a hearty highlight. I felt as though my temples were being sandblasted from within. The garbage taste on my tongue offset the throbbing ache in my bladder and threatening nausea. I hurtled in the curtains-drawn darkness for the loo. After I relieved myself, the nausea passed. I tried to perform scouring magic with a plastic-wrapped toothbrush. I finally emerged, still queasy. Judy, drowsy but aware and tender, felt that a popper of amyl nitrate and a pill might help. I agreed; we were quickly off again, rocking and tumbling from the bed to the floor like weak-willed adolescents, adrift momentarily in a guilty, giggling haze of euphoria. In no time, this fresh combination of goodies brought me to my knees in the bathroom again. This time successfully. Madame Gumm sat on the floor beside me. She held cold washcloth compress against my forehead and attempted to pat clean my splattered white dress shirt. She hugged and clutched and told me that there was no reason to be embarrassed. I saw that she was starting to fall back asleep. I was relieved for both of us; she had to perform that night and I longed to be alone. My own bed at home seemed very far away indeed. I helped her back to bed, arranged her pillows, and was careful to air-kiss her goodbye upon her fluttering eyelids. I crept into the living room to finish dressing. The wilted flowers, empty glasses, and stale party debris made me hurry as best I could to escape the stagnant air conditioning. Before I left, I gobbled a few pears, grapes, and peaches from a couple of gift arrangements. My stomach lurched in the fresh air and on the flight that I boarded home to Los Angeles. Having made it back alive, seeing Maggie and Judy on Norma Place calmed me before I crashed into a ten-hour stretch of oblivion.

On December 4, the night that her beloved Cowardly Lion Bert Lahr died, *Daily Variety* made much of Judy being too grief-stricken to perform. I called to console her and found myself promising to return for her closing night. Chuck and Tucker were game—again— and off we flew on the afternoon of Saturday the 16th. The two who were my support system swore that on this trip they would not leave Las Vegas without me.

There proved no need this time to fret over wearing out my welcome. Tom Greene had suddenly flown back into the picture from New York to play house with Judy. This development fostered my usual nose-out-of-joint jealousy. I could not stay with Judy, but I resented the others who tried. I kept my irrational thoughts to myself because I knew not only that Tom's position was temporary, but that the lady he was with enjoyed keeping the hats of as many people spinning in the air as possible. Besides, it was not my being impersonal that piqued Judy now.

She was desperate to finish the Caesar's Palace engagement. She seemed tired and preoccupied, as was evident in her final, ragged-voiced midnight performance. Danny Thomas, another Vegas headliner who had finished his own show, took the stage to give her a few moments to rest. He extolled Judy Garland's legend, instructed that the house lights be darkened and suggested that each audience member hold aloft a lighted match or cigarette lighter while they sang "Auld Lang Syne" to their cherished trouper. We did. Judy, crumpled low, resting on the edge of the orchestra platform, brushed away tears in laughing spasms of gratitude. In return for our tribute, she sang "Swanee" and "Somewhere Over the Rainbow" with some of her old gusto and artistry. I stood to applaud her as hard as I had at the Palace and many another venue. I had no thought that my tears at seeing Judy Garland in concert would be my last.

Our romping in the star suite afterward was desultory and not prolonged. Judy had it in her mind that Caesar's was neither paying her on time nor enough. She unscrewed every light bulb that surrounded her dressing room mirror. "They docked me for the night my darling Bert died!" She began to smash the bulbs one by one into a shopping bag. The procedure was nerve-racking. Judy was veering away from manic mischief-making toward some sort of verbal explosion or a plunge of escape into sleep. I was familiar with those deadening pupils and that dark expression. I also knew that she did not like the idea of my leaving Tom to deal with whatever would be the result of her edgy mood. But he was a good fellow and I knew that he would—gently. Chuck and Tucker ran interference as I departed for the airport with as much affection as Judy allowed before she clapped the door closed behind us.

We flew in near silence into Los Angeles with the dawn. Our second trip to Las Vegas marked the final time that Chuck and Tucker partook—sparingly—of my amphetamines. We had not quite landed when the plane did, so we headed for the Four Star instead of home. Judy had already punctured our high. A 6 A.M. pick-me-up, one round only, seemed in order—to allay our Sabbath sadness.

Speaking of pick-me-ups, I had a coping strategy for dealing with the holidays in this same era, when I lived alone and thought I liked it. My friend Oren Curtis and I would go to a movie on Christmas Day. Then we enjoyed a long cocktail time before our dinner at the Cock 'n' Bull on Sunset Strip, a hangout Henry Willson had introduced me to. It was around the corner from his office on Carol Drive. The pub-like atmosphere lifted Oren's and my lachrymose spirits in 1967 after the final Hepburn–Tracy turn in *Guess Who's Coming to Dinner*. We jostled for barstools on which to await our table. It had to be in the thick of things in the front room—adjacent to the chock-full bar. That is where the truly hard drinkers of the motion picture business gathered to seriously celebrate Yule or anything else. In our day, good-natured '30s and '40s movie star Sonny Tufts toppled off his perch and Johnny Weissmuller was escorted out to the street while attempting to repeat his ear-splitting Tarzan yell. No doubt they had hoisted too many Moscow Mules, the house specialty drunk from an icy tankard filled with lime, ginger, and, for the regular customer, a hell of a lot of vodka. Errol Flynn was the predecessor of gentlemen like Mr. Tufts and Mr. Weissmuller. Indeed, the entire British character-actor contingent, from C. Aubrey Smith to David Niven, made the Cock 'n' Bull their watering hole during World War II. In the decades to come, many more actors and civilians would follow until family ownership sadly decreed that it close in 1988.

One night in the early '70s when my sister and her husband were visiting, we found our way to the Cock 'n' Bull. After a few, their eyes glazed over, and not just from the Moscow Mules. It was difficult to shut me up about Judy, especially during those turbulent, doomed days. The true English Cock 'n' Bull buffet was as exalted as the toasts—all the courses one could eat at no extra charge. Baked ham, roast beef, and Yorkshire pudding, turkey with chestnut dressing; together with every conceivable accompanying side dish, followed by mince pie, plum pudding, or trifle for dessert. The Welsh rarebit appetizer was so strong that it could keep you awake. The restaurant's hallowed walls were yellowed with smoke, adorned with faded V-for-Victory signs, war flags, Morse code signals, and photographs of gloried squadrons—all amidst most of the formal portraits of Queen Elizabeth that were ever taken. The noisy, jolly setting was one in which to relax and overeat, which Oren and I always did.

My "respectability" in those days came from my role as landlord with my Lloyd Place duplex. The tedious act of managing and maintaining it took some effort, though I preferred leching to being a landlord. I also spent some time scrounging around for abbreviated television roles and doing the fairy story presentations to fend off ennui. *The Picture of Dorian Gray*, with me in the title role, was to be added to our fairy tale repertoire for a more fulsome "Evening with Oscar Wilde"—when Judy telephoned me from Boston in July 1968. She was enjoying the company and quarters of a male musicologist after a stay—which she could not afford—at the Peter Bent Brigham Hospital. For "fatigue and malnutrition," she repeated, in the pauses when I would not comment on her new friend.

Her convoluted existence had become too complex to keep track of, much less question. I tracked her through intermittent press mentions and sightings of her uneasy, high-strung appearances slurring through small talk and songs on the television shows hosted by the likes of Mike Douglas, Merv Griffin, and Johnny Carson. Now dear Judy, adrift, wanted to alight—on my doorstep. Joey and Lorna were in the custody of their father at his apartment in Westwood, and she missed them terribly. Could she come to see me in California? Just for a couple of days? She missed Norma Place too, she said. I said of course. Then, she dropped a bomb: "Darling, will you help me kidnap Joey? I want him back East with me!" I thought of car chases, guns being drawn, and of Sid Luft. I replied that we would have to talk about that when she got here.

She looked wan coming off the plane on July 31. She wore a blue-striped sailor blouse and a white pleated skirt, carried an overnight case and a shopping bag that she said was full of vitamins. She took to rattling this mixture immediately, vowing like a pale and chastened child how good she was going to be to get back her strength. She had to work, after all, to pay the damn taxes, and she had promised the doctors at Peter Bent Brigham to take better care of herself. My heart melted. I held her on the way home in a taxi. Judy could not quite see that there was no ashtray, so she snuffed out her cigarette on the taxi door handle. "You did that because we're passing MGM," our smiling driver deadpanned. He lowered another window and continued down Washington Boulevard toward Robertson. We looked out the window at the crumbling MGM and back at each other and howled, happy to be together again.

Judy began her final, whirligig spin through Los Angeles with an interminable phone call to Sid Luft, pleading and placating. I left her on my living room sofa, to putter about on small pretenses, not wanting to butt in with advice on what seemed to be becoming my business. The upshot when she hung up was dinner plans with Joey that evening. Lorna's whereabouts were vague, but we would pick up her brother at Sid's apartment. I waffled and dared not commit to Judy's serious urgings to make off with him to the airport after dinner. We lay down to nap, were close when we could not sleep, and we drove to Westwood in the late afternoon. Unflappable Sid made us feel at home. Joey, a beach towel around his shoulders, appeared like a handsome sprite fresh from a swim in a schoolmate's pool. He flung himself into Mama's arms, wet bathing suit and all.

"She wants to kidnap him," I told Sid, when Judy went to fix her face and Joey left to dress.

"I figured something like that. I know you'll bring him home safely, John," my host replied.

I was proper in Sid's eyes. Whenever he checked our whereabouts, Judy stressed my Baltimore WASP background, which made me a suitable companion. I rolled my eyes and allowed him to classify me in that prosaic pigeonhole. He thought that no one loved or knew Judy as well as he did, which was his prerogative. At least his run was the longest. Rumor also had it that the charming Mr. Luft could be anything but when he was ticked off, so his son's later homecoming was assured.

We took Joey back into town to Por Favor. The waiter John refrained from doing nip-ups at seeing Judy again. Diahann Carroll, then at the height of her television *Julia* fame, stopped at our table for one of those huggy Hollywood hellos.

"Give me a job," said Judy, in the middle of an air-kiss, "on your show."

"Are you serious?" asked Miss Carroll.

"You're damn right. And no singing!"

Ms. Carroll, delighted, said that she would do everything that she could. Of course, the offer of a straight role never materialized.

The other Por Favor diners enjoyed surreptitiously watching the three of us have a good time. Repeatedly, I pointed out to Judy that it was a Wednesday night and Joey had school the next day. It was her son's apparent contentment that finally satisfied her. Her "oh, all right" attitude toward my status quo position on abduction softened further when we made plans to get together with him again—in Los Angeles. We had him back at Sid's on Manning Avenue in Westwood at a decent hour—as promised.

Then we spent a light-hearted, indecently late night at Chuck and Tucker's house. Judy looked as though she might burst trying to reach her recorded high notes at Carnegie Hall. She told vaudeville stories about the tribulations of the Gumm Sisters in fleabag theatres. She gave hilariously lethal impersonations of Deanna Durbin and Marlene Dietrich. She skewered Joan Fontaine, whom she could not fathom my liking, with an exaggerated debutante slouch, arched eyebrows, a demure one-sided smile, and a plummy Mayfair accent. More than once she admired the snug guest quarters that Chuck and

Tucker had added to Warbler Way. She asked me if she could stay there. I told her to ask our hosts. They agreed that Judy should have a private bath. At the front door, the morning light traced fresh shadows on the depleted faces of my acquiescent friends. Plans were made for their house guest to move in after our foursome reconvened for drinks on Norma Place and dinner at Por Favor. Judy and I drove off down Doheny. Garland hours were upon me. I had finagled the help I knew I would need.

After Por Favor, the night's climax was earlier, but memorable. Chuck sat bright-eyed on my barstool intent on prolonging the evening. Judy, unaccountably waxing lyrical again about my marrying her, gathered up her things. Fatigue and talk of matrimony made my nerves as niggling as they could be. Chuck, covering old ground like a rabid dog, pushed the wrong button. "You both have such a good time together! Why don't you marry her, John?" I wanted to end this discussion. "John! Do it! Why not?"

"Because I'm homosexual! That's why!" I slapped him hard, nearly knocking him off his perch. I rushed for the bathroom but Judy barred my way.

"Stop it! Now just stop it!" she screamed. "I've had enough violence in my life!"

"Well, I am!"

"Well, what difference does it make?" The quintessence of Garland, that remark; she was a Don Quixote for romance. Chuck, already off and running, and Tucker, carrying Judy's things, escorted her down the stairs.

"Nobody's perfect. Good night, darling." She walked out the door, and they were gone.

I never felt an iota of guilt at being gay, but the cataclysmic lady who could modify my bent was the one person I could not allow to. I was afraid that she was no longer a survivor, and I had to be. I finished my drink and, done in, went off to bed.

My friends enjoyed having their hands full with Judy—at least in hindsight. She ran out of Ritalin and puffed up like a red-faced adder in her nerve-end need for more. Tucker was obliged to cajole an admiring pharmacist on Sunset Strip into an illicit refill. The dry cleaners located next to the Shermart agreed, on short notice, to press a white pleated traveling skirt only as a favor to Miss Garland. While Tucker drove up and down Doheny running her errands, Judy attempted to concentrate on soap operas. She imitated the angst-ridden daytime leading ladies for Chuck's amusement. She lulled herself to sleep reading dictionaries, taking special delight in the new Random House because she was an entry in it. Tucker was not able to sleep until her downstairs light went out; he walked on eggshells with Madame Gumm under the same roof. One mid-morning, Judy found her hosts pretending to concentrate on their reading. "My god, this is like the Christian Science Reading Room!" she proclaimed, trying to liven things up.

I wish that I had not taken a night off while my two friends took Judy and Joey to the "in" disco, the Factory. It would be the last night together for mother and son, who, according to Chuck and Tucker, stole the show on the dance floor. Back on Warbler Way, Tucker had a difficult time extricating Joey from his mother to return him to Westwood. Judy held her son close, beseeching him to stay with her, at least until she slept. Joey, the most gentle of souls, piped "Good night, Mama" for the final time, crept quietly out of the house, and walked down the front path to Tucker's car.

The three of us made plans to take Judy to Tony Bennett's opening at Cocoanut Grove. I rang the Warbler Way doorbell on August 6 to keep Judy company while Chuck and Tucker attended a long-accepted dinner party. She greeted me with the news that she had made reservations on the 11:45 TWA flight to Boston! She was dressed for traveling and removing curlers in her hair. She said that Chuck and Tucker were on their way home. Their host's butler had announced a call from Miss Garland and they were as stunned as I was. When they got home, Judy insisted again that she could take a cab to the airport. We repeated that that was out of the question. We would drive her to the airport. She said she was "expected" back in

Boston. She said the children were fine for now with their father. We were sweet to want her to stay, but her plans were final.

Of course we should never have left Judy alone, and we knew it. I had made her feel that she had worn out her welcome on Norma Place. In her diminished professional and financial capacity, she could not cope with the idea of the hoopla of Tony Bennett's opening— much less without a proper dress. Her fears had taken over.

We got into the car. Chuck sat in front with our reluctant driver, Tucker. Judy leaned against me in the back seat. I kept my arm around her all the way to the airport. It was the least I could do.

At the reservations desk, the clerk greeted her rapturously. He told her how well she looked. He supervised her left-handed awkward scrawl on her traveler's checks. He summoned a passenger cart. We rode it in forced merriment to the VIP lounge. Her plane was ready for boarding before we could order a drink. Judy thanked us profusely, held each of us hard, and kissed me goodbye.

"I'll be back, darling. Soon."

I believed it as we waved, watching her walk down the ramp. She placed one pretty ankle directly in front of the other, carefully, like a farsighted showgirl. The three of us rehashed her short-lived trip again and again on the wilted drive home.

I paid more attention to Judy's last marriage than I did to my father's. Dad had married Jean Atkins when his divorce from Mother became final in 1962. He met Jean in his new safe harbor and my anathema, Alcoholics Anonymous. I thought the organization had robbed him of his joie de vivre and sapped his style, but it was more complicated than that. Jean, plainer than his three previous wives and more compliant than Mother, served as his mature companion and nurse through his bout with emphysema. This, with one collapsed lung from tuberculosis, made his last years a physical struggle.

My third stepmother was understandably nervous on the night I went to meet her. I was merely curious and glad that my father had given me permission to bring my own liquor to their apartment. The newest Mrs. Posey seemed a decent but colorless woman. The thought that her affection for my father was slightly overacted crossed my mind more than once. But it was too late in both of our lives to take the trouble to get to know one another.

Judy called me, and we talked about her impending marriage to Mickey Deans. "You never had enough time for me" was her rebuke on the telephone when I asked if she was certain about marrying him. Mickey was a nightclub manager in New York that my piano-playing friend Charlie Cochran should not have introduced to Judy. Well, I barely knew Mickey; let us just say that I was biased. She did not share my superior attitude. When the forlorn ceremony actually did take place amidst a flea-circus atmosphere in London, there was nothing to be done about it.

She came with her groom of six months to New York in June 1969. The bridal pair, in a nebulous quest, at best, to keep the Judy Garland business afloat, aimed to profit from Judy's name on a chain of movie theatres. They stayed at Charlie Cochran's apartment on Lexington Avenue. Prudent Charlie bunked down in a nearby hotel. I called Judy in her fly-by-night quarters on June 10 to wish her a happy birthday. She was forty-seven. She was also in bed and alone.

"I've lost my audience." She sounded almost resigned.

"No, love, you haven't! You never will." I changed the subject to a book that had just been published, *The Films and Career of Judy Garland*. It was comprehensive, and I wanted to cheer her up. She thought it was a lovely compliment. Then she said, "Oh, darling, let me come to California."

"You're a married lady now. I would, you know I would. You must try to get stronger. You've got to take care of yourself." I spoke carefully; I was in no position to lecture. "Judy, your audience is always there for you! So am I, sweetheart. You know that."

"Darling, how's little Judy?"

I told her that my eighteen-year-old cat was very ill. She had enteritis, and she did not have much longer to live.

"Oh, darling, put her by the phone."

I did. Judy sang "Somewhere Over the Rainbow" to her namesake, softly, like a lullaby. It was the last time I heard her sing.

"Get well, Judy, darling," she crooned, "for John and me, please get well."

We spoke a little longer. She seemed so tired.

"Good night, love," she said, and we hung up.

I cradled my cat Judy helplessly. She was weak from shots and throwing up and would survive only months beyond my lady friend.

When the Judy Garland movie theatre project fell through, Charlie's houseguests flew back to London. Retiring Charlie felt that he had been in the wake of a hurricane. He was in sudden limbo. Impulsively, he came to Los Angeles for a change of scene and climate. I met him in the San Fernando Valley and we drank at various jazz joints through the Saturday evening of June 21. Page Cavanaugh and the other performers we watched took a back seat to our—my—compulsive talk of Judy. Charlie was still punch-drunk from the newlyweds, but I missed Judy. I insisted on going back to his motel and calling her at my expense. Charlie was peckish but obliging.

He placed the call from his room. He gave my CRestview 4-6801 number to the overseas operator and handed me the receiver. The time was two A.M. in Los Angeles. Mickey's voice was sleepy when I woke him at ten A.M. London time. He was by himself in bed in the mews house they had rented in Cadogan Street. He said that he did not know where Judy was. He guessed she was in the bathroom.

"Well, go and get her," I commanded. My liquor gave me more than normal assurance.

"Well, all right." Mickey didn't mind—not really. "Hold on," he said. I did, for two or three minutes before he came back on the line. "Look, she can't talk to you right this second. Give me your number and she'll call you back in half an hour."

Charlie and I waited. We nursed nightcaps on lumpy twin beds, paying scant attention to the *Late, Late Show* movie flickering on a snowy motel television set.

The phone rang. I picked it up with "Judy, I miss you!" But it was not Judy. It was Mickey.

"John, Judy's dead."

"You're kidding." What he had said did not register.

"John, she's dead. She's in the bathroom."

"You've got to be kidding." I was paralyzed.

"John, if you say that once more, I'll kill *you*." This to a suddenly-sobered automaton.

"Oh, Jesus, Mickey," I said, finally comprehending. "I'm so sorry. Oh, God, I'm sorry. What can we do? I'm with Charlie." Charlie sat up on his bed, staring. He knew.

"Tell the children. They can't hear it on the news. Go to Westwood. Please." He hung up. To contend with God knows what. Scotland Yard? The press? A grieving world that loved her?

I drove, babbling to Charlie in shock and disbelief all the way to Westwood. I vowed to attend Judy's funeral—wherever it might be. Charlie held fast to my door handle in those days before seat belts. When we got to the apartment building on Manning Avenue, I rang Sid Luft's doorbell repeatedly. He did not answer, so we doubled back to Norma Place. Sid did not answer his phone either, so I called Vern Alves. Vern was incredulous but calm when I told him. He promised to find Sid so that Lorna and Joey could be notified by their father. There was nothing more to be done. I made Charlie and myself whopping drinks and turned on the radio. Some part of me still doubted, and I dreaded official verification. There came the sound of her glorious singing. It trailed off. The announcer said, "That voice was stilled last night."

Enraged and hysterical because she was gone, I kicked out the screen on one of my balcony doors. I hated her desertion, her bringing it about. I sobbed for her absence, cried for her company, and I choked on the knowledge that I would never hear her wondrous laughter again. No loss, before or since, has been as grievous. I remembered: shopping with Judy for Liza's wedding present for her marriage to Peter Allen. We did not have enough money between us for the Irish linen tablecloth Judy chose. We rejoiced when the saleslady at Maison Blanc in Beverly Hills said: "Oh, but Miss Garland, you have an account with us." Judy, caring nothing about space exploration, pointing to the night sky above Malibu, her fist clenched and threatening, just beyond tide's reach, crying, "Don't you dare fool around with our moon! Don't you dare!" Madame Gumm prancing down the middle of Norma Place like Dorothy on the Yellow Brick Road chanting "I'm a star, I'm a star, I'm a star." Munching popcorn and drinking vodka during screenings of *The Clock* and *Meet Me in St. Louis* in the Thalberg Building at MGM. The elderly guard had said: "Welcome home, Miss Garland!" Those grateful brown eyes when I held her in my arms on Norma Place. We moved to Tony Newley's "Look at That Face," the record scratched from my playing it for—to—Judy. Her furies, her machinations, her affection; her touching! Above all, those tremulous, tender fingers touching, always touching—understanding the need.

I had no one left to call upon before the sun rose. In 1969, I did not yet know that that was for the best. Besides, all my life and after I knew her, she was so much more than a playmate. Sometimes I think she plunged a stake in my heart and calcified it by leaving. I have missed her every day, and I believe she was my soulmate.

Judy's funeral was in New York; it should have been in Los Angeles. I decided not to attend. I did not want to be beholden to Charlie, who generously offered to pay for my ticket, nor did I care to approach Sid Luft for preferential treatment among the throngs gathered at Campbell's Funeral Home. The family's chaos was their own; Judy and I were close in ways unknown to young children and former husbands. I sent red roses, which were duly noted by the *New York Post* when they were placed beside her bier. Thoughtful telephone calls ranged from my concerned father in Baltimore to Chuck and Tucker, who were on holiday in Cannes.

The kindest tribute in my sympathetic mail came from John, our waiter at Por Favor: *In this time of deep sorrow,* he wrote, *may I take the opportunity to say that I cannot thank you enough for sharing with me in some small way, your close relationship with the Mightiest Lady of our time. There are no words.*

He was right. The only words more comforting were Judy's excessive own, written to me—thank God—on the flyleaf of a cheap edition of *Dorothy and The Wizard of Oz* on February 15, 1967: "To my beloved John—who makes all dreams and hopes, not only wishes—but true and happy and real—I love you, darling. Judy. 'Dorothy.'"

CHAPTER FOURTEEN

A GENTLEMAN INHERITS HIS WEALTH

NINETEEN SIXTY-NINE and nineteen seventy were not banner years. On August 28, 1969, I accepted the fact that I could not maintain my cat Judy's comfort through shots and pills. She could only sustain her extraordinary devotion, which made more painful my decision to have her put to sleep. I made my resolution known in a strangled whisper, handed her over to Dr. Miller, and fled for my car. I did not pick up my carrier until the following day—which was the start of surviving Maggie's extended, befuddled bliss at becoming the solitary object of my affection.

In November '69, after exhaustive rehearsals, *Another Picture of Dorian Gray* was scheduled to round out our "Evening with Oscar Wilde" at Beckman Auditorium in Pasadena. This *Dorian*, adapted by William Barton, was a memorized reading staged with a series of sketched, representational slides that hung behind the company to illustrate my aging process in the title role. The nuances of Dorian's disintegration and final decayed collapse were up to me. My State Repertory friends in artfully combined character roles bolstered my growth in this egoistic delight.

We broke for dinner following a long day's technical rehearsal in the imposingly expansive Beckman. In the restaurant where we dined, I decided to alleviate my fatigue and terror with an upper. Performers frequently do their very best work when wiped out, but I had to learn the hard way. On that opening night, my overwrought, perspiring energy raced unharnessed toward Dorian's demise. *Playbills* fluttered from restless hands in the sold-out audience. My out-of-sync performance alarmed my supporting cast and infuriated my director, Robert Laning. Molly Dodd sat silent at her makeup table afterward, refusing to glance in my direction. I removed the smudged makeup on my enlarged Dorian Gray mouth and wanted to run for the hills.

The next day when I read my review in *Daily Variety* at the Shermart magazine rack, I did not believe I could bring myself to go back on stage at the Beckman. "John Carlyle," it said, "has a tremendous burden to bear, and it is too heavy for him." I did return, of course, independent of chemicals. I had to in order to redeem myself with fellow cast members, and for the benefit of the *Hollywood Reporter* critic who, praise be, attended the second night. Pills or booze before a performance were a no-no after my Dorian Gray came unhinged.

There is strength in an actor being another kind of blockhead: being tough. My thin skin hardened slowly, but my career languished. I changed agents frequently and frantically. I became demanding in my frustration as even smaller role offers became infrequent. New young people unfamiliar with my work took over the casting and production ranks. Then, as now, their scripts no longer featured aristocratic playboys, consumptive poets, or dissolute WASPs. Good looks were becoming passé, even as mine had begun to fade. My chutzpah came and went. But more looseness and honesty, and less intellectualizing, crept into my work after *Another Dorian Gray*, and I persevered.

In May 1970, Paul Millard and I took an eighteen-day pilgrimage through the illusions of our past. The MGM auction was an escape into fantasy. Its countless assorted treasures ranged from Captain Bligh's tricorner hat and gold-buttoned naval uniforms to the hand-sewn gossamer gowns created for Garbo in *Camille*, from ormolu-laden mantel clocks in *Marie Antoinette* to *Showboat's* phantasmal paddle steamer built on a man-made lake in the middle of Lot Three. The gold catalogue, with its four different colored supplements, cost ten dollars, a picayune amount to pay for the privilege of roaming the grandest studio of them all. Every majestic soundstage, crammed with artifacts from legendary films, resembled the final overhead traveling shot of the interior of "Xanadu" in *Citizen Kane*. The antiques, covering every period and every nook and corner and trestle table, were real.

The costumes in the "Star Wardrobe," listed by each item in the rose supplement, were proudly paraded on Stage 27. Their painstaking workmanship and familiarity caused pandemonium among more ordinary mortals gathered on the old lot than were ever present in the heaven of MGM's heyday. Bedlam mounted as flailing auction cards were held aloft to bid—mind you, sixteen years before Mrs. Onassis and Wallis Windsor inflated things— $450 for Margaret Hamilton's peaked witch's hat, $450 for one of Norma Shearer's silk taffeta *Marie Antoinette* costumes, $500 for a beaded Adrian gown worn by Katharine Hepburn in *The Philadelphia Story*, $250 for Fred Astaire's *Easter Parade* hobo hat, and $175 for a chapeau created by Cecil Beaton for *Gigi*. Debbie Reynolds confronted a flummoxed producer. He denied wanting to wear Tarzan's loincloth and brought his arm and the house down. The hyper Miss Reynolds outbid collectors and millionaires in her spirited effort to amass the most pieces of famous clothing—opulent and otherwise—for a Hollywood museum that never happened. Paul and I gasped, applauded, and gaped, went in and out to relieve ourselves and roam the other lots and soundstages, waiting for the Ruby Slippers.

My emotions ran the highest walking along the pride of Lot Three, the *Meet Me in St. Louis* street. I strolled, disbelieving, in and out the Smith residence front door. I stood on Esther's gingerbread-laden front porch to gaze at 5133 Kensington Avenue next door—and at the seven adjacent houses, wondrous Victorian confections all, still immaculately kept. They appeared lost in another time, like their visitor.

Dorothy's Ruby Slippers were the climax back on Stage 27 on Sunday night, May 17. The mayor of Culver City spoke for them first, on behalf of the local schoolchildren. *The Wizard of Oz* had, after all, been created where he stood. The slippers were then brought forth, tilted toward us on a velvet cushion by a delirious auction attendant. There was a small hush before the mayor's plea was swept away in a frenzy of waving arms, my own included. The furious bidding had escalated to $18,000 before Paul managed to grapple my frozen appendage back into my lap. Clamor and television news crews surrounded the anonymous buyer's representative when the slippers went for $22,000, a fraction of what they would go for today. There were six or eight pairs made for Judy originally. The authenticity of the Ruby Slippers that I saw sold has been bickered about ever since. The auction was controversial too, a desperate, garage-sale end to the bankrupt MGM. The studio no longer exists on the lot we drove sadly off that Sunday night. Condominiums rose in the dust of the *Meet Me in St. Louis* street. There is a Garland–Astaire street intersection in the smoggy, residential area where, on Lot Five, in Metro's very own train station, Garbo jumped onto the tracks in *Anna Karenina*. The locomotive that did her in was another auction item. One item that I could afford, for $125, was a bamboo étagère that I have yet to glimpse in *White Cargo* on television. I pictured Hedy undulating in front of it as Tondelyo. I lined its shelves, which proved to be top-heavy, with fabric, and placed my KLH stereo equipment inside. The sound was not contained, the bamboo legs were not enough to keep the stylus from wobbling, and I soon sold it at a tiny profit in a neighborhood garage sale. Real life prevailed outside MGM.

• • •

I came home very late, thankfully alone, from an after-hours bar on November 1, 1970. A telegram had been pushed through my mail slot at the bottom of the stairs. It was from my brother-in-law Stuart. He informed me that my father had died that morning in Baltimore. He was sixty-two. The racking emphysema had finally devastated a body weakened by tuberculosis and the removal of a lung. Before that, alcohol had diminished his vaunted reputation as a trial lawyer. He had turned to writing plays, which, like his second and third marriages, failed. His seven unproduced plays, surely not totally insignificant, are still, I presume, the property of his last wife Jean. He was resistant to, or incapable of, rewriting one, *The Hair of the Dog*, that the William Morris Agency had optioned. Illness beset him, sapping all but his fine mind and even his interest in the theatre. Even his shriveled handwriting, peculiar at best, told me that his spirit had subsided. It seemed that only sobriety and Jean's companionship had made his long last years meaningful.

I had recently been home for a visit—staying at my sister's—and Dad and I had also talked on the telephone the week before. So the deep sadness in his tired voice was not new. Our last conversations, with Jean in another room, fell into uncomfortable silences that were too late to rectify. His support of my career was still unflagging, but our companionship had lapsed into staleness. I should have pretended to be more interested in Jean and in their AA meetings and sober way of life—to repay my father for the rare understanding that he gave me in the formative years when I needed it. He told me on the phone that he longed to see me again, but he understood that my finances precluded a visit more than once a year.

After I got some sleep, I called Ann to say that she and Jean should proceed with funeral arrangements, and I bought a ticket to fly to Baltimore. Mother telephoned too. She mourned my father more than she admitted. She was torn because of travel plans she and her new husband, James M. Sill, had made to go to Bermuda. I said of course she should go on their trip. I did not burden her with how much I would miss seeing her in Baltimore. Paul Millard said he would take me to the airport. Oren Curtis agreed to Maggie-sit. I pulled myself together to wear the well-mannered mantle of Baltimore bereavement and not fall apart.

The evening funeral service at the Church of St. David's was filled. I thought of Sunday school in the basement, and Mum at worship beside me as a child. I could smell her perfume and recall the feel of her furs. Her elderly maid and final chauffeur, Louise and Bagwell, were at St. David's together. They clucked affectionately over me, as did many old family friends. When they introduced themselves, I only remembered a few of them. I was amazed that the congregation was comprised primarily and overwhelmingly of friends of my father's from Alcoholics Anonymous. They paid little heed to me, and I tried to disregard them. Jean was the teary widow from within their ranks. Mother's trip to Bermuda was fortuitous.

I stared straight ahead while readings from Bill W. were interpolated into the Episcopalian service. So were black gospel singers—to raise the eyebrows of the hidebound WASPs. I imagined toe-tapping in the coffin that was closed in front of me. Ann and Stuart and Jimmy Grieves sat to my right in the front pew. My baleful fourth mother clutched a damp hanky beside me on the aisle. She had followed my father's wishes, I supposed, for the service. He had actually professed belief at the end, and not just in AA. At the conclusion, we stood for the reading of the simple words in John 6:37–40. Suddenly I crumbled, crying loudly like my father sometimes did when he still drank. My sobs were for his raucous horse laughter, the warmth of his arm around me in his den where—both of us wearing plaid bathrobes with piping and fringed sashes—we listened to Fred Allen on the radio. Jimmy Grieves, startled, leaned forward to look at me. I regained my composure.

The next morning, I tried not to be skeptical while Jean verbalized her loss in the cortège from St. David's in Roland Park all the way to Druid Ridge Cemetery. She was the quintessential stepmother, nervous and uncertain riding to a late husband's resting place—with his children from previous marriages. Ann and I, both possessed of a certain arrogance, made the requisite polite remarks that our strained stepmother might have felt were patronizing. They were not meant to be. The two of us were under a strain too and impatient for this funereal gathering of so many non-acquaintances to hurry up and disperse. The tent that protected the drizzly gravesite made them cluster closer. I concentrated on the headstones in front of me. A grief-stricken stab of panic shot through me on seeing my father's casket lowered into the hard winter ground beside my mother Carlyle and my grandmother Mum. This time I clenched my teeth to check my emotions.

"When are we going to see you again on television, Carlyle?" I was asked in my father's apartment at Jean's reception. "My girlfriend went to school with Lee Remick! What's she really like?" "Why did poor Judy Garland turn into a drunk?" The last question strained my forced conviviality, but I remained cordial. Jean presented me with Dad's gold watch. She said she understood my reluctance to snoop through the rest of his belongings. I was glad she promised to have his handsome set of leather-bound Dickens shipped to me, but I had no interest in carrying clothing or other articles back to California. I should have asked for his plays, but my only preoccupation was his will which, Jean informed us sotto voce, would be read to Ann and me in Dad's lawyer's office the following day. Our hostess exhausted her hors d'oeuvres, the gathering remained moribund, and my sister and I, after a look to one another to signal that duty had been done, took our leave.

That evening was cozy at Ann's. Stuart lit a fire. We ate heartily and were glad to be rid of dresses and ties and solicitous people. I drank my amiable brother-in-law's liquor at leisure, and Baby Sister and I escaped into squeals of laughter. Her donkey bray is as ear-piercing as my father's horselaugh.

The scene the next morning in attorney William F. Grimes's office, with its panoramic view of downtown Baltimore, was out of a movie. Jean's, Ann's, and my expressions were as covered as any covey of poker-faced actors. The proceedings were civilized and too polite, except that Ann and I indulged in some discreet eyeball-rolling when we learned that our father had a good deal more loot than he had let on. The Widow Posey, in on the secret, received a sizable marital bequest—as well as one half of the residuary estate. In turn, because there was no stipulation that it revert back to Ann and me, she could leave it to relatives in Wisconsin or anyone else she pleased. I felt intense gratitude that my quarter share was more than I expected. The reality of the inequity of how Jean's bounty had been doled out sank in long after it was too late. Besides, contesting wills and complaining publicly about such matters is anathema to well-bred WASPs. My father felt that Ann had made a prosperous marriage, that both of us already had sufficient benefits from Mum and, in my case, the Boones. His opinion when the will was drawn up in the '60s was understandable, if exaggerated. Ann in fact found a more giving second husband in Dr. Jerrie Cherry twenty-one years later. Instead of genuflecting in Mr. Grimes's office, Ann and I went to lunch with our maverick stepmother.

"Your father wanted both of you to be well provided for," she repeated, picking up the check.

At the top of the stairs on Norma Place, I proclaimed to Oren that I could pay my property taxes. Mr. Grimes had suggested that I retain certain blue-chip securities and convert only a few to cash. I followed his good advice and invested most of the cash that I did receive into a conservative mutual fund. Chuck and Tucker did not have to twist my arm to talk me into going on another trip to Europe with what remained of my filthy lucre.

"A gentleman inherits his wealth," according to the stuffed-shirt observation. The saying is also facetious and lynch-provoking. Too bad; I regret that the wills that I am named in are evaporating—like the inheritances I received in the first place. I dismiss the odious thought that I am becoming too long in the tooth to be a beneficiary and remain grasping. A friend, sounding like an IRS agent, labels inherited income "un-earned excrement." Hats off to whatever one wants to call it.

• • •

I *flew* to Europe the second time. Chuck and Tucker sat in front of me on the plane. They were able to sleep during our fourteen hours of cramped discomfort to London. I reasoned that a sleeping pill would mean missing something, and I did not want to be groggy when we landed. So I popped a Dexamyl mid-flight. The woman on the aisle opposite me glared whenever I lit a cigarette. I smoked more and glared back at her in the dark. We were, after all, in that dinosaur, the smoking section.

A customs official at Heathrow observed my bugged eyes and flushed out my toilet-kit cache of pills. He questioned each and every prescription while Chuck and Tucker looked on in alarm. Twenty minutes later, when I convinced my inquisitor that the labels were bona fide and on doctor's orders, we were free to hail a cab. My nerve-end state intensified when the Europa Hotel desk clerk announced that our rooms would not be ready until late afternoon. At the new Europa, off Grosvenor Square, the service was cursory and the plumbing problematic. My room, when it was finally ready, was like a hutch under a crippling eave. Chuck and Tucker settled into a more accommodating double directly across the hall. I managed a spiraling-down nap before we met to have a delicious dinner that was almost revivifying at the Provence Restaurant in Chelsea. In the early '70s, Chelsea was the in-vogue, eclectic borough for travelers to London.

Overrun Kings Road offered grab-bag shops, the hippie hoi polloi, Mary Quant–clothed young things, and, near the cash register in another small restaurant we frequented, ex-screen siren Veronica Lake's name posted on the bad-check list.

We queued for tickets to the magical London theatre in as many historical box offices as our schedule would allow. Mellifluous Coral Browne arched her eyebrows above disdainful stares through Shaw's *Mrs. Warren's Profession.* Sir Laurence Olivier brought tears and raised our hackles with his final scream as Shylock in *The Merchant of Venice* at the Old Vic. The consummate Gladys Cooper, silvery beautiful, crowned her career as the definitive Mrs. St. Maugham in Enid Bagnold's *Chalk Garden* at the Haymarket.

A new ballet in homage to Sir Noel Coward was world-premiered at the Drury Lane. His music was featured, Princess Margaret attended, and the Master himself sat beside her in the royal box. I was too shy and shaken—because I was sober—by the throng of titled, eminent well-wishers, and by his frailty, to try to approach him afterward. I should have said hello. Instead, riding atop a London bus to Chelsea with Chuck and Tucker for an after-theatre supper, I held back tears over a friendship I had not meant to abandon.

Slag was an embarrassing new play at the venerable Royal Court in Sloane Square. It starred Anna Massey and Lynn Redgrave. At one point during the otherwise forgotten counter-culture proceedings, Miss Massey knelt by the apron to lick the toes of another actress. The clenched expression of Adrienne Ames, Miss Massey's mother, sitting further along in our row, sticks in my mind in place of the text.

I was given a freebie to the endlessly running *Canterbury Tales*. I had come upon the juvenile lead in a London bathhouse—along with Rudolph Nureyev, who was *not dancing*—and the English actor arranged for me to have a choice stall seat. There, fellow cast members could check out through their peephole his American conquest. I sat up straight, smiled a lot, and applauded wildly.

On my last morning at the Europa, my toilet overflowed. Despite several smoldering calls of complaint to housekeeping, there was still no sign of a plumber, so I packed and was delighted to depart the swampy bathroom. I carried my own luggage downstairs, paid my bill, slammed down my key, and assured the desk clerk that management could count on being certain to receive the form that he gave me, requesting my opinions on the Europa. Chuck and Tucker had just departed for Rome; I would rejoin them in Cannes for our final week in Europe.

Peter de Merritt waited for me in the lobby. He was peevish and impatient for us to leave for Paris. From there, we would visit one of his wealthy benefactors in Switzerland, and then fly to Athens to board the Piraeus-berthed boat of yet another of his admirers, Harry Blackmer, to begin a four-week cruise among the Greek islands. Harry was a bald, soft-spoken billionaire-expatriate who was besotted with Peter. He worked every *New York Times* crossword puzzle and voraciously read all imported biographies—to avoid learning Greek to better communicate with the tight-lipped servants who padded about to dust around his notable collection of bibelots and treasured antiquities. Polyglot Peter, who visited often, was the surrogate scourge of the staff, correcting their mistakes and putting them through diffident Harry's paces. The princely Peter, sartorial in personally-tailored Savile Row attire, looked casual and handsome in a custom snakeskin jacket. It was form-fitting and Tennessee Williams–sexy, with the same sheen as Peter's sandy colored hair.

Peter was my friend from furniture-refinishing days with the other Peter, Hartshorne. My fellow apprentice was lackadaisical gold-leafing or staining, and we never wanted to sleep with the same man, which was a good thing because Peter would have won out, hands down. He was engrossed by the possibility of either a motion picture studio contract, or, preferably, the patronage of an older rich gentleman, and, unaccountably, the fatter the better. Lines formed to fill the position.

My peripatetic friend now maintained a small flat in Paris. He was bored with being well kept, so he had taken up sports-car racing. He assured me on the ferryboat from London that this hobby was on hold. That was not apparent on our hell-bent drive from Paris to Milan. Peter's breakneck speed reduced me to jelly and left Frenchmen cursing as we sped through their villages. We tore across the Alps through the world's longest tunnel under Mont Blanc. We swung around breathless caracole turns with Peter driving the way he lived: with impetuous impatience on some fractious spree, with stops to dispense magnetism along the way.

His fluent French intimidated me when he ordered entrées for the two of us at La Galiote in Paris or pills in Pharmacie Principale in Geneva. But I was experimenting on my own by the time I was in the vaulted glass structure of the Galleria of Milan. Peter was delighted when he strolled by the elegant restaurant Savini in the Galleria with a Milanese politician. He found me with the proper food on my plate, and attempting to converse—flirt?—with my Italian waiter.

The American traveler who makes an effort to communicate with charm rather than demands is the one who is respected. Peter's sporadic bulldozer tactics brought this home more clearly. But he was my guide, better company being my teacher, and it was advantageous to please him. I become discombobulated when rushed. In our frenzied early mornings, I recall Peter's crabby haste to move on. For instance, he had me out of the Hotel alla Scalla like a churlish shot, too foggy and furious to note for the last time La Scala across the street, and left to vigilant, mouth-shut wakefulness during our March-hare drive to the Milano airport.

Peter beamed at successfully transporting suppositories filled with marijuana into Athens—where the animated, free and easy customs officials paid no attention to my prescription drugs. A rotund official who was a de Merritt enthusiast actually waved us with gold-toothed delight and effusive fanny-patting through the airport. Touching of some kind, especially among the men, seemed to be everywhere—when they were not busy gesticulating expansively, re-adjusting their private parts, or merely chattering loudly in the white Greek sunlight in a language that sounded to me like boisterous animals chattering. The consuming summer heat was made worse by breathing the red dust through the open windows of our taxi. It was a cool relief to go inside the thick walls of Harry Blackmer's four-story villa on a secluded Domboli Street hillside overlooking an Athens cemetery.

I was grateful to the ample woman who, aproned and expressionless, clattered her sandaled way down the stone stairs to show me to my guest room on the ground floor. The double bed in whitewashed sparse quarters looked welcoming. I most appreciated my own adjoining bathroom. That was tiled in Greek fashion throughout, with a central drain in the middle of the floor; all well and good until one showered with no curtains, soaked the fresh towels, threatened to flood the entire chamber, and stepped out upon sopping bath mats. But it was nice to be able to stand up in the shower. Squatting with the hand-held variety installed in most European tubs turns this tourist into an improperly rinsed contortionist.

The hot-blooded days of my travels were the ones relaxing in Athens before boarding Harry's boat. The city was easy to get around in and seemed like a small town. I took to the cheap tavernas and the friendly, craving Greeks. Comely soldiers short on drachmas were everywhere, looking for a good time. They wolfed down the room-temperature food and threw back their ouzo in a toast to any traveler delighted—like myself—to be a sucker. I was shown through the Athens Museum, the shops and bars of the Plaka, and to the top of the Acropolis. My first sight of the Parthenon, in the moonlight, made me weep—to the perplexity of the uniformed stranger with me. My downstairs traffic in Harry's villa was a too-brief repeat of the Hotel Wilcox in Hollywood. I departed for Piraeus before my host's canny servants fathomed the reasons for my accelerating phone calls from the natives.

The *Meroë* was a graceful black-hulled schooner with red sails. She slept six, in addition to our Greek crew of five that included our chef. They carried out all preparations and cast us off while Harry sat below playing solitaire in the main salon. He came aloft to arrange himself on deck only when he became aware of our movement out to sea, a new book, sunscreen, and a gourmet luncheon close at hand. My own mind as I gazed at the Aegean Sea emptied into the bluest water I have ever seen. Peter, like some lithe, spread-eagled figurehead, stood poised in the prow lines to scan for approaching shorelines. The three of us swam off the *Meroë* when it was feasible, and Peter liked to maneuver its small speedboat like an attack vehicle toward the curves of deserted coves.

Harry descended again to his solitaire whenever we went through the process of docking to visit Syros, Poros, Hydra, Patmos, or Mykonos. From the *Meroë*, each island appeared dotted with sun-baked white houses and innumerable tiny churches built of stone. The buildings sprang out of inaccessible, sprawling hills splotched with bleached rocks and olive trees. The eerie terrain that had looked sparse and monotonous turned into barbarous beauty when we landed. We were berthed in lolling comfort, and, on shore, the attendant Greeks peddled gifts: jellabas, baskets, trinkets, and the offerings in more tavernas. In those, they joined muscular arms and endeavored to lead us in their dances, before we slammed and smashed our dishes, emptied of moussaka, upon the reverberating floor.

Well-known Mykonos was aswarm with bars and tourists. One excessively festive, medicated night, tanned and colorful in a newly acquired jellaba, I escaped with two Germans to a less-populated opposite shore. When I got there in their car, the idea of isolated fun and games and a threesome made me more paranoid. The two turned as harsh as their language when I said an abrupt good night. I was obliged to wait in the lobby of their outlying hotel for the only late working taxi on the island to pick me up.

When I was finally delivered back to the principal harbor, I discovered something else the region was famous for. The Greek "malteme," or bad wind, roared from the sea. It blasted me across the deserted town square and into the arch of a storefront doorway. The swirling Mykonos sand blinded my eyes and added to my panic. The sun was rising as my vision cleared. I could make out the fishermen below the seawall slithering about like eels trying to secure their boats. Panic turned to fear when I saw that the *Meroë* was no longer docked where I had left her the night before. I stepped forward, tilted my body into the Herculean air currents, and plunged toward the quay, where the knowledgeable harbor folk pointed out the *Meroë*. She lay in the distance, her anchor dropped farther out to sea, secure from being buffeted by the smaller boats tethered closer in near the rocks of the jetty. I knew Harry could not have the speedboat cast off for me on such choppy waters. I had to get to the *Meroë* on my own. I had no desire to reel about Mykonos, hung over and unkempt, for the threatening hours that it might take for the wind to subside. I began to dart from boat to boat using supplicating sign language, offering drachmas to better my chances, to negotiate a lift from one of the puzzled fishermen. My ankle-length attire prohibited fluid movement almost as much as the wind—but the long orange and white stripes of my jellaba did command attention. God knows what amount I offered an eventual benefactor; I sank like a crumpled signal flag to the bottom of his boat as we bounced up and down, crashing our bruising way toward the *Meroë*. When we came alongside, Harry, Peter, and the entire crew were leaning over the hull. Their faces were like seagoing revelers in a silent movie, their laughter lost on the ferocious wind. The ladder was lowered; I was hauled aboard and dropped to the deck in a fiery-colored lump. I tottered below, accepted two aspirins with a slug of Harry's vintage brandy, and collapsed on my bunk for the rest of a very long day.

The *Meroë* returned to Piraeus, and it was hard to leave her. So was saying goodbye to my consummate host Harry and to Peter, who had been responsible for my once-in-a-lifetime cruise. The two restless rakes, bored with the Mediterranean, and perhaps with their guest as well, were off to London. At first I was nervous at being left on my own in Athens. I found a middle-priced, air-conditioned hotel, the Galaxia, on centrally located Adkademias Street, near Constitution Square, the primary gathering place for the Athenian cognoscenti. I had a haircut at the Grand Bretaigne and one meal at the King George. Both esteemed hotels overlooked the outdoor cafés of Constitution Square. In one of these sat Tasos, handsome, black-eyed, and on the lookout. We smiled and nodded at one another. I shook his husky hand, sat down, and he offered to be my guide. I stopped feeling forlorn.

The ebullient, quintessential Greek attractiveness of Tasos was as transfixing as the ambience of Athens. We wandered the city, more crannies of the Plaka, and the time-worn excavations at the base of the Parthenon. He introduced me to native restaurants where I bought our inexpensive meals. I tried to outlast him, at least by being admiring, while he danced with the prettiest girls, showing off, in his

favorite all-night discotheque, the Architectoniki. He put his arm
around me in the Acropolis just like the Greek soldier had, trying not
to laugh at my emotion. I felt as if I was showing the Acropolis to
Tasos. He stood and pranced impatiently upon the stones—while I
froze forever in my head the view that lay below. He explained—like
the jaded New Yorker who never looks up at the Empire State
Building—that the temple was something that he had always known
and never paid attention to. Tasos was already jaded, and crafty, too—
at, what, eighteen? But so what. His charm made up for it in our brief
encounter. I gave him what drachma I could spare to take home to
his family, and I asked no questions. Our communication flourished,
despite ignorance of one another's language. Tasos preened with my
lavish use of "efharisto," meaning thanks, and I thanked him a lot for
his company. I was more grateful for his affection. Like all Greeks, he
did not keep his hands to himself, and I followed suit. We walked like
teenagers, arm over arm or shoulder, even swinging hands. On my
last day in Greece with my companion, I was in the doldrums. My
memory of seeing Tasos through the rear window of my departing
taxi waving goodbye is a melancholy one. His white, dazzling smile
seemed the brightest in all of Athens.

Above all else, Tasos dreamed of coming to the United States.
For a time I thought of sending him a ticket. But I could not afford
it, and eventually reality and the phrase of an acerbic friend sank
in. "The Greeks don't travel well," said he. There was one other
thing. I was afraid that Tasos would not make love, so we never
went to bed together. Not really. We hugged and massaged and
slept; that is all—dammit. I thought, as with Jordan Street so many
years ago at Christchurch, that trying to have sex would spoil
things.

I flew to Nice and was half awake in the taxi to Cannes, barely
glancing at the scenery of the Côte d'Azur along the corniche. Chuck
and Tucker were resuscitating company for twenty-four hours, but I
surprised all of us on our final night in Europe. After dinner, I went
back to the Hôtel Provence, another converted villa, and fell into

bed. Athens had sated me. I wanted to sleep and forget the next day's long jaunt home to America.

Oren was relieved to have me back on Norma Place and determined never again to housesit. Faraway Maggie, approaching feline senility, had not been the problem. Cranky Mr. Curtis had dealt with my downstairs tenant on Lloyd Place, a helpless woman who could not change a light bulb, much less deal with backed-up pipes. She expected Oren to produce a plumber within an hour. Her high-pitched voice to Oren the actor had become as offensive as her shrill demands. He was delighted at our reunion over a homecoming drink, but he flinched when the telephone rang. The Auto Club was calling me back to verify my address. They had to jump-start the new car in my garage. Yes, it was courtesy of Dad, a four-door Datsun.

After I drove Oren home, I parked it on the street opposite my balcony. My garage was at the bottom of the driveway next to Paul Millard's building—on a piece of property that Christopher Isherwood owned. Christopher, by the way, sometimes appeared in person to collect his garage rent on the exact day it was due—both before and after the Garland–Carlyle nocturnal intrusion. His bushy brows came together, piteously, but during the rainy season, he ignored my complaints of having to wade in to retrieve my car.

I went back inside to Maggie. As always, I first unpacked the contents of my all-important toilet kit. I opened the drawer in the bathroom where I stashed my pills. There, in the bottom of their empty cardboard box, Oren had left a note, printed in his small and careful hand: "O, ye of little faith."

CHAPTER FIFTEEN

IN THE PROGRAM AND IN LOVE

IN THE EARLY '70s, I was in a final glide path in thrall to my medication. Even Oren shared my nostrums when I insisted, so that he could sustain our—my—all-night forays into excessive behavior. It was I who drove us home from the bathhouse. At the same time, he was the bulwark that prevented me from sailing off into oblivion. He was realistic in his judgments, but unstinting in his friendship. One night, draining my sixth bullshot, I removed my dinner from the oven and fell backward to the floor. My dinner and I were both okay, but after I had eaten, I called Oren to ask if he thought I was an alcoholic. "That's a very good possibility," he replied. I resolved to eat earlier.

During this holding pattern, the closest I came to acting was doing recordings for the blind. I drove to a tiny studio in Hollywood to volunteer my talents twice a week. The urbane character actor John Hoyt was often scheduled to read in another booth at the same time. His career had also hit a snag, because of a publicized morals charge, not addiction. Behind his glass partition, his thin smile was sadly

guarded. Instead of du Maurier or Dickens, I was generally assigned
Ayn Rand, Saul Bellow, or a high school geography textbook. But I
adjusted my earphones and microphone to ham it up anyway. I
enjoyed the sessions until the scholastic material and the scheduled
trek into the run-down section of East Tinseltown along Santa
Monica Boulevard bored me — like such tasks often did, too easily.

Norma Triangle had already gone downhill. Not from decay, but from
the loss of its leading lights. Dorothy Parker was long gone; in 1967,
she was interred in Ferncliff Cemetery in Hartsdale, New York, which
I became familiar with through two aching visits to Judy's grave. Nina
Foch moved, first into a house in the hills off Doheny Drive and then
to the flats of Beverly Hills. Screenwriter Hagar Wilde died of alcoholism. Carleton Carpenter lived in Warwick, New York. The dear,
depressed John Dall was a suicide in 1971 over the loss of his career.
Now and then Estelle Winwood's maid Obelia served me tea in the
pristine little white house that Estelle had moved to in the San Fernando Valley. Paul Millard relocated to another piece of property that
he owned one block away on Keith Avenue. Costume designer Noel
Taylor took his downstairs apartment in the lovely building where I
lived. Goateed, whispery Noel, with a voice that only dogs could hear,
promptly installed swank marble floors that were formidable in a
rental unit. Other properties changed hands and were, thankfully,
maintained, as they escalated outrageously in real estate value. It has
seemed through the years that ball-breaking lady agents, tough
lawyers, personal managers of both sexes, and neighbors who never
nod hello make up the majority of what I consider newcomers to
Norma Triangle.

Stephen Bellon was an exception. He lived beneath me for a time
in Estelle's former apartment. With his Vandyke beard and Prince
Valiant hair, Stephen resembled a stringbean hippie. He was in fact
a whimsical, erudite teacher of English and history at the respected
Oakwood School in Los Angeles. His good conversation was non-
stop, he was a wizard in his kitchen, and his cackling laughter was

persistent. He also directed productions at the Company Theatre when on hiatus from Oakwood—when a project moved him. One play did, for some reason. *Mary Stuart*, by Wolfgang Hildesheimer, was a ninety-minute one-act of gothic pretentiousness that read like Greek to me. The Company was avant-garde, popular for staging street theatre and having its members fondle a blindfolded audience. None of this appealed to me either. But I chalked up my intolerant attitude to my increased bewilderment in the taste of the young. And, being like the average actor who cannot see the forest for the trees, I agreed to appear in *Mary Stuart* because generous Stephen offered me a part in it.

Gervais, unctuous servant to the queen, was my first characterization of a flat-out homosexual. Barriers, after all, were falling. Our audience, which would not be blindfolded, might possibly be filled with au courant casting directors, or so I hoped. Oren, in a more androgynous turn as another court dignitary, was an added incentive to join the cast, marking our first theatrical reunion since we had become acquainted sixteen years earlier doing *Twelfth Night*.

We were strangers to the assemblage. From day one of rehearsals, we were regarded as outsiders by the tight-knit, original initiates of the cat's-meow Company. They were churlish, undisciplined, and overrated. Stephen's friendship, more ameliorating than his direction, and one or two other recruits who came on the scene, were all that kept us plodding away in a piece better written by Schiller than by Hildesheimer. Wolfgang remained a mystery, as did his play to our audiences. The leading lady with her Tudor features had her moments preparing for her execution, but the supremacy of Nina Foch could not have mesmerized with the White Queen's convoluted monologues. The ensemble, despite its disparate styles, was lauded for its efforts. My own were included, in that fell-swoop listing of the cast that does not fortify an actor's ego.

The obsolete *Mary Stuart* remained so. After its production, so did the Company Theatre. The style of the tyro troupe fell from vogue like the disappearing flower children who had cluttered Sunset

Strip. Robert Redding, formerly one of the latter and a robust member of our cast, had cheered us by singing in our smelly and rickety co-ed dressing room a camp version of "Tangerine" at the top of his lungs. I missed the irrepressible six-footer all over again when I read his obituary in *Daily Variety*. He was a victim of AIDS. Reading about his death, I recalled a moment at the start of my doing time at the Company Theatre. I was bending over my kitchen sink on Norma Place. I straightened up, astonished to be wet-eyed with gratitude toward my neighbor downstairs for giving me the opportunity to act again, even if it was in such a forgettable play.

Morris Evans was one of the guests at a cocktail party a friend gave. The party was in the old Hollywood splendor of Sunset Towers, the only apotheosis to art deco that survives, with another name, on the Strip. It makes me shy to stand alone at a cocktail party, so I was well fortified when I got there. I was dressed in a size-too-large pale yellow cashmere sweater, and I grew clammy from more nervous imbibing. My Dexamyl seemed to be backfiring, my mouth was dry despite the sipping, and I hoped my blue-streak chatter was brilliant. It was in this perturbable state that Mr. Evans sought me out.

He was fire-hydrant muscular, with thinning blond hair, California-casual in Boy's Department jeans, and the possessor of enough charm to sell snake oil. He suggested that we leave the gay one-upmanship of the party and go on together to dinner. The usual mediocre gay-restaurant fare smothered in exotic sauces did not fuel my sparse appetite. Nor was Mr. Evans able to get many words in about being a children's television show producer while I talked about myself. We left the restaurant on La Cienega and returned to Norma Place anyway. After we went to bed, I continued in my wound-up mode by playing Judy Garland records. My guest's blue eyes grew wary. He announced that the hour was very late—for him. We exchanged telephone numbers, said good night, and I locked the front door after he left. I went back upstairs to pour a final nightcap—to toast another one-night stand.

But it was not to be a single dalliance. The assertive Mr. Evans did telephone, and a relationship ensued that continued throughout 1973 and beyond. My deep need for such a partnership surprised me. I accepted the commitment and hung on, too tightly, to a lifeline.

Morris was a disciplined, self-made man whose parents had been alcoholics in Ohio. His concern for my drinking curbed it in the beginning. I took fewer uppers. To be helpful through a long per-spiring day, I did pop a Dexamyl to help him move from a Lake Hol-lywood house to his new one on Outpost Drive. It was hard to shut up, transporting his library of children's books and all his Early American furniture. He was too naïve to suspect that I sustained my energy artificially. When he taught me to take naps, I put my pills away. Then the daily drift-off became a necessity.

His tactile affection, love of laughter, and vast curiosity were a boon. His companionship calmed me as his energy wore me out. No day was fuller than one with Morris. A sleeping pill would have been superfluous on our trip to San Francisco. We stayed at the Hunt-ington Hotel on Nob Hill. We trudged and explored, up and down every hill. I huffed and puffed beside my non-smoking friend. I was thankful for every respite to sit down in the restaurants or on the cable cars, at the Top of the Mark, or on the ferry to look at Alcatraz. I was a wiped-out lover at the end of each day at the Huntington.

Back in Los Angeles, I grappled with a bicycle while Morris rode one. He reminded me of Jimmy Grieves speeding along in front of me in my childhood. Morris was competitive and ferocious in his zest for life and fierce and unyielding in his maintenance of a healthy one.

For months I adhered to his standards and tuned in to his domes-ticity. He taught me how to sear pork chops in a ribbed, salted iron skillet and sauté perfect calf's liver in his gourmet kitchen. He made me appreciate the clay pots laden with seashells sold at half price in godforsaken Rosarita Beach. Morris salivated for a bargain. So with barely room for me to put my head in his lap while he drove, we lugged the striking containers back across the Mexican border to Out-post Drive. I helped fill them with impatiens and azaleas. I volunteered to strip and refinish his mantelpiece, and, pooped, wished I hadn't when I finished.

Morris and his art director took me on trips to San Diego and San Bernardino to scout locations for his television shows. We covered miles on such forays to find the proper storefront or vintage house. Sometimes I was perverse enough to order a martini when we stopped for lunch. More often than not, I returned to sleep for the night on Norma Place. Maggie was not the only reason. Morris, who could be awakened at the sound of a moth, complained that I snored. He owned a Scottie, Shasta, who did not induce tranquility when I did stay over. Shasta barked in my face in the morning. He tore at my socks and sneaker laces when I went to sneak a nightcap. Nonetheless I continued to hold both dog and master in high esteem.

There was a red-letter outing with Morris to the Alouette on Santa Monica Boulevard. The restaurant was small and moderate, family-run, and served authentic French food. Morris took note of the occupants of a table below ours and across the aisle. He cautioned me not to stare, but who could help it? There sat the actor Ralph Bellamy and his wife with their friends Mr. and Mrs. James Cagney. Yankee Doodle Dandy's red hair was now white, he cupped one hand to his ear to follow the happy conversation, and the sound of his voice made me remember sneaking off to the movies as a teenager in Baltimore. I thought I had gotten over being star-struck, but my feet tingled. Whether Morris liked it or not, I clicked my wine glass against his to toast the jackpot of seeing Mr. Cagney.

Then, not so suddenly, a large fly loomed in the ointment. An actor is quick to recognize faint praise for his profession. I began to realize from his negating so many plays, movies, and the people in them that Morris held actors in contempt. His short stature, small talent, and having to kowtow to superiors had curtailed his own early yen to perform. It was top-dog position and his-way-or-the-highway with Morris. So he rose through the ranks of the theatre as a stage manager. That led to his producing national touring companies assembled and mounted out of New York. He masked his intolerance of the insecurities of performers as he became a Napoleonic hands-on producer. No production's detail escaped him. But he grew more disdainful of the childish ego clashes and displays of one-upmanship and infighting that were de rigueur and then forgotten by his cast members. His caustic comments about my peers, in television now, produced a curled lip and a change of subject when I called him on an attitude that I did not want to accept.

I saw that Morris's obsession was making a profit. Few perks, a non-union crew, and the lowest possible actor's salary were the rule on his sets. I was a reluctant visitor to these low-budget affairs, and phony-ebullient to the actor playing the part that I should have had. Finally, after some not-so-judicious nudging, a couple of bones were tossed my way. The first was galling, but I was still enamored. Morris declared the small voice-over role important, praised my reading of it, and did not pay me. For the second, I officiated, in front of the camera at least, as a cleric at a funeral. I did play one lead for Morris—later on, when we were trying for a friendship. That ballet-instructor role was a stretch to say the least; off-screen I dance like St. Vitus. My instructions, à la Balanchine, were shot in flaring nostril close-ups at the Wilshire Ebell Theatre. The amused corps of the real Los Angeles Ballet looked on. They concentrated on my acting.

But in 1974, on the downside of being smitten, Morris was merely intrigued by my background, polite about my acting aspirations, and relieved that I owned a building. His sweeping dismissal of other people's work became infuriating and intimidating. It was he who swam in the mainstream, not I. When I found the performances by Bernadette Peters and Robert Preston moving in the world premiere of *Mack and Mabel*, Morris denigrated the entire production. Angela Lansbury was more honest and realistic than the theatrical Ethel Merman in the revival of *Gypsy* at the Shubert, but Morris pronounced her Mama Rose "forced." I found much to admire in the film of *The Great Gatsby* with Robert Redford; Morris muttered about walking out before it was over. We went to a revival of

Casablanca at the Los Angeles County Museum. Morris had never seen it. He scoffed at the miniature sets in the film and was disappointed. I found my voice but did not yet use it.

I reverted to old ways when Morris's attentions wavered. His heightened focus on his work and, I believed, whatever pretty actor was involved, were tolerable until he became a shit. One day he was overseeing the editing on one of his productions. The fury that is often in me had been held back. It was triggered by his sneering orders at his technicians as though they were slow-witted. I sprang from my guest's chair, told him that he was acting like an ugly prick, slammed the door of the control booth, and drove home. Shortly after that episode, he went on location for his next show with a most attractive cast that I was not a part of. While he was away, I drank heavily and ignored the telephone.

One regrettable midnight on my way to bed, I stumbled headlong into a ceramic cachepot that sat upon my bedroom bureau. I crashed to the floor with both plant and container. I finally awoke after having passed out for hours in the debris. My first concern was for my bureau. It was my best antique, sold to me for a song by Fred Astaire's daughter, Ava. I saw that the bureau was unscathed, but I was not. My face was covered in dirt and blood. Blood was still flowing from a gash above my right eye. I bathed the cuts and open gash with hot washcloths, then peroxide. I was afraid I had damaged my eyeball, of going to a doctor, and of how to explain my appearance. I took half a Seconal to sleep off my terror. When I awoke, my bloodstains had soaked through a towel onto my pillow. But I thanked God that my vision was intact. I was too ashamed to go for sutures above my eyelid. During the next rocky days, I announced to one and all that I had been mugged while I walked out of my garage. My story, in a time when such casualties were becoming disquieting, became firmer with each telling.

"Oh, my god, John!" Morris cried when he saw me after he returned from location. His shocked concern was what I was looking for. Yet in the end, it did no good that I had gone to his house for dinner looking and acting the battered victim.

A few days later, he asked me to return his house key. He wanted to put "some distance between us for the time being." He told me again about his alcoholic parents. They were not, he said, "a pretty sight." Quite frankly, he thought I drank too much.

I was filled with mixed emotions. One moment, I deified the severed relationship. The next I thought: "So what?" The comfort of booze brings conflicting attitudes. I had tried to stop smoking, to drink less, and to be monogamous for Morris, for Christ's sake. But I missed his companionship and good cooking. And the early laughter. I wondered, bleary-eyed from a number of things, including tears, how to redeem myself to regain our fellowship—Shasta's, too. I missed Shasta more than Morris. I could not confront being alone again.

The flesh above my right eyelid drooped for too long, but my scars healed quickly. Facial wounds always do. But inwardly, as the Good Witch would make clear, I had reached my bottom.

John—If you keep drinking and using the way you are, you will die like Judy did.

The note shoved through my mail slot in the front door was anonymous. I sat on my stairs and re-read it. At first I was angry, and then enraged. I was tired of telling people that I only drank after six o'clock, which was true, after all. I had not been using much. I cursed the gutless bastard who had not had the decency to sign the note. The words made me sweat—from fear of having been watched. They also planted the seed.

Very soon afterward, I was sitting stone sober at my desk to pay my bills. Pride in my handwriting was about all I had left. Now, for the first time, my checks were difficult to write. Normal coordination in my hands seemed to be beyond my control. I remembered my Christmas shopping discomfort. I had steadied my checkbook and imagined that the saleslady was smirking. My signature was that of a trembling old man. My tendency toward the shakes, which now seemed to be becoming permanent, alarmed me enough to compel me to pick up the telephone. That is what did it; not passing out, indiscriminate sex, or falling down, mind you; merely my clumsy handwriting. I asked a friend—who spoke of little else—to take me to one of his AA meetings. He was delighted to oblige. I stressed that I was just curious. I mentioned that my father had belonged. I only wanted to see what it was like.

It was awful. The gloomy church assembly room in Hollywood was filled with what appeared to be vagrants. They were gulping cup after cup of hot coffee, mingling merrily, and chain-smoking. The atmosphere was thick with haze. The walls were peppered with placards, lettered large. SURRENDER, they read, LET GO—LET GOD, TURN IT OVER, POWERLESS, and EASY DOES IT. I was urged to hold hands with the stranger next to me as we stood for the Serenity Prayer: "God grant me the serenity to accept the things I cannot change, the courage to change the things that I can, and the wisdom to know the difference." We sat back down on wooden chairs for a reading from Chapter Five from the Alcoholics Anonymous Big Book, the chapter about the Twelve Steps. All of them sailed over my head into the umber region above the ceiling's rafters.

My friend, stabbing away at a piece of macramé, appeared permanently settled. He listened and knitted while two speakers shared their separate descents into hell and alcoholic degradation. Between their two horror stories, there was a stampede to get in line for still more coffee. Familiarity bred more skittishness at the close of the meeting. Again I clutched hands and stood to murmur the Lord's Prayer that I barely remembered. One or two people welcomed me into their ranks while we were leaving. I thought of my father and tried to be gracious.

I was never a joiner. God was by no means paramount in my thoughts. Susan Hayward was. As the reformed Lillian Roth in *I'll Cry Tomorrow*, Susan soaked up AA plain speaking. I felt more patronizing than Lillian toward the seemingly humble crowd. Only the simplicity of the Serenity Prayer struck home. But I did stop drinking. That night. Cold turkey. Because I was frightened.

Abstinence was more boring than difficult, although my accelerated intake of caffeine made me almost as wired as Dexamyls—which I never took again. They were ten times harder to give up than liquor, but to make my instant sobriety easier, I decided to further explore the support system of Alcoholics Anonymous. My macramé-fashioning friend had given me a booklet of scheduled meetings and their locations. I thought it best to seek out the bluebloods, and hopefully some casting people, by going to a gathering in Beverly Hills. I went alone so I could scram in case of second thoughts.

Another, grander, church community hall, complete with a velvet-curtained proscenium stage and more SURRENDER signs, was SRO. This one on Rodeo Drive had its share of people in my profession, if not in casting. Two or three well-known actors and actresses looked purposeful and peaceful pretending not to be seen. Knitting needles in the manicured hands of a preponderance of Beverly Hills matrons clattered at a furious rate. Some were pale and lonely widows who had turned into souses in their baronial, barren homes. Many of them, courtesy of their plastic surgeons, had the same face.

The formula of the meeting was the same—always. At this one's coffee break, a tall, very thin man with a short beard approached me. His long, aristocratic neck was like one glorified in a Modigliani painting. His hands shook slightly as he refilled his coffee. His outstanding features were his straight back and nose and, most of all, his kind brown eyes. In greeting me as a newcomer, he was ill at ease. He introduced himself as John Paul Davis. He asked me to go with him to a nearby AA birthday party after the second speaker and the Lord's Prayer. John Paul's reserved artlessness compelled me to accept his invitation.

Our hostess's Beverly Hills home burst with hospitable people busy helping themselves to an impressive display of food. The party was jollier than my companion. His social diffidence was tough going—in the face of the manic nature that in my new surroundings

I was attempting to suppress. Drawing out Mr. Davis was like gently prying open a clamshell. It took time to discover that he was the son of undemonstrative alcoholic parents. He had come to Hollywood from Fort Walton Beach, Florida to become an actor. He had done office work for years at Paramount Studios to support his acting efforts in workshops and little theatres. Oh, woe, I groaned, tempted to try to go and work the party—another actor. But he told me—warily and with regret—that he was about to embark upon a career in real estate. Good thinking, I thought, relieved. On the night of the party, he was happier to celebrate completing nearly three AA years than being two weeks shy of his fortieth birthday.

My significant other, the surrogate that the Good Witch sent, would have been slighted if I had not asked him back to Norma Place. It was Maggie who cottoned immediately to his trembling attentions. She maneuvered her way into place upon his lap while he hesitantly muttered more about himself. After leaving Paramount, he had lived in Europe in 1969. He tended bar in a London pub before going to his beloved Rome—where Franco Zeffirelli, teasing and screen-testing, finally decided not to cast him in *Brother Sun, Sister Moon*. He stayed on in the Eternal City, studying acting and living like an Italian hippie in a communal nest of friends. But the expatriate without a trust fund had to come home, whereupon he broke his leg skiing in Mammoth, California. Associates, culled from AA by then, rallied around to help him through his year-long itching recuperation in a thigh-to-ankle cast.

His accessibility guaranteed John Paul companionship. His nature is supportive. I had the impression that he was drawn to AA because of an inner isolation, not the damage done by drinking. There did not seem to be any. He told me that he drank heavily to break through, to communicate more easily, and, often, to be the diplomatic mediator in a gathering threatened with mayhem. Now he was becoming freer through natural means in abstemious company. He began to try, in the most lenient and thoughtful manner, to clarify their way to me.

The Saturday night after we met, he drove me to an Alcoholics Anonymous meeting in Malibu. Like my father, I pretended to remain blasé at the sight of more movie stars. Some were garden-fresh and others nearly forgotten. Dad had divulged seeing a royal couple from the silents, Vilma Banky and Rod La Roque, at a meeting chaired by Robert Young. My current companion and the presence of creative people in all walks of life shored up my uncertainties. After Malibu, John Paul continued to point out celebrities at other meetings nearly every night—to re-ignite my interest.

At more than one meeting, I was welcomed by acquaintances. I thought they had left Los Angeles. One friend announced, at the top of his lungs, "John! We've been saving a seat here for you for years!"

John Paul presented me with the Big Book with its Twelve Steps and, in a tiny volume, the "Good Thoughts for Twenty-Four Hours a Day." I didn't pay as much attention to either as he would have liked. He looked dour when I told him that he was my sponsor. I was not prepared to dump on someone else. A new member was expected to tell all to a patron in a written inventory. I never did. I told John Paul everything. This tardy testament must stand as my written inventory.

The Twelve Steps put me off. I did not trust God or understand Him well enough to turn over my life or will to Him. Forgive me, dear Mum; since childhood, He had not provided the need. This lapsed soul would more likely surrender to Him in the Episcopalian or even Catholic Church instead of to a "higher power" in AA. Or if I'm lucky enough to be in one, on my deathbed. I do still use the Serenity Prayer. I respected one other AA tenet, the most difficult for me to follow: One Day At A Time. Still I wake in the night to fret—about next week's groceries, what will or will not come in the mail, living long enough to get a book published, and being too judgmental or abrupt.

There continued to be no drinking; just cigarettes and coffee at regular meetings, and birthday cakes with more coffee at parties. With John Paul's help, and despite my hidebound disbelief, the dogma of Alcoholics Anonymous became my way of life.

When I had been sober for six months, the secretary of the Beverly Hills meeting asked me to be a first speaker the following Friday night. I would have sooner played Hamlet in the nude in the middle of Rodeo Drive, but one was instructed not to refuse. My screenwriter friend Stewart Stern was the complete observer, gung-ho on self-help groups, and he asked to accompany me so that he could listen. I said yes—Stewart had been putting forth calming vibrations since the days of *Rebel Without a Cause*—because I needed moral support and did not see enough of him. He took me to the Konditori in Beverly Hills for dinner. His bovine brown eyes were reassuring as he watched me pick over my food. He drove me to the meeting after dinner and sat against a side wall on a folding chair while "John C." was introduced. There was no script, and, under the terrifying circumstances, an actor's artifice was out of the question.

I could not admit to being powerless over alcohol, but I did speak of the many wrongs in a life that had grown unmanageable. I did not drop Judy's name or play the total debauché in a narrative that Stewart told me afterward was straightforward and revealing. How revealing, I had no idea. In appeasing the Good Witch, I forgot everything that I had said. She must have been listening because, by the end of my half-hour, there were some laughs that relaxed me. I closed with something soppy about using brighter light bulbs at home and sat down. The applause was gratifying, but from that night on I avoided any further requests to speak. My soul had been glimpsed—not bared—and I wanted to keep it that way.

Stewart drove me home. He refused a nightcap from the stock that I still served drinking friends. Had I been, I asked him, a shallow show-off? Absolutely not, said he. Then he broached the idea of undergoing EST, together with AA. My eyes crossed, and we said good night.

Many of the Hollywood mighty had fallen, Henry Willson among them. He was forgotten, bankrupt, and more paranoid then ever as a resident of the Motion Picture Country Home. Most retirees who were truly eligible to live in the beautiful Woodland Hills facility counted their blessings. Not agent Henry, for whom strings had been pulled and possessions sold. He believed that his phone was being tapped and that one of the Chicano gardeners was trying to kill him. Had Henry made a pass at him? I didn't ask. Mary Astor and Henry were the two unhappiest people there, two mean-spirited charges that the obliging staff found the most difficult to deal with. Henry was not alone in complaining that the reclusive Miss Astor would not speak to him. He hissed that the actress would not even accept calls from her friend Bette Davis. He was venomous too about his ungrateful clients—as he always had been. Now, except that there were none, he had some reason. The faithful Chad Everett, Edd Byrnes, Tom Irish, Troy Donahue, and John Smith visited him anyway. They drove him to futile lawyer meetings, haircut appointments, and paid for his dinner in the city. The others—Tab Hunter, Rory Calhoun, Guy Madison, and Rock Hudson—had long since deserted him. Alas, I never saw Mary Astor, but I took Henry to lunch whenever I was up to braving that most unnerving phenomenon, the California freeway.

Henry was lucky to live in one of the small, attached cottages that afforded residents some privacy. But I usually found him at a side entrance talking on a pay phone, watchful, literally sniffing the air, his hands like pudgy tentacles thrusting in and out of his stained and baggy change pocket. There were no more deals to negotiate, but this outside telephone that no one eavesdropped on was life-giving. He dressed, as he did when he *was* an agent, in suit and tie, which was now a rumpled uniform. He was always glad to see me. The feeling was mutual.

He made me laugh over lunch at the Calabasas Inn when he insisted that I give him my champagne. His small brown eyes grew brighter and his perspiring jowls turned pinker as he enjoyed the complimentary bubbly, a beverage that I didn't care for even when I did drink. His protruding lower lip looked more petulant when he spoke of unpaid commissions, his Bel-Air house on Stone Canyon

Road being sold for a pittance, and of getting back on his feet again just as soon as he could afford to live somewhere else. That was his pipe dream.

I urged him to write a book. He waffled, terrified like always of litigation. Henry's truths were not being told in the '70s. The slime reporting being perpetrated twenty or so years later would have made Henry's tales of homosexual myth-making look tame. Besides, it would have been impossible for Henry to admit his lascivious business dealings, much less write about them. He was actually from an Old Philadelphia family and trained in good manners — until the tarnishing rot of Hollywood advanced his sullied name. Before he entered the Motion Picture Country Home, while Henry held court at Robaire's and not Frascati's, with hustlers instead of hopefuls, Hollywood had already moved on.

While I was off trying to entertain the Mormons — that should get your attention — I sent Henry the dinner theatre program from Salt Lake City. I was touched that he should respond. His letter extolled the excitement of it all, of how certain he was that I would "knock 'em dead," and ended by asking me to be sure to call him as soon as I got home. When I returned to Los Angeles, it was too late. I was told that not long after the time of our lunches, he had begun to give up. When he died, a few manicured paths away from his cottage, he was ill and distended, and dismissed by the outside world. He had been moved to the Motion Picture Country House Hospital, the last stop for all the residents, including Mary Astor.

Since AA precluded my drowning my sorrows over lackadaisical agents and lack of work, I took them to Theatre East, a prestigious actors' workshop. It was located over Joe Kirkwood's Bowling Alleys in the San Fernando Valley. The board of Theatre East accepted me because of my résumé and my letter of intent, which made clear my dedication — easy enough to overstate in writing. I lived up to their expectations spasmodically. My input averaged two scenes a year, I was inhibited as a commentator, and I refused to participate in the politics of Theatre East. Those were myriad and sacrosanct and at the whim of the ruling egos. One learned by doing, and the pursuit of perfection in the eyes of my Theatre East peers was killing. The only reward on Tuesday nights was talk. And more talk, under the guise of discussion and not-so-objective critique after viewing one's work. It was less trying when I received hosannas. My scenes from *The Night of the Iguana* and *The Dresser* were personal triumphs. I drove home in glory, in love with acting again, my ambition renewed by praise. Was that why I did not work? Why I was not a star?

There were kudos, too, for my acerbic playwright in *Deathtrap*, my playing against type with a New York accent in *The Gingerbread Lady*, and for rising above some infrequent new material that would never be produced. Some scattered gurus carped that my nuances had gone haywire when I tore theatrically into chunks of *Winter's Tale* and *Tiny Alice*. One actor raised his hand to wish that I had displayed more of my "natural charm" when I vented my mocking spleen as George in *Who's Afraid of Virginia Woolf?* So it went. At home I made notes of the "objectives" that the actors were expected to state after these exercises. The performer was not allowed to talk back during his critique, which was just as well. To analyze and expound on the struggle to seem real is a bore.

Theatre East gave me the heart to flex my acting muscles again in the real world. Jon Epstein was that rare Hollywood producer who hired his friends. Jon's joyful piano playing and leering, Groucho Marx-like personality had been one of life's pleasures since my work long before on the sets of his *Men of Annapolis* and *King of Diamonds*. The only thing he required before signing me to play a minister on his new miniseries *Rich Man, Poor Man* was that I have a short haircut. I was to marry two of the leads, Susan Blakely and Peter Strauss, in a mock-'40s ceremony.

The location was at a pretty church somewhere in the flats of Burbank. My bit did not merit a limousine ride, in the eyes of Universal Studios. I had to drive to find the site on my own—a common practice to further unhinge actors in the bare-bones motion picture and television economy of today. My lines, when I got to the church on time, were barely the words of a non-denominational wedding service. Suddenly, director David Greene bade me improvise on the joy of joining the families of Miss Blakely and Mr. Strauss—to William Windom, Helen Craig, and Ray Milland gazing at me with beatific faces from the congregation. Somehow I did. I did it again for the celestial Dorothy McGuire. She wept instant tears into a lace hanky throughout her close-up. Peter Strauss's compliments on my ability were more than welcome as I spread blessedness throughout the day as each star's kisser was lovingly photographed. My own face was last. I was pleasantly surprised a few weeks later when I saw on television—briefly—that it had not fallen.

My craving for more acting than I ever got was totally self-centered and brooked no competition in the home. It was enough to contend in the marketplace. One night I made this clear in savage fashion to John Paul. He was struggling at the Castagna Real Estate office, working part-time at night and on weekends at Brentano's Books in the Beverly Wilshire Hotel, and living with me on Norma Place. We were having a conversation about agents. He murmured something about my helping him find one. His tack was incendiary, and I was instantly enraged. There could be no rehash of anyone's old ambition except my own.

"You worry about your own goddamned career!" I growled. To make my point, I hurled a heavy glass ashtray against the marble-topped coffee table. The table cracked down its center with the impact. Shards of rose-hued glass splintered in every direction, luckily missing John Paul's hurt, incredulous eyes. His hands, with the tremor that he'd had since childhood, were his shields, shocked into stillness in front of his face. Numbing guilt came over me. My wails of apology flew as fast as the glass had. I made certain that Maggie was safe under the king-sized bed, hugged my forgiving friend incessantly, and did penance crawling on my hands and knees to pick up the splinters. John Paul stuck to real estate. Yes, I was relieved.

CHAPTER SIXTEEN

HE'S A LOT BETTER
THAN JUDY GARLAND

MY WHOPPING PROPERTY taxes for Lloyd Place were becoming more and more outrageous. So, at the risk of leaving Maggie, John Paul, and California, I auditioned for the new Tiffany's Attic Dinner Theatre in Salt Lake City. *Catch Me If You Can* was to be the first production. I read at the casting lady's house in Sherman Oaks for the Utah producers. They were two frosty hotshots young enough to be my sons. After a mercifully brief wait in the lady's dining room, they offered me my old Gallery Theatre role. Twelve weeks, they said, four in rehearsal. I stalled; they gave me until six o'clock to make my decision. I drove home to telephone John Paul at work. I told him that such a long contract was out of the question unless he cared for Maggie on Norma Place. He said that he would, and I agreed to travel to Utah, where I would proudly entertain the Mormon masses.

I drove to Utah because I wanted the freedom my car could afford me in Salt Lake City. My glove compartment was stocked with a mammoth supply of Trident gum. But after six weeks of Chinese torture forgoing the wicked weed, I stopped in Barstow for a pack of cigarettes. I told myself I would throw it away before I finished it. There had to be something to do other than chew gum while fending off homesickness and stage fright crossing the California desert. In the trunk of my Datsun, packed as carefully as my manual typewriter and luggage, there was a batch of the latest movie-star biographies. I had hoarded them through John Paul's purchasing discount at Brentano's.

During rehearsals for *Catch Me If You Can*, neither the details of Doris Day's hyperventilating nor quitting again after each fresh pack were distractions enough to keep me from wanting to throw in my notice. Only by opening night through the companionship of my leading lady did I force myself to focus on holding my own in what had become a combat zone upon the stage of Tiffany's Attic.

From day one, the comic Al Lewis had made my work on the show catastrophic. He was the nominal dinner-theatre star of *Catch Me If You Can* because of his sight-gag turn as Grandpa on the old *Munsters* television series. At our first reading, I found that my character, Corban, had been trimmed to favor his Inspector Levine. I ate crow in silence in rehearsals too far away from home and at my most dismal apartment in the suburbs of pristine Salt Lake City. The apartment did not have a working lock on the front door. So while I was off slogging through daily repression, I trusted in Mormon probity.

The bland director was an uncommunicative traffic cop intimidated by Mr. Lewis's rights of way. This Inspector Levine was a squinty-eyed ham, merciless in his rapacious desire for laughs and vulgar in his efforts to discomfit the actor on stage with him. He tweaked cheeks, poked at our clothing, and leered delightedly behind our backs at the waiters, carpenters, and Tiffany's Attic technical people. He was, unfortunately, very funny in his time-dishonored shtick, leaving the rest of us with egg on our faces.

Our leading lady, Tani Guthrie, was as appalled as I was. Our budding friendship saved my sanity. I used the excuse that the backstage construction was not yet completed in order to finagle out of sharing

Al's single shower; Tani graciously obliged, allowing me to share her space. After our abysmal technical rehearsal, the stony-faced producers repaired to their front office, seldom to be seen again. Tani and I hid out to frantically run lines while she sewed pads into the underarms of my white T-shirts—to absorb the flop sweat.

The opening night audience, which included the Governor of Utah, was my savior. Their laughter steadied my equilibrium and gave me the moments in acting time to take stage. I reveled in Mr. Lewis's astonishment, maybe even his relief, as we gradually began to share his howls and my own laughs. He saw, too, the new rage in my eyes when he pawed my face for what proved to be the last time. His grandstanding continued, as it would for eight weeks, and he left them in stitches at the final curtain. But my own reception was warm and generous enough to renew the confidence of an insecure actor on the brink of becoming a mediocre stooge to the top banana. I grew with each workhorse performance into Mr. Lewis's worthy opponent instead of, alas, his straight man. My Corban held his own—hopefully without resorting to Mr. Lewis's tricks. Of course one could not be certain in out-of-town Utah—my one and only baptism in the high art of dinner theatre's low comedy.

Tani was a lovely, talkative godsend, save on the one day a week when she fasted. At that night's performance, she would drift trance-like into unexpected places on the stage. But I valued her company too much offstage not to adapt during our scenes together to her unfamiliar and sometimes better blocking. Like me, Tani found her housing wanting, so the two of us bitched enough to be moved after the opening week into modern, air-conditioned units in a new Salt Lake City apartment complex. From there I drove her to and from the theatre. We had supper together after each performance. We shopped for our own linens at the ZZMI department store that seemed as large as Harrods, observed rehearsals for the enriching Mormon Tabernacle Choir, and visited the industrious Brigham Young's small house on Salt Lake City's wide main street. Tani packed us picnics of health food to enjoy in the clear, clean air on a

grassy bank beside a stream in an unhazardous Salt Lake City park.
If all the young Mormon men who jogged by looked like skiers, it's
because they were. Tani laughed at my panting after them. We marveled most at the primal beauty of Utah on the bicentennial Fourth
of July. We drove to the Alta Ski Lodge for more buffet at the gala
holiday brunch than we could ever manage. After we gorged, we sat
out on the stone terrace overlooking the breathtaking summer
slopes, filled as much with the love of country as with food.

A mutual friend cared for Maggie long enough for John Paul to fly to
Salt Lake City to see the last show and to spell me on the return drive
home. From the airport, I took him to lunch in Trolley Square with
Tani and her identical twin sister Dran, who had also arrived for the
closing. Our deafening conversational level made my usually quiet
companion even more so. My own babble was not only to cover John
Paul's shyness; it also betrayed my nerves at the prospect of performing for him. Like any show, *Catch Me If You Can* was more fun to
be abandoned in before less-exacting strangers. It had seemed in mid-
run to be never-ending; now, with the actuality of our final night, our
emotions were bittersweet. Mine were hyper during my last whirligig
performance. Upon glimpsing my poker-faced friend in the audience,
I played as though I were on a pogo stick until, during intermission, I
took some deep breaths to calm down for a redeeming second act.

In the dressing room after the show, John Paul, as is his habit,
downplayed the congratulations I could never get enough of. A
bawling Al Lewis lumbered in, arms outstretched, to strangle Tani
and me with maudlin goodbyes. Dumbfounded, we almost forgot
what had gone on before.

On the trip home, the soaring coppery crags of Arizona's Grand
Canyon rendered John Paul and me speechless; so did being charged
twenty-four dollars to split a plump plastic bottle of Coca-Cola
plopped into an ice bucket in the Caesar's Palace showroom. The Las
Vegas stop was at my insistence and was meant to be a treat for John
Paul. But the swaggering derring-do of Siegfried and Roy with their

majestic wild animals did not quite make up for the patronizing maître d' or our cheap motel off the strip that Sam Spade would have deemed grubby.

The congested freeways as we entered smoggy Los Angeles produced the familiar sinking spell that comes over me being forced to face reality again at the end of a trip. I just looked forward to seeing my declining cat Maggie again. The feeling was not mutual when I lay on my belly to try to coax her out from under the bed. She was either too old to recognize me or angry at my desertion. On October 4, 1976, John Paul and I watched a late show of *The 39 Steps*. Maggie came out of the bathroom at one A.M. She looked puzzled and walked in front of us across the living room toward the bedroom. I followed her. When I picked her up, her gold eyes widened clear—like a kitten's— to stare at me while she had a massive heart attack. The next day at Dr. Miller's, she was cremated. She was twenty-three years old.

Less than six weeks and one flea bomb later, on Sunday, November 14, to be exact, John Paul and I drove to Ellen Wallace's remote house beyond Malibu in Latigo Canyon to pick up cats six and seven. They were eight-week-old brother and sister kittens. Wallis and Dulcie were given over after Ellen's thorough physical inspection. My Bessie Watty from *The Corn Is Green*, who understood the wrench of animal loss, had offered Maggie's replacements from her own menagerie. The force of Dulcie was with us until she succumbed, at fifteen, to cancer. I dare not dwell on Wallis. He was my shadow. If there is a cat heaven, he is surely in it. He survived on love until he was seventeen, a courageous gray ghost with failing kidneys.

During this period, I helped out an AA friend, a young filmmaker, when he was working on a student film in his freshman year. My scenes took place in the old Doheny mansion, Greystone, which was the original home of the American Film Institute. I returned to the mansion a little while later for an audience with one of the last household names worth crossing the street to see, Bette Davis, who was on hand for a question-and-answer session. The young directing student suggested that I might enjoy the evening. I was only permitted to attend under his aegis. He did not have to ask me twice.

The penultimate screen star and self-described "New England broad" came to Greystone after a screening of *The Little Foxes* for AFI students. I was as agog as they were when the star, wearing a gray flannel skirt and tailored shirt, made her entrance into the packed great hall. Middle-aged and sturdy still, with her own gray-brown hair in a pageboy, she proceeded to answer our questions in her agreeable staccato speech patterns, gesticulating with the omnipresent cigarette in her right hand to punctuate her opinions, which were plentiful and forthright in regard to her films, directors, and co-stars. Her large eyes were surprisingly blue and beautiful behind slightly tinted glasses.

Our mutual friend Robert Osborne had suggested beforehand that I ask her why she had not switched roles with Olivia de Havilland to make *In This Our Life* more interesting. She answered that she had discussed the exact casting with director John Huston. She had prodded Warner Brothers to make the switch. Their verdict was that the public would not accept her as the "*good* sister!" There was a great cackle and the clang of her bracelets in a swirl of smoke. The writer Paul Monette, another exhilarated interloper, gave me a congratulatory wink, and all of us joined in her laughter.

Twilight was approaching through Greystone's tall windows when Miss Davis stood up to leave. She wished every one of us good luck in the industry that she had conquered, threw us a mighty Bette Davis kiss, and was gone. I was a movie-struck kid for the last time. I drove down Doheny toward Norma Place to rehash the afternoon's high with John Paul.

God smiled on me when John Paul was unable to sell my Lloyd Place duplex in 1976. The asking price was $89,500. The two of us had some idea of joining forces in a condominium with the proceeds. Paul Millard did sell his building Norma Place, and he told me the new owner wanted to take over my apartment. I reluctantly gave actor James Ray, my downstairs tenant, nearly five months' notice to vacate Lloyd Place. I moved with John Paul—reluctantly too, in the beginning; sharing is not my thing—to Lloyd Place on September 3, 1977. A bucket brigade that included Chuck, Tucker, Oren, and even Morris Evans made the change easier. We transported everything except the kittens across the street within four hours. My helpful friends placed my methodically packed boxes and belongings where I had blueprinted a dozen times and I sent them to lunch. I returned alone to Norma Place to put a deranged looking Dulcie and Wallis in their carrier. Paul was there and I gave him my keys. Our footsteps echoed in the empty space as we circled one another. I asked him not to say anything for fear I would cry. I picked up the carrier, went down the stairs and through the open front door, and walked to my first new address in eighteen years.

The Lloyd Place faucets dripped, the stained toilet sounded like Niagara Falls, and the loose and rusty shower head had a mind of its own. A couple of the dirty windowpanes were cracked, and termites hung out in the service porch. You needed a seeing-eye dog to walk into the patio and garage, as there was no outdoor lighting. Queen Elizabeth was visiting California that winter; she was not the only one inconvenienced by the Los Angeles monsoons. More than a few Lloyd Place windows seeped in the ferocious winds. A bucket had to be placed under a leak in the dining room ceiling. We were hard put to slam shut the swollen front door.

So, after the termites were zapped and the panes were caulked and the Spanish tile roof and the plumbing were repaired, new interior paint was in order. I undertook that job myself. The passé "decorator wallpaper" in the kitchen had to be removed professionally. I managed to strip the plaid pattern off the bathroom walls myself. One day I lifted the garage door. The steel spring that supported it catapulted through the air, sailing just past my head. It bounced off the back door of the garage and landed at my feet on the cement floor. Luckily, the deep dents it left were in the back door and not in my head or a preceding tenant's. Later, in addition to new springs, I was able to have a Genie automatic door opener installed—from my salary for an *Amazing Stories* television episode. There were landscaping improvements and the myriad host of ongoing repairs, patch-ups, and projects that, when economics allow, are never-ending with every homeowner. Nevertheless, it would be agreeable to be carried feet-first and fully dressed out of my home on Lloyd Place. John Paul can sell it if he wishes—for a helluva lot more than $89,500.

I celebrated the passage of Proposition 13, that blessed piece of legislation that cut my property taxes in half, with a respite from Lloyd Place and AA meetings on a trip with J. P. to see my family in Baltimore and to see some theatre and my Aunt Camilla in New York. In the Royalton Hotel, for the first time that season, the heat was turned on. The din of the clanging old pipes sent an exhausted John Paul and me out for more Big Apple adrenaline in streets that automatically jump-start the nervous system.

So did the hit musical *Ain't Misbehavin'*. John Paul had to sit with his date, the writer Elizabeth Kaye, two rows in front of Aunt Camilla and me. Before the curtain, I asked Auntie Camilla how she liked J. P.

"He is a lot better than Judy Garland, dear," she replied as the houselights dimmed.

After the show, we went to the Russian Tea Room for supper. I excused myself to go to the men's room. I was wearing a brand new black-and-red plaid sport coat from Carroll and Co. With dark gray flannel trousers, I might add.

"What on earth is Binky wearing? It looks like a horse blanket," said Auntie Camilla to J. P. and Elizabeth.

All the Boones called me Binky from my childhood. I have forgotten why. I wonder if my mother Carlyle was as adept at discharging trenchant ripostes as Camilla and the rest of them. Zingers come easily for me too. The Carroll sport coat hasn't left its garment bag since that trip.

On a later family trip, John Paul went home to Fort Walton Beach to visit his sister during a hot spell. He returned to California looking like an egg. I opened the front door and there stood a stranger to get used to. No beard, no warning, and it took a while.

The MGM Grand Hotel on the outskirts of Reno, Nevada was the site of another getaway—one that I got paid for. At an audition in the foyer of the Huntington-Hartford Theatre in Hollywood, I was asked to expound, from a couple of pages of hyperbolical hieroglyphics, on the merits of Jeeps and four-wheel-drives. That evening, my commercial agent notified me that I had been hired to be the spokesman for American Motors at their annual trade show. The generous salary was a godsend, but the $500 bonus that was offered, urging me to memorize the script, was cause for hives. It turned out to be twenty pages. I dare say Lord Olivier in his prime would not have retained such a lengthy discourse on the joys of off-road driving in the spiffiest new AMC models. The night before John Paul drove me to the airport, I could barely sleep.

The new MGM Grand loomed up like a modern fortress against the skyline of the Nevada mountains. Inside its cocoon-city only one gewgaw among thousands registered: an enormous framed blowup of an MGM Garland smiling at me from one wall of my opulent room. I was summoned downstairs and shown out onto the largest stage in the world. That was more jolting than Judy. I tapped my stage-left microphone and began to babble to the bobbing, silhouetted heads in the distant control room my desperate need for a podium on which to place my script. My circumspect producer, wary of recasting, acquiesced from on high in a disembodied voice. From the cavernous wings, a handsome stagehand appeared carrying a solid stand. I wanted to hug him.

From the moment that I could refer to the script in front of me, I enjoyed saying all those words throughout rehearsals and later at the shows we presented at ten each morning. Sixty gypsies from the MGM Grand's nightly "Hallelujah Hollywood" danced to throbbing disco music among the new Jeeps and four-door sedans between slick film clips of the same shining wonders overhead. A curtain of rain fell on cue across the vast stage. During this extravaganza, I talked and talked to wake up and galvanize what seemed to be every American Motors dealer in the western hemisphere. The job that I had lost sleep over turned into a lark.

My co-worker Deanne McKinstry almost added a love affair to the gig. Deanne extolled the glories of new sedans as they glided by her great legs at stage right. She used a podium too, as she charmed our audience—and me along with it—on sight. The warmth and wit of her company soon made us inseparable offstage. We learned about each other's lives through breakfast, lunch, dinner, and, huddled in one corner or another of the teeming casinos, late into the night. She had the incandescence of a star, large brown eyes brimming with understanding, and I came as close to being capable of falling in love with her as I had been with Judy. But I only kissed her good night on the cheek and wished that I could do more as she gently closed her door.

Deanne had a discipline that was earthbound, healthy, and iron-willed. She was also a vegetarian; she meditated, had never dreamed of smoking, and drank like a canary. She firmly believed that a beneficent Prince Charming with like virtues was on her horizon. That let me off the hook, but I did make her laugh. She made me seek fresh air outside the hotel sanctuary—even our meals were provided—that I began to luxuriate in. We took long moonlit walks around the MGM Grand and rented a car to see the honky-tonk town of Reno. I told her about my second mother Estelle establishing residence there to divorce my father. Deanne showed me snapshots of her mother, who lived alone outside Boston. She also showed me photos of Shanti, her golden retriever at home in Hollywood, so we bonded as pet lovers. We were hushed by the splendor of undomesticated nature when we parked on our drive around Lake Tahoe, and we were sad when our easygoing job was completed.

We flew together on the same plane back to Los Angeles. Our whopping paychecks, despite the absence of a bonus for memorization, mitigated our melancholy. It was typical of Deanne to begin to mumble about using a portion of hers to send our producer a small thank-you gift. I told her to forget that, to deposit her salary and hope the check didn't bounce. Of course the money was good because American Motors was—then—in fine fettle. For a time after the splendiferousness of our MGM Grand surroundings, Lloyd Place seemed awfully small. I missed Deanne and could not wait to introduce her to John Paul. Today she is a married, treasured friend. We always laughed together, but too few of our shared acting dreams came true. Like me, she is preoccupied with writing now—and with the dogs that came after Shanti.

My new-found love of nature after Reno carried me to further adventures. Morris Evans purchased a cabin in the deep woods of Sky Forest above Lake Arrowhead. We were allies on the surface at his insistence. John Paul particularly liked to drive up into the San Bernardino Mountains where we were house guests in Morris's truly rustic retreat. Twenty-four hours of Mother Nature's bounty is enough for me, never for John Paul. At the cabin, the cold crept through the logs in the wall beside my twin bed. A nocturnal pee meant creeping downstairs to the bathroom. The all-night sounds, such as snow melting off the pine branches upon the tin roof, were reason enough to sneak a valium—and, soon enough, to drink again. When the white stuff made the driveway impassable, we had to walk out. We slogged up and down the hill behind the cabin to Morris's Jeep to unload groceries. The Jeep was parked on the main road above, which had been plowed.

Admittedly, the rewards for less than Waldorf-Astoria amenities were many. Morris, who did not like cats and grew bored with dogs, filled bird and squirrel feeders to satisfy all comers in the profound isolation outside. We stuffed ourselves on fine stored food at the country dining table in the wood-beamed kitchen. There were bickering Scrabble games before the flames in the stone fireplace and quiet hikes over soft pine needles when the weather was warmer.

I was happier in the spring and summer high altitude, and never more so than on the day when button-eyed John Paul ran in from

the front porch whispering for Morris and me to look out the
kitchen window—quickly! We rushed to the same sill that we had
just slopped our lunch over—the customary means of disposal for
cabin garbage. These particular leftovers were being gobbled up on
the sloping bank by a Volkswagen-sized brown bear with glinting
Norma Shearer eyes. Bantam Morris flew outside with his camera.
He appeared below us to take his pictures barely twenty feet uphill
from the bear. Big Norma glanced toward the clicking camera
shutter. She continued to loll sideways on furry flanks, savoring
peach pits in enormous paws. John Paul and I, transfixed, watched
the animal take its sweet time to finish eating. Then it stood to shake
itself and began to amble, swaying from side to side, up the hill and
into the trees. Cool-headed Morris had prudently vanished. We
thought we could hear the bear walking, crunching on pinecones in
the distance. Our host came inside to triumphantly brandish his
camera. The three of us chortled in amazement over what we had
seen. But back in the city Morris found that he had no pictures of
the intruder because he had had no film in his camera. We repeated
the Big Norma story anyhow, but I didn't walk alone again into the
wildlife beyond that cabin.

Another long-standing friendship like Deanne's came about when I
did Enid Bagnold's brilliantly loquacious play *The Chalk Garden* at a
grubby little theatre in Burbank. My role, as the butler Maitland, and
the chance to co-star with the enthusiastic Patience Cleveland, who
played Miss Madrigal, were the reasons I embarked on the show. Maitland's mistress, Mrs. St. Maugham, was taken up by Gertrude Flynn,
a mildly accomplished character actress then entering into senility.
She blew her lines with savage consistency during the long luncheon
scene, forcing me to serve up new dialogue with the food. Except for
the gifted Patience, the others in the amateur, amiable cast were concrete in the hands of our maladroit director, a fretful, failed actress
who threatened to fire Patience and me for giggling during rehearsals.
She had good reason. Ms. Cleveland and I dared not look at one

another for fear of embarrassed spasms of uncontrolled laughter. Our friendship grew as we became terrified of succumbing to hysteria in front of an audience. In coffee shops and on the telephone and during frantic cigarette breaks in an alleyway behind the theatre, we vowed to behave and to pull our combustible selves together. We finally did, but the struggle was mighty. Patience's New Hampshire discipline and her contact lenses came to the rescue. I admitted to Patience that her intent blue eyes darting off in panic behind thick rehearsal glasses to look at the ceiling, floor, or the back wall instead of at recalcitrant me had set me off. She forgave me, and we connected skillfully in actual performance and left the merriment to the audiences. We have laughed together ever since, but never on stage.

It was after *The Chalk Garden* that the drip-drip-drip of the rain-drops on Morris's tin roof during an unexpected summer cloudburst kept me awake on a return visit to the cabin. The pummeling sound of the rain became harder and more nerve-racking as I thrashed about in my twin bed. Two A.M. came and went on the clock radio. I reached for my robe. John Paul slept fitfully on the other bed as I opened our bedroom door to creep downstairs. Outside, the creaking wail of the swaying trees drowned out any sound that my bare feet made on the wooden floorboards. Lightning illuminated the bottle of vodka sitting on a shelf of the tall pine cabinet in the living room. I reached for it. I took it into the bathroom, shut the door, and took a swig. Then, without thought or conscience, I drank another. I replaced the bottle and went woozily back upstairs. I passed the closed door of Morris's master bedroom and crawled into bed. John Paul dozed on. The nightcap was a knockout.

That was the first of several sneaks in subsequent months. I enjoyed them in secret as I became more and more determined to depart the unvaried ranks of Alcoholics Anonymous. I longed to drink again—moderately. There had to be something left in life to flatten out my fears, to buttress my joys. If immaturity breeds boredom, I stood guilty. The doctrine set forth in meeting after AA meeting left me impervious and kvetching and unwilling to do battle with my flawed psyche. Quitting amphetamines was enough. I banished my guilt at this self-knowledge. My deep apprehension was at the prospect of lost friends in the program, and, above all, at confessing to John Paul the feelings brought on by my faltering.

He was aware of my turbulence. There were signs that he would follow me. That decision, which I both feared and wanted, had to be his own. While we were on a plane to visit his sister in Florida in October 1982, I admitted to John Paul that I had "taken a drink." His understanding was absolute, but he dismissed my "slip" as a thing of the past. I knew better, and I proceeded with caution.

The Florida Panhandle, according to my companion, is ordinarily mild and breezy in October. It was, to put it politely, sticky and still for our visit. His Aunt Lillis's single-story house, where we stayed in Fort Walton Beach, had grown weary like its owner. There was sand between the bedsheets, the smell of fish being defrosted on the old wooden pantry counter, and the grit of sediment dribbled from the water pipes. The informality—tank tops and shorts—was extreme. I sat most of the time, clammy after a shower, gulping like a toadfish for a breeze off the Gulf.

Sue, John Paul's handsome sister, pricklier with the heat than when I had met her in California, did what she could to make us comfortable. She had given up her room at Aunt Lillis's to us and was staying nearby with younger friends. She came to drive us on baked roads between miles of scrub pines to look at what few sights there were to see. The exception was the clean, blinding sand on the region's beaches. It was so white that even through dark glasses its glare was like staring into the sun.

Aunt Lillis's delicate lemon cake was refreshing, but I became more and more concentrated on Sue's unquenchable thirst. Her capacity for beer was so remarkable that I poured a vodka martini of my own to beat the heat. It was our last evening in Florida. We were seated around the kitchen table. John Paul looked stricken. Sue said that I should do what I wanted to do. I did, and supper was so convivial that Aunt Lillis toasted us goodbye with bourbon.

We left the Alligator State, heading for Maryland. The next night before dinner in Baltimore, I had another cocktail in the Egerton den. Ann took it in stride. Stuart was my jovial host. John Paul remained perturbed—until he joined me in a drink on our final night in Baltimore, and every night after that when we have been together. In private, he swore that he had poured one himself in Florida. I wanted him to repeat his assurances that he was drinking again because he wanted to and not to keep our peace, and he did.

I came to believe him, but there were some in the program who never did. We had chalked up seventeen years between us in a valuable fellowship where defection could not be tolerated. We were out and imbibing and a few turned their backs. Therefore, so did I.

I would say that I am a *controlled* alcoholic. I have overindulged and pursued the past. But the pain of doing damage to myself is no longer worth it. It is rare now that John Paul sticks around to hear Judy yell "We'll stay all night and sing 'em all!" at Carnegie Hall. When he does, he climbs the stairs, two at a time, to go to bed. Nevertheless it is sad that the past is just that; receding, farther and farther away. I must chase mine down with words instead of liquor, before it evaporates, like Dopey's soap bubbles.

Speaking of the stairs, I was fortunate enough to have my Lloyd Place tenant vacate the upstairs apartment seconds before the newly incorporated City of West Hollywood decreed a relocation fee. I was able to convert my duplex into a single house. I became less vexatious the moment that John Paul and I could enjoy the privacy of separate bathrooms. That particular room and other spaces of one's own sustain the sanity of friends who dwell in close proximity. The next best benefit to prolong equanimity is separation, and John Paul loves to travel.

Aunt Camilla coaxed me to fly to Baltimore for Uncle Herbert's funeral. I declined her offer to raise the coffin lid so that I could look at him lying in state in an Oak Hill drawing room. Auntie said that his strawberry-colored hair dye would surely run in the condensed soup air of my hometown, where the mercury soared to 103 degrees. In the imposing Boone family home with its thick stone walls, there were only air-conditioning window units in the upstairs bedrooms. I chose the comfort of one on the third floor—instead of departed Aunt Muriel's stately bedroom. There I would have been required to share the adjacent marble bathtub with Uncle Herbert's female secretary. His mournful peacocks peered in at his bier; his family at their end of the flagstone terrace amused themselves by talking about everything except his money. We sat in shirtsleeves and summer bathrobes waiting for the will to be read after the next day's funeral.

Ann and Stuart were forced to miss the ceremony. They were vacationing in Maine with my niece and nephew. But a great many older Baltimoreans sweltered on the steps of Mary Our Queen Cathedral, waiting for the immediate family to drive up in the funeral procession. They included Mother, who admitted she would not have missed the event for the world. The rest wondered who I was as I enjoyed escorting Aunt Camilla down the aisle just behind the casket. I wore my lightweight beige poplin suit, tried to keep in stride with the apple-cheeked acolytes swinging their incense, and knelt to enjoy the theatricality of a high Catholic Mass.

Beside the Boone plot in the old Loudon Park Cemetery afterward, as Uncle Herbert's coffin was being placed directly above the one occupied by Aunt Muriel, my cousin, Judge Gordon Boone, was heard to say, most audibly, "On top for the very first time."

My old nanny Gertrude assisted in the lavish reception that we returned to at Oak Hill. Mother urged me to help solve my identity by introducing myself as Carlyle Fairfax Posey to the various surviving friends of my birth mother Carlyle who were there. I did. Some were startled, some were ailing, and I welcomed each introduction. I was warmed by every fragile show of reawakened affection. The Maryland humidity became unimportant in the beauty of Oak Hill and the tranquility of its grounds. At a distance, the scattered peacocks stared from the trees. For a little while, I felt like a fool for ever leaving.

Twenty-four hours later, upon hearing Aunt Camilla's announcement, I felt like a fool for coming back.

"We are not wealthy!" she intoned with a flourish. Her arch Boone
inflections echoed from the front door through the great Oak Hill
entry hall. She and my Uncle Teen, Gordon's father, had just
returned from the attorney's office. Her words seemed to reverberate
off the paneled walls and bounce around in my head.

The bulk of Herbert's vastly depleted estate—including Oak Hill
and the treasures therein—was left to Johns Hopkins University. The
twenty-two-room apartment on Park Avenue and the house on Oahu
had been sold. Medical expenses, private nurses around the clock—
one wishful thinker was fired after trying for a proposal of marriage
from the cancer-ridden, asexual Mr. Boone—residential developers,
and the all-encompassing IRS had further whittled away the estate
and Oak Hill acreage. The most generous cash bequest was left to the
lady secretary and, for the time being, we got nothing.

The family began to make up for that, that very day. A locust-like
assault on Oak Hill commenced. Station wagons were loaded with
silver, china, and pieces of furniture, cars with linen, clothing, and
more silver. The family-owned Audubon books were carted off to be
stored and appraised. The Miró, the tapestries, the other art and
objects had to be left for strangers to inventory, but we executed as
thorough a legal swipe as possible. I made an awkward trip back to
California carrying one of the striking Wemyss Scottish china pigs
that sat on the hearth of each Oak Hill fireplace. Gertrude wrapped
it for me in a large box of thick bath towels. The towels were labeled,
as in summer camp, "James R. Herbert Boone." I carried some sterling pieces in my suitcase.

It would have behooved me to rent a car and pack it to the max
like my Maryland family members, but I did not. There is a salutary
postscript to my whirlwind round-trip flight: "Herbert," my Honda
Accord, bought through the courtesy of the Audubon books and
Johns Hopkins. The university, thanks to the nettlesome efforts of
Uncle Teen, finally settled too small a share of the booty on each one

of us. After new counter tiles and wallpaper in the kitchen on Lloyd Place, and "Herbert," that was the end of it. Oak Hill, the house that my Grandfather Boone built, now sits for sale like an empty stone elephant surrounded by a subdivision of what my sister calls "vulgar villas."

I wonder what the life span of the iridescent peacock is. I hope that some of Uncle Herbert's brood are still enjoying the comforts of the Baltimore Zoo.

CHAPTER SEVENTEEN

SHOOTING STARS

APPROACHING JOAN FONTAINE became realistic again in 1978. Our friendship grew cordial, so long as it was on Joan's terms. There could be no screen goddess claptrap with this armadillo beauty. I always walked on eggs and I was always loyal.

Joan began by asking Robert Osborne and me to dinner at the Beverly Hills Hotel. She had a suite there while filming a mini-series. Robert had become the new columnist for the *Hollywood Reporter*, and he was a friend of her sister. Olivia de Havilland was a topic to avoid at our dinner at La Loggia. She remained so, unless Joan brought her up. Robert's flattery was brushed aside when Joan said that she had nothing to do with her good looks, that she had inherited good genes. She had firm political opinions, and intelligent talk of travel, world figures, or food sparked her vivacity. Shop talk did not. Her bemused blue lynx eyes became bothered in the patrician profile, a signal not to dwell on her film work, as though the discussion of past laurels was painful. Curious ladies and other diners still paid discreet heed. Hopefully my moistened brow went unnoticed when Joan, with her Mona Lisa smile, acknowledged that since the '40s, I had imitated her singular handwriting. She added that many people had; I stressed firmly that my variation was now my own. Otherwise the evening was smooth sailing, and it was astonishing to be in her company. Our hostess would not even allow Robert and me to leave the tip.

Joan's generosity has always been magnanimous. She asked me to houseguest with the late actor Murray Matheson, a mutual friend, when she had a summer rental in Carmel—before she moved from her apartment in New York to her own home in Carmel Highlands, California. Joan cooked, sped us around the gorgeous Seventeen-Mile Drive, and pointed out Jean Arthur's house. She drove us into the John Steinbeck country of old fisheries in Monterey, showed us the chapel in Del Mar where she had married Brian Aherne, and took us to lunch at Pebble Beach Golf Club overlooking the very cliffs that doubled for the coast of Cornwall in *Rebecca*.

Joan played solitaire, worked every crossword puzzle, and cleaned the absentee owner's oven while Murray and I took long walks over the most beautiful bluffs in California. Murray was an enchanting man who had done film and theatre with Joan and nearly every other female screen goddess who had taken to the stage. Mischievously, he claimed that his silver hair caught the light, so no one looked at the ladies. His tales of these leading ladies and other show-business stories were often so funny that I almost toppled into the sea with laughter. He was a matchless raconteur.

When we took Joan to a restaurant in Carmel for dinner, Murray excused himself to go to the men's room. While he was gone, Joan explained that he had failed to become a top character actor because of his lingering Australian accent, a barely noticeable trait that seemed attractive to me. He returned to the table, and the three of us discussed the work of current actresses. I regressed, and raised my wine glass to toast the memory of Joan's performance in *The Constant Nymph*. Joan chalked my preference up to "arrested development" and changed the subject.

I drove Joan with John Paul to Claremont College where Joan was to do a lecture. Our picking her up in Hollywood where she was staying with my old friend Carroll Righter gave me a brief reunion with Pappy. He beamed and poked like always, well into his eighties. On the living room wall, his puss was celebrated on a cover of *Time*.

Beginning with our drive to Claremont, Joan took to John Paul's "contemplative nature." Later he located the perfect rental house for her north of Sunset in Beverly Hills. It was, she said, "the only location in Los Angeles, according to Ronald Colman." She took a long lease on the Miradero Road hideaway after she starred in a new pilot for television. The script was as inept as the supporting cast, and the pilot was a failure. Joan's hopes, too high too soon, were dashed. John Paul was left to sublet Miradero to another actress, Polly Bergen. The necessary arrangements for this turnaround, though not as remunerative, were almost as monumental for him as closing an escrow. Joan was appreciative, which helped our friendship. J. P. and I then began to visit her in her new home in Carmel Highlands.

What does one give Joan Fontaine as a token housewarming gift? She sent my choice back to me by return mail. It was two samplers stenciled TO BE RICH IS NO LONGER A SIN, IT'S A MIRACLE and PLEASE DON'T SPRINKLE WHEN YOU TINKLE. She wrote that she would have to needlepoint for years in order to finish decorating her "glorious new house," and that "scatological bathroom humor" was not her style. I switched to Rigaud candles, hand-delivered, to much better effect.

Fang, Fury, and Muldoon regulated the proceedings at Villa Fontana, together with their mistress. They were Joan's German shepherd, golden retriever, and Alaskan husky that exercised her house guests in the wooded and remote Carmel Highlands countryside. They also had the run of a private beach below Highway One. The five of us returned panting to the house with its light wood-paneled library, two separate guest quarters on the first and second floors, a formal living room that is seldom used, and a panoramic view of the Pacific. The view is best from the pentagonal window in the dining area that Joan designed off the kitchen. We unwound in front of Joan's double fireplace with our feet propped up on Fang. The dogs were fine company and a source of solace in their fog-enshrouded retreat. Joan chases the sun in Carmel Valley. Her burnished Oscar beckons in the downstairs stairwell as though to another life, where the framed memorabilia of her career leads the way along the corridor.

"I've got a copy of *The Constant Nymph!*" Joan's plummy tone from the back of her station wagon was conspiratorial. John Paul, who would have preferred her Bentley, was driving us to the house in the lady's humdrum station wagon after Joan had met us at Monterey Airport. Lord knows, she knew my affinity for the film, which had not been released to television. A fan had sent her a bootleg cassette. I was surprised and delighted when she told me.

Joan served us thick French onion soup and lamb chops for lunch, instructed us how to operate the video player in our guest suite downstairs, and left us until the cocktail hour. We drew the brocaded drapes, and John Paul went along for the ride while I tripped-out, again, on soulful Charles Boyer, the melancholy music of Korngold, and, most poignant of all, the lingering death of Joan's fragile Tessa. At six o'clock, my eyes wisely dried, I approached the determinedly alive star of *The Constant Nymph* with words to the effect that I was glad that she had not been downstairs to witness the wistful spell that the film still cast. Joan's hands rose in front of her as if to physically halt my praise. "Have we got the sound? Does the picture reception leave too much to be desired?" she asked. I retreated to the vodka decanter on the round antique table in the library to talk about the sunset.

The safe ground fell out from under me on our next long weekend. This time we drove. John Paul's Mercedes sat behind the gates in Joan's driveway. The three of us were comfortable by the fire, feet up on Fang and the footstools beside the floor-to-ceiling bookshelves, perhaps too relaxed from after-dinner drinks. Some barriers were down. Joan was speaking about Olivia, displaying the photographs of her niece Giselle in the French magazine *Paris-Match*.

There was talk of the two sisters' legend, but the sequence and my own input is blotted out. Joan was suddenly on her feet. John Paul looked alarmed.

"John, stop talking about my career. We can discuss anything else, anything at all. But not that." She walked past me toward the hallway.

"Joan, I don't remember what I said, I only want your career to go on as long as Olivia's."

That made it worse and she left the room. John Paul whispered to me to go after her and apologize. For what, I wondered?

But I did, from the doorway of the kitchen where Joan was rinsing glasses and the dinner dishes. Coldly, she murmured an acceptance and we said our good-nights. I went downstairs to have a breakdown.

I was, behind two pairs of closed double doors to our guest quarters, truly stricken. I cried and ranted at Joan's abrasiveness, about my lifelong absorption with her, at John Paul for not understanding. He too was a member of the generation of movie idols, after all. Why should my idol have to be so guarded, so very different from what she seemed on film? Is *anyone* privy to Joan's vulnerability? Judy Garland had loved me, for God's sake! I drank more vodka from the downstairs bar. I slugged myself to sleep with a Halcion.

The next morning, the fog inside my head was denser than it was outdoors. I lost a contact lens when I dropped it on the bathroom floor. I wore my glasses, but the day was still a blur. Joan reappeared to go with us for lunch at the Ventana Inn further down the coast. She acted as though she were oblivious of the night before. After a long disappearing act to nap, our dinner had to be gotten through— at a posh new restaurant in Monterey. Joan, blonde and impenetrable by candlelight, sat with our waiter staring at her. I had a forced time keeping up my end of the fitful conversation. In a feeble attempt to rally when we got home, I called attention to the stars that seemed at arm's length above Joan's courtyard. She did not look up. She waved us good night, retreating to her bedroom.

When we departed for Los Angeles earlier than usual on Monday morning, Joan was distracted by a visiting neighbor. His small talk made our exit less awkward. I wanted to vanish and was relieved to drive away. On the drive and over lunch in Cambria, I babbled my sad saga of the star I could not talk to. I did not get it all out all over again at dinner in Santa Barbara. John Paul was cross-eyed when we arrived home, and not just from driving.

I—almost—came to terms with the lost-illusion department on that particular Villa Fontana visit. My relationship after that weekend visit was mostly by telephone. Joan Fontaine is the better for learning to leave the sorcery of, say, *Letter from an Unknown Woman,* to the VCR. But, dear Joan, sometimes I am still the schoolboy who wrote to you, too easily flummoxed. I hope that you will read this, and understand.

And what of my own work in those days? There was some. My interview with the producers for the role of the butler to Lloyd Bridges in the glitzy new series *Paper Dolls* went well. Talk about expectations! I was ecstatic. I visualized Paul being given more and more dialogue, and perhaps marrying the housekeeper to enlarge his focus during the second successful season. In the first sequence I did, I announced to Nancy Olson that her luggage was ready. For viewer identification, I asked Ms. Olson to address me by my character name. During her eleventh take, I was still nameless, so I left being identified to my billing. Leo Penn, Sean's accomplished father, directed. He was charming in declining my request to pad my part. I turned my tailored white jacket back over to Wardrobe to await my next assignment in the series.

That came four months later. The critics had massacred the show, which was already zilch in the ratings. The summer day was broiling on location at a Hancock Park mansion with no air-conditioning. Throughout the morning, Lloyd Bridges climbed the formal stairway without complaint to repeat his scene. I stood by at the bottom of the stairs machine-gunning something brief to him. Between setups, Makeup aired my face and jacket with a blow dryer.

Of all people, Ralph Senensky was the director of this episode. He had guided me in something more substantial in Pasadena years before, *The Iceman Cometh*. Before lunch, the principal *Paper Dolls* seated themselves to rehearse around the dining-room table where I was to serve them in the afternoon. Ralph, meaning to be gracious, made my white collar more wilted when he touted me and our Eugene O'Neill triumph to each and every one. They weren't interested. Nor was the public in the canceled *Paper Dolls*.

When I reported for work on "Shatterday," the premier episode of the revival of the *Twilight Zone* series, I was instructed to park my Honda behind steel mesh and motorcycle guards in downtown Los Angeles. We shot in the once-fashionable Alexandria Hotel. The denizens of the lobby and the derelicts in the men's room bore no resemblance to the traffic of Charlie Chaplin's day. The mild-mannered horror maven Wes Craven directed "Shatterday," which starred a friendly and unassuming newcomer from New York, Bruce Willis. My agitated hotel manager became more and more pompous as we rehearsed our scene together. Popping from my ornate cubbyhole behind my antique desk to startle our star was a pleasure. For once, I looked forward to viewing my work as much as receiving my paycheck.

I telephoned everyone I knew. I mailed cards with the airdate to possible employers. On the night of the debut of the new *Twilight Zone*, John Paul and I were in place in front of the television set in the Lloyd Place living room. On the screen, Bruce Willis left the hotel elevator. Next we saw him in an *exterior* scene on the street. No one had harassed him to pay his bill; my scene had been cut. Shades of *A Star Is Born*, with the rage to match! There was my name—still featured prominently in the end credits. That meant residuals, but it did nothing to pick up my spirits or dispel my embarrassment. That night, I had a drink to fortify myself *after* the show instead of before.

CHAPTER EIGHTEEN

IF THE SHOE FITS

BECAUSE I DECIDED that being housebound couldn't always make memories, John Paul persuaded me to go to Europe with him in June 1986. The flight to New York and the endless one to Rome made me wish I'd had a change of heart. Upon landing and entering Italy, a surly official slammed my passport shut. He nodded me through Customs without looking up. After twenty-four sleepless hours, I was gaga in the taxi that drove us into the city, and I was certainly bad company waiting in the bright sun on the roof terrace of Scalinata di Spagna for our room to be made up downstairs. When the room was finally ready, I collapsed for the afternoon. I began to revive when we joined Chuck and Tucker at their hotel, the Ingleterra, to have a drink and go out for dinner on their last night in Rome. A reunion with my old friends on my third trip to Europe was appropriate. After eating al fresco, we strolled to the extraordinary Piazza Navona, less inhabited by the ill-bred than now, to sit and linger over a lemon ice. The square's sere surrounding buildings reflected the light of its three magnificent fountains. Fatigued or not, I was moved by the heart-stopping beauty into the spirit of the trip.

By day, Rome seemed marred by vandalism, dirt, and decay—and the thieving gypsies who picked the pockets of unsuspecting tourists. In the softer light of night, though, the city's vibrant vistas lived up to their ancient legend. So did its ebullient beautiful people, who sprang to life after dark. I stared at the extraordinary men. Most smiled; some winked. I ached, but who wants to pay for it?

The harried Italian waiter doesn't assist the tourist at any hour. So at lunch I admit I digested the more easily understood food in an English teashop beside the Spanish Steps. The fountain at the bottom of the Spanish Steps was closed and under construction. The Trevi Fountain was dry as well, but it was home to an Italian cat. John Paul and I watched it streak and dart over one ornate figure to another, the entire length of the fountain. We saw it disappear into what was surely a waterspout. How on earth did it fare when the fountain was on?

We took the train to Venice. The Venetian menus were also indecipherable, and, like the prices for everything else in that city, the items were at triple the lire—but the environs made them worth it. It is true that Venice is nothing less than rapturous. I was overwhelmed from my first boat ride from the train station by the colors and sights along the Grand Canal. We alighted at Pensione Academia. The water, into which I nearly dropped my wallet, lapped gently up the stone steps of the enclosed courtyard that lay beneath our room. In the small hotel's remote location off the canal, I felt a tranquility that I had never known while traveling. I was blanketed, too, by the extreme silence. The canal bridges along the narrow back streets echoed our footfalls when we walked home at night instead of taking a gondola.

A Venetian epiphany occurred as we departed Piazza San Marco on our last evening. A group of young musicians sang Gregorian chants a cappella in an archway. The vaulted stone ceiling afforded perfect acoustics. Their glowing, passionate faces were silhouetted in the deepening shadows. The pure sound of their voices reverberated across the moonlit square into the air that smelled of the sea. We clustered to listen with the other spellbound onlookers. Mahler would have wept for joy as I did.

Chuck and Tucker were waiting to meet us again in Cannes. There, on the beach in front of the restaurant Ondine, half the gentlemen of West Hollywood seemed to be gossiping over lunch. Today, gays are discouraged at Ondine—after we put it on the map. The Provence had no available rooms, but the Molière, another converted villa next door, proved as comfortable as the former had been in 1971. We drove our rented car out of rarefied Cannes past the elegant villas of Somerset Maugham territory to see the consummate sanctuary in Antibes, the Hôtel du Cap.

We had a drink on the terrace of the authentically grand hotel. Then we strolled down its sloping, palm-lined parc to go to dinner at the Eden Roc. The Eden Roc, overlooking the Hôtel du Cap's private beach and cabanas, lived up to its beau monde reputation with a leisurely, epicurean meal. The maître d' touched a button to raise the outside awnings—to present his gawkers, pretending to be blasé, with a stunning view of the sunset over the Mediterranean. Later, when we left the parking area of the Hôtel du Cap after a brandy back in the lobby, it seemed that all my delusions of grandeur had been fulfilled in a single evening. Well, almost.

Overdeveloped, overcrowded Monte Carlo was a far cry from the civilized oasis of gambling bluebloods that François Reichenbach had introduced me to. Only the old casino and royal palace remained the same. John Paul walked with me through tiny Monaco to where I wanted to go, the principality's chapel, to stand before the grave of Princess Grace. She lay at our feet behind the nave that was encircled by the tombs of the Grimaldis. In sadness I wondered if the family welcomed the solitude of night when the shuffling tread of the tourists stopped. It was more eerie to imagine what Judy's reaction would have been if she had been standing there beside me. We would have gone outside, wiped away our tears, and whispered that Grace Kelly had still not deserved that Oscar for *The Country Girl*.

Paris stunned us with a stifling heat wave. The Lenox Hotel on the Left Bank gave us a converted attic room fit for acrobatic Munchkins. We could only stand erect to look out one dormer window. The sweltering bathroom under the slanted tin roof was at the top of a narrow stairway. I complained vociferously in my pidgin French until we were moved to a floor below, where we could at least unpack on one level—and at our full height.

At lunchtime and during the summer showers that drove people off its avenues, St. Germain retained its charm. Too much of the world congregated there at night. They elbowed one another for a better view of the street peddlers and the performing American expatriates attempting to recreate the street theatre of the '60s—to bag enough francs to return home.

The new Picasso Museum was formidable, if you like Picasso. Its stone chateau structure was as elegant as, if less venerable than, the Hotel Lancaster's, where Harry Blackmer and Peter de Merritt were ensconced. My father had stayed there on European hegiras in the '20s with Mum and Grandfather Posey; now, in his well-appointed suite, Harry poured us martinis from his monogrammed sterling pitcher. He took us to a Right Bank restaurant within walking distance for the best French food I have ever eaten. I used to collect matchbooks, and I wish that I had collected theirs because I have forgotten the name of the place. I shall search for it again sometime, but never, sadly, with Peter. The next day, Harry withdrew to hibernate in Athens and aboard the *Meroë*. John Paul and I made plans to see Peter the following week in London.

Stupefied Englishmen relished every rare minute of the sun as they lay about in London's grassy parks in their shirtsleeves. Tickets to see *Les Misérables* were almost as hot as the climate. We lucked out through a South Kensington scalper. He was close by to our hotel, which Joan Fontaine had recommended, the Number Sixteen. It was converted from Sumner Place row houses, private, and very nearly perfect. So, to my amazement, was *Les Misérables*. I am not an opera buff, and opera is all I had expected. The production was glorious and moving, worth climbing the stalled escalators in the tube from South Kensington to get there, and definitely worth every pound of its inflated ticket price.

There was no air-conditioning in any West End theatre. The ladies glistened and the gentlemen removed their jackets. Each time we went, I hoped that the sea of fanning programs did not distract the wilted cast. It did not appear to. The London theatre still seemed to this Anglophile to be the most accomplished in the world.

In London, our friend Peter de Merritt was fêted like a handsome lapdog on the occasion of his fiftieth birthday. Age became him at the party John Paul and I attended in a genteel flat with a dozen or so other admiring gentlemen. Peter, debonair in his Tommy Nutter blazer, was fundamentally mirthless in the celebration of what would be his final birthday. Back in the United States, Peter had refurbished a small farm in Tiverton, Rhode Island. John Paul and I had had a brief and uncomfortable stay there after a visit to Baltimore in 1985. Not one piece of Peter's extreme and quintessential art deco furniture was fit to sleep in or sit on, but we did not tell him that. The valuable objets d'art that he liked to collect were incongruous in the farm's rustic setting—on land that demanded a hard upkeep to fend off, we presumed, Peter's chronic ennui. When he went abroad, Harry and one or two well-heeled others provided him with well-kept respites from being a gentleman farmer.

Not long after we had returned to the United States, Tucker telephoned to tell me that Peter had killed himself. Not wanting to lower the property value of his farm, Peter had checked into a motel in Newport, Rhode Island. He spent his last day alternating the ingestion of the proper pills that he had hoarded with liquor and ginger ale. He wrote a long suicide letter and notes of apology to his family, his older companion, even the police and the desk clerk; then he lay down dressed in his silk pajamas to die. His companion in Tiverton

told me later that Peter's boredom, ill temper, and all-inclusive dis-
pleasure in the rigors of life had grown terminal. He was also said to
be heartsick at the death of his two closest friends on the East Coast
from AIDS. He helped to nurse them, convinced that he himself was
a carrier of the virus. None of these facts made any difference to me.
I was so shocked at the news of Peter's death that I would have
slugged his lifeless face in the Newport morgue.

For five months in 1987, I played Uncle Freddie, the aristocratic
"closet fluff," in Martin Sherman's Holocaust-themed gay drama
Bent. I made the ten-minute drive to the Coast Playhouse on Santa
Monica Boulevard, changed into my 1934 suit, scarf, fur-collared
greatcoat, and a homburg and went onstage to sit on a park bench to
play my ten-minute scene that brought the house down—or else.
Then I retired backstage to read until the company curtain call. I
read many books during the run of the smash West Hollywood production that the critics called stunning. We played it through thick
and thin. The phrase is applicable to our cast and its changes, not the
capacity audiences.

The all-male communal dressing room was an antic combination
of loony bin and gym basement before, during, and after each performance. I was the senior character actor of the company—time
gallops—and neither a sports freak nor an underwear fetishist, so a
book was the ideal escape to tune out the bedlam. David Wells
played Greta, the proprietor of a gay nightclub who sang "Streets of
Berlin" in drag. He prepared for his entrance by singing it backstage
as well—off key, about seventy times a night. Many homosexuals
came to see the handsome nude actor featured in *Bent*. He fluffed up
his private parts behind a flat of scenery. The contest to catch him at
it became maniacal. Another less-bashful young actor relieved himself in a dressing room wastebasket if the men's room was occupied.
Talk of scores and scoring became epic until shushed by our director
and leading man, David Marshall Grant. David, who professed to be
high on his own confidence, had to leave the show several weeks into

the run to make a movie in Manila. Our expectations and the *Bent* box office soared because he was to be replaced by an actor of some renown.

The new Max had sensual good looks and prodigious talent, with a cocaine habit to match. The latter was not evident in his rehearsals and first performances. We did not, in the beginning, carp on a certain languor and a tendency to grimace because he was a pleasure to play with, and the play seemed the better for him. But shortly he began to arrive at the theatre at seven fifty-five for an eight o'clock curtain; not endearing to the conscientious Tate Donovan, who liked a bit more preparation time to partner their opening scene together. Max was never off stage, and his tempo grew more and more lethargic until the show ran a full twenty minutes longer than it should have. After two or three such tedious performances, the anxious producers gave him copious notes that bordered on threats, all to no avail.

Our star's arrival time approached five past eight or later; spirits in the dressing room were no longer tumultuous. The culmination of this corroding course of events came when he did not appear at all. He slept through the Sunday matinee. The horny girls and boys who had come to see him in person milled about outside the box office to get their money back. He was abject in his apologies when he arrived for the second show, blowing his nose all the while. The refunding producers, now apoplectic, threatened to fire him over lunch the next day.

His charm prevailed, and, to the fury of his understudy, he was allowed to play on. The cocaine was common knowledge by then, and, because I was the resident elder, one night after everyone had departed I tried to counsel my "nephew." I praised his ability and urged him not to squander it and throw away his career. I warned him that a bad reputation was lethal in the small town of Hollywood. I told him that I was no stranger to the joys of getting wasted. I mentioned Judy and recounted my own addiction to pills. He listened with soulful eyes, fidgeted with his earring, gave me a hug, and muttered thanks and empty promises.

Bent was videotaped by the star's secretary. Our addresses were carefully collected because a copy was to be sent to each member of the cast. The promised cassette never materialized. Neither, for one evening performance, did Max. That was his shame-faced end. The star's understudy had his day until Mr. Grant returned to complete the run.

Our final performances were tight and David Marshall Grant disciplined, but the company levity was lost. I worried for the future of our wayward star and missed the animal immediacy with which he galvanized Uncle Freddie—and the man who played him. We soon closed, and the *Bent* cast went their separate ways. They claimed to have made me young again—and they were right.

Television pickings remained so slim that I began to be less certain that I wanted to pluck them. I was a smooth-talking auctioneer in *Amazing Stories*, a suave maître d' on *The Colbys*, and a crazed caterer on *General Hospital*. There were actually three energetic scenes on the soap opera, with the usual murmured intimations from the casting office that the role would recur. I stopped holding my breath some time ago. An interview for one more job did get my attention, though.

Ken Russell, a director whose work I had admired in the past, wanted to see me for a part in an actual feature film. I could believe neither the title nor the script pages when I picked them up at the studio to peruse my role the night before the audition. It was not easy to get to sleep as I mulled over how to improvise my assignment.

The following morning, looking—but not feeling—urbane in my understated Carroll's suit and regimental tie, I drove to the house that Mr. Russell had rented on the hill above the storied Château Marmont. He sat, a deranged and pudgy imp with white hair, in a California '50s-style living room that the owners had rightfully rushed to lease. His casting director, Linda Francis, and one of the film's producers looked on from a mustard-colored sectional sofa while I launched into the first dirty audition of my life—or my second, if you count my meeting with Mae West.

The attractive actress who was assisting Mr. Russell by being my partner took the note that I had copied from the script and written down at home. She read me what I wanted to hear. She told me what a naughty boy I'd been. I begged "Mommy" to say it again, and louder. While she obliged, I gestured for her to give me one of her shoes. She did. I slipped my free hand with my folded pocket-handkerchief into my unzipped fly. She increased her volume while I pantomimed licking her shoe. I nearly passed out against the cork-covered wall taking my time to feign an ecstatic ejaculation in my trousers. When I, ahem, *finished*, Mr. Russell gurgled "very good indeed." I recovered my balance and admonished Ms. Francis that this was not to result in typecasting. There was laughter all around. I meant it when I told the British imp that I had admired his film *The Savage Messiah*. He replied that not enough other people had and thanked me. I drove home to change out of my disheveled suit.

Any voyeuristic cinema addict will know by now that the film was *Whore*. I did play, fully clothed mind you, Theresa Russell's shoe fetishist. The stranger-voyeur would not know that it was I because Ken Russell photographed me sideways lying on the bed, and the producers did not give cast members role identification in their billing. That's for the best in a film that turned out to be one of the British imp's shoddier efforts.

When we shot my scene downtown at the Park Plaza Hotel, Mr. Russell urged me on in high, lascivious tones to "keep sucking." Theresa's scarlet high heels were fresh from a shoebox, not from her feet. A grip held my knees—the beginning of my torn meniscus, or the end?—to keep me from sliding off the bed. I sniggered and tossed the shoe over my shoulder when I supposedly climaxed. Miss Russell's eyes rolled. It seemed that all of the crew filled the seedy hotel room, looking on like clowns stuffed in a circus car. Between takes, I concentrated on the bucolic view from the fire escape. MacArthur Park looked safe and serene—from a distance. I also mused on the knowledge that I no longer gave a damn what I did on camera—short of frontal nudity. It was a bit late for that.

I wrestled with something more. There was a painful irony in working with abandoned inhibitions on *Whore* and, at the same time, relinquishing ambition. Tortuously, I accepted the fact that my name might never sweep on with the music above the title. My impossible dream was too damaging not to die. I had to be realistic in order to survive. I told myself that I was like so many, most, in my profession. We missed the brass ring. The miracle was that I had not succumbed, like my innumerable peers, to sloth, alcoholism, drugs and illness, or despair. Close, certainly, on some accounts, but no cigar. Being orderly has saved me, and, yes, electing, much of the time, to be shallow. Life must be neat. I am compelled to straighten it up, like I did my cubicle at Christchurch.

I saw the truth in an erudite friend's long-ago remark. I was tight and cantankerous, sitting in front of an after-dinner fire at William's on Avondale. I was railing for a role, an Oscar, a series. I was pleading and angry for fame and its accompanying praise.

"So. No approbation, no recognition. That's what's wrong with you," the friend observed.

The harder truth is that I was a sexual sybarite, desperate for distraction and for being loved. Acting was not my life. The admission, when I made it, was a sort of relief. Once I did, I welcomed work. But the effort not to shrivel up and self-destruct for the lack of being loved—or for the lack of sex—is not, finally, so gigantic. At least the former is not out of the question.

There is also companionship to keep me sane—or insane, depending on John Paul's point of view. Leap and Pinto are cats eight and nine. They are male and female, respectively. I also have my home, and Madame Gumm would still recognize the neighborhood.

When senility sets in, I would do well to emulate the lady who came the closest to raising me. Fat chance. Mother's composure improved with retirement homes. Her fourth, a countryside spread in Baltimore named Pickersgill—which, to amuse my nephew Stuart, I called Peckersgill—was her last. On the telephone, she agreed with my platitudinous observance that aging was "interesting." She said that of course she had some arthritis. So she took a hot shower and "thought of other things." After a heart attack and a broken hip, at ninety-seven she went off to the races with equanimity. To steady my own composure at her gravesite in Baltimore's Green Mount cemetery, I wondered if John Wilkes Booth was close by. The point is that Mother accepted giving up her home and her possessions. Her resignation to her own reality astonished her admiring family.

They, too, have changed, as have some of their partners. My sister Ann is in a condominium with her second husband, Dr. Jerrie Cherry. Good thinking, her marrying a doctor, and the spelling and rhyme are not his fault. Her children Ann and Stuart have apartments of their own. Stuart's daughter Meg has made me a granduncle. Their father remarried and lives another life. They are like upscale rabbits. When I go home, if John Paul is not behind the wheel of our rental car, one of them has to drive me to visit their different warrens. Sometimes I succeed in looking straight ahead if Oak Hill is along the way.

I remember the old wooden terrace at Oak Hill that I ran across as a child. The one that Uncle Herbert replaced with flagstone and that my mother Carlyle crashed against when she was a young girl. "Look, Mother," she called to Grandmother Boone from her stalled roadster, "I can drive!"

That, like Peckersgill instead of Pickersgill, is funny. Humor is all. It sustains interest and fragments boredom. It can bring you up short and take you by surprise—like life. Oh, to crack up laughing instead of battling! I vacillate toward both too rapidly. I hope that mirth wins out. Comedy at one's own expense is healthful too. Maybe the best of all. As at a Jimmy Grieves dinner party in his Maryland home: my stepbrother and I are civil, and I held forth at his table. I was the Hollywood raconteur and a feast for all ears—that is, until my actor's instinct told me to turn the conversational reins over to someone else before they got away from me. I said that I grew tired of being charming. Mrs. Grieves answered from her kitchen, and she held for her laugh. Mine was the loudest, as my father's would have been. "Don't worry," she said, "you're not *that* charming."

Who says?

TO THE LEFT OF THE RAINBOW

What do I remember of John Carlyle? I don't want to romanticize things, but that's hard, since I'm talking about a romantic original. To begin with, he had a nickname for me: Taya-Bithiah. Bithiah was name of the character Nina Foch played in Cecil B. DeMille's *The Ten Commandments*. Ms. Foch, an old pal of John's, is the former owner of my house.

Looking back on the time that he's been gone, I realize that what I miss most is John's absolute comic intensity. When I round the corner and pull in my driveway, I sometimes think I will see him, that he will invite me over to watch the evening news and have vodka with him and J. P. On those regular occasions, he would always tell me some extraordinary thing I did not know about James Dean, Marilyn Monroe, Marlon Brando, Bobby Kennedy, or the Jaguar-driving real estate lady who lives three doors down.

John was a guide and a touchstone for me. He was the beacon that we all must have as we navigate through life. I learned from his humor and from his mistakes. I learned by his example how a gentleman lives his life, and I learned that we just shouldn't take any of this too seriously. Life goes on — we are beautiful, we age, we die, just like John did.

Thirty years ago, when I was a teenager in Beverly Hills, it all seemed downright magical to me as I walked through these very streets on my journey up to the Comedy Store on Sunset Boulevard. The cozy houses were just as they are now: tasteful and quiet with nicely polished windows. In that long-ago time, if I walked past any house with the door opened just right, I could hear the soft voice of Barbra Streisand or the harder voice of Elaine Stritch. The air was tinged with a heady mixture of jasmine, roses, and poppers.

In those turtlenecked, bell-bottomed, hair-parted-down-the-middle days, this part of West Hollywood was considered a "gay ghetto." Back then, I understood "gay" to mean dignity and good taste, not shirtless boys and tweakers. Now, looking back, I see that it was an era of thoroughly self-created American taste — like jazz and hot dogs — invented out of necessity, developed in order to survive in a world filled with terrible, unfair things like vice-squad raids, double lives, and blacklisting.

This highly developed taste, most likely inherited from Edwardian grandparents of a certain class and from the movies, was exemplified in John. It served as a life raft for men of a certain "persuasion," allowing them to float through the treacherous currents of their lives, lives that have, for the most part, vanished. For a young man like myself, the feeling back then was enchanting.

The first time I met John set the tone for our friendship. I came outside early one morning and saw a handsome older man standing ramrod-straight, dressed in slacks and a sweater, sweeping the part of the street in front of his door. He looked over at me with clear eyes and said: "Oh, you have caught me doing my Duchess of Windsor impersonation." "Pardon?" "Well, even when Mrs. Simpson lived in Baltimore, before she married the Duke of Windsor, she always swept in front of her door . . . in her jewelry." Then he let out that serious laugh of his, clear, loud, and as authentic as Christmas in Connecticut. John's winning, self-deprecating laugh allowed his humane intelligence to show through.

Here was the man who was clearly the star of my new neighborhood. He was also its historian. He told me: "You know, Taylor, Joan Fontaine almost bought your house. I told her about it. She came and walked through it. Stayed a long time in the kitchen. Came right up that driveway and said: 'It's not for me!' Joan knows what she likes."

Then he told me, in his crisp, r-less mid-Atlantic way, "Dorothy Parker lived here on this street; she nicknamed West Hollywood 'The Swish Alps.' She has been face-down in every clump of ivy from here down to Doheny. Good old Dottie. Her husband, Alan Campbell, died right there." John pointed his broom toward the spot on the driveway of a stucco bungalow on Norma Place. "Horrible. They took Alan away in an ambulance, and Dottie looked so devastated. I asked if there was anything I could do. She turned around and said: 'Get me another husband.'"

Los Angeles is a city of dreamers, where the line between fantasy and reality is especially blurry. I have seen people come here and thrive in the fantasy—some of them live forever on the side of the fantasy, perhaps because they know deep inside that the reality ride will be too rough and require too much from them, as it takes valuable time away from long lunches that lead to sexy, moonlit evenings. Nonetheless, those lives are just as authentic and vital, in some cases more so, than those who have followed the path of hard reality. They become stars in their own life, cultivating their personality as carefully as their iconic counterparts do. John Carlyle was one of those people, criminally wicked in creating his aura out of necessity.

Rumor had it that Judy Garland once lived on our street. Because I was not a fan of Miss Garland, John worked tirelessly to convince me of her merits. In doing so, he convinced me of his. While he explained how their friendship defined his life—she was the woman that got away—I realized that I was the neighbor that got in, and here was where I belonged. We became a team. To know John was to know Judy. In fact, I now know more about Judy Garland than anyone *should* know. But more importantly and thankfully, I know a lot about the life of John Carlyle. I thank my lucky stars every day that I found and bought my little cottage here on this fabled block filled with so many ghosts.

One evening, John said: "Please come with me to see the little Judy sprite perform." I asked him: "Who is the Judy Sprite?" "Why, Little Lorna! She is performing a private concert for friends of the family. You must come." As we drove down Sunset Boulevard, there was excitement in the air. John said: "You know, I miss Judy so much. The laughter. The laughter! Judy would laugh." John looked at me and smiled. "It would come from the bottom of her feet. Why do they make such a big deal out of the fact that she took forty Ritalin a day?" John cackled with ironic affection.

Lorna sounds so much like her mother. I felt like I was at a séance. I expected to see Judy coming toward us. But it was Lorna who came right up to us. She hugged John and they looked sad together. John's crying was magnified by his thick glasses.

As we drove home down the blighted streets of Hollywood, John stared out the window. No one said anything for the longest time. Then John told a story: "I tackled Judy once. She came at me. She was out of control, she snapped. She was screaming at me. 'You don't love me! You don't love me!' She was hitting me. I was nude. I had just come out of the shower at her house in Brentwood. I struggled with her right in front of the fireplace. You had to stand up to Judy, or she would walk all over you. I tackled her, and when we realized what was happening, we just started to laugh."

I gazed out the window as the ensuing silence evaporated the image he had just conjured. I couldn't get the picture of John and Judy on the floor in front of her fireplace out of my mind. Judy got him. Life didn't. He bounced back, he survived because of his taste and the restraint and quiet elemental dignity that were his life raft. But John is gone now, and the street is different. Leaves have gathered at John's door. We don't hear Judy or Elaine much any more. The boys run by chattering on their cell phones, rushing off to buy fifteen-dollar martinis and get laid. John Carlyle did more than his share of that sort of thing, of course, but I believe in my heart of hearts that these people are not savoring life as deeply as John and Judy and all their cohorts did. That era is gone, replaced by the house-techno music thumping at 128 beats per minute that blares up from the queer lounges around Santa Monica Boulevard. Sometimes it's so loud that the china cups tap gently against the glass in my cabinets.

On the occasion of John's seventieth birthday, J. P. and I threw him a surprise party at my house. All his friends gathered, toasting and laughing with John. After the last guest left, John and I sat in front of the fire. He said: "You fit here. You are the energy that was this neighborhood." And then he asked: "Do you have a joint?" He giggled devilishly as I went to my stash box and rolled the birthday boy a fatty. We smoked and giggled the night away. But that's a long time ago. Writing these words, I understand something now. Life is not symmetrical; one has to go forward courageously in the borderless space that we all inhabit. They say beauty is wasted on the young, that the young have the fringe benefits. But those benefits can be compounded when life is lived fully. All the beauty, the kisses, and the all-night parties are not wasted. They live on in our memory rooms—and on the pages of John's life story. They affect all of us when we pay attention.

On that long-ago birthday night, John and I talked about his accomplishments, how happy his life was, and about how he enjoyed the life he had carved out with John Paul here on our little stretch of domesticity on the Norma Triangle. Maybe John Carlyle didn't go very far up the snowy mountain of life. I think he preferred to stay down at the lodge on the base of the mountain, cozy in front of the fire, drinking rum toddies and entertaining us all. But I believe that his life, the one he made, was just as real as a handful of old Golden Globes or a wall of dusty gold records.

When I walked John home that night, we were both a little wobbly. He slipped on a wet brick and went down, taking me with him. I braced him so he could fall on me. There was one silent moment and then he let loose that laugh, part cackle, part secret handshake. "Judy would have loved you!" I don't think I ever felt such a compliment. It was his way saying he loved me.

A couple of years after that memorable evening, John called me on my cell phone, something he never did. He said: "Taya-Bithiah, I have cancer. The doctor told me I am dying. I am only telling the people I love." His tone was soothing and protective. Gob-smacked, I told him it would be fine and tried to make a joke. Then we hung up. That was that.

John and J. P. became my trusted friends, my gay dads. I miss John. I miss him sweeping and making proclamations about the new movies and popular culture. I miss him lying on top of me, laughing. He was an absolute treat. So, here's to John, the gentle man across the street. Here's to the laughter. That's what I remember most.

—Taylor Negron, from the Norma Triangle, West Hollywood

ACKNOWLEDGMENTS

Friends—some famous, some infamous—mentors, lovers, and other actors have given up and disappeared, self-destructed, died. I have been lucky. For that I am grateful—and to my father and his third wife, my sister, my cats, and laughter. And, of course, to John Paul Davis.

—John Carlyle

I would like to thank John Paul Davis for trusting me with *Under the Rainbow*. It has been an honor to see this book into print. My thanks go out to Taylor Negron, Stephen Bellon, Robert Osborne, Tom Irish, Bob Hofler, Don Weise and the folks at Carroll and Graf, The Maryland Historical Society, Warner Bros. (especially Peter Steckelman, Darlene Grodske, and Marlene Eastman), Don Bachardy, Ann Posey Cherry, Stuart Egerton III, Annette Atkins, Beverly Radaich, Norma Koetter, Stephanie Aitken, and Saint John's University for the sabbatical time and support.

—Chris Freeman

I would like to acknowledge John's talent as an actor. Much has been said about his desire to be a movie star, even by John himself. Having helped him prepare for many roles over the years, I have a different perspective. John had a desire to be the best he could be, even in workshop productions. Hours would be spent by both of us deep into the night for days until he felt he had gotten the role just right. His performances in *The Dresser, The Night of the Iguana,* and *Death Trap* earned him raves from his fellow actors, even years later when he'd run into someone who had seen a performance. He was a very talented and dedicated actor.

I'd like to thank Chris Freeman for his hard work editing *Under the Rainbow* and for finding a publisher who is as excited about the book as we are. Without his efforts, the book would still be languishing in a closet in West Hollywood. I'd also like to thank Gerald Clarke, the late Gavin Lambert, Barbara Rush, Ramona Rush Hennesy, Oren Curtis, Tucker Fleming, the late Charles Williamson, Stephen Bellon, Don Bachardy, Ann Posey Cherry, Bob Hofler, Bobbie Phillips, Taylor Negron, Robert Osborne, Marci Miller, Joanna Heathcote, Deanne McKinstry, and David and Carolynn Wells.

—John Paul Davis

INDEX

NOTE: JC is used as an abbreviation for John Carlyle.